T0338592

Cases on Edge Computing and Analytics

Paranthaman Ambika
Impact Analysis, India

A. Cecil Donald
Kristu Jayanti College, India

A. Dalvin Vinoth Kumar
Kristu Jayanti College, India

A volume in the Advances in
Computational Intelligence and
Robotics (ACIR) Book Series

Published in the United States of America by
IGI Global
Engineering Science Reference (an imprint of IGI Global)
701 E. Chocolate Avenue
Hershey PA, USA 17033
Tel: 717-533-8845
Fax: 717-533-8661
E-mail: cust@igi-global.com
Web site: http://www.igi-global.com

Library of Congress Cataloging-in-Publication Data

Names: Ambika, Paranthaman, 1982- editor. | Donald, A. Cecil, 1990- editor.
| Kumar, A. Dalvin Vinoth, 1989- editor.
Title: Cases on edge computing / Paranthaman Ambika, A. Cecil Donald, and
A. Dalvin Vinoth Kumar, editors.
Description: Hershey, PA : Engineering Science Reference, an imprint of IGI
Global, [2021] | Includes bibliographical references and index. |
Summary: "This book provides a practical approach to edge computing and
analytics, its architecture and the building blocks for edge computing
implementations. It address many characteristics of edge computing, such
as key drivers for implementation, computing capabilities, use-cases,
etc. case studies "-- Provided by publisher.
Identifiers: LCCN 2020018692 (print) | LCCN 2020018693 (ebook) | ISBN
9781799848738 (hardcover) | ISBN 9781799858294 (paperback) | ISBN
9781799848745 (ebook)
Subjects: LCSH: Edge computing--Case studies. | Internet of things--Case
studies.
Classification: LCC QA76.583 .C37 2021 (print) | LCC QA76.583 (ebook) |
DDC 004.67/8--dc23
LC record available at https://lccn.loc.gov/2020018692
LC ebook record available at https://lccn.loc.gov/2020018693

This book is published in the IGI Global book series Advances in Computational Intelligence and Robotics (ACIR) (ISSN: 2327-0411; eISSN: 2327-042X)

British Cataloguing in Publication Data
A Cataloguing in Publication record for this book is available from the British Library.

All work contributed to this book is new, previously-unpublished material.
The views expressed in this book are those of the authors, but not necessarily of the publisher.

For electronic access to this publication, please contact: eresources@igi-global.com.

Advances in Computational Intelligence and Robotics (ACIR) Book Series

ISSN:2327-0411
EISSN:2327-042X

Editor-in-Chief: Ivan Giannoccaro,University of Salento, Italy

MISSION

While intelligence is traditionally a term applied to humans and human cognition, technology has progressed in such a way to allow for the development of intelligent systems able to simulate many human traits. With this new era of simulated and artificial intelligence, much research is needed in order to continue to advance the field and also to evaluate the ethical and societal concerns of the existence of artificial life and machine learning.

The **Advances in Computational Intelligence and Robotics (ACIR) Book Series** encourages scholarly discourse on all topics pertaining to evolutionary computing, artificial life, computational intelligence, machine learning, and robotics. ACIR presents the latest research being conducted on diverse topics in intelligence technologies with the goal of advancing knowledge and applications in this rapidly evolving field.

COVERAGE

- Fuzzy Systems
- Evolutionary Computing
- Artificial Intelligence
- Adaptive and Complex Systems
- Intelligent control
- Synthetic Emotions
- Algorithmic Learning
- Cyborgs
- Machine Learning
- Neural Networks

IGI Global is currently accepting manuscripts for publication within this series. To submit a proposal for a volume in this series, please contact our Acquisition Editors at Acquisitions@igi-global.com or visit: http://www.igi-global.com/publish/.

Titles in this Series

For a list of additional titles in this series, please visit: http://www.igi-global.com/book-series

Artificial Neural Network Applications in Business and Engineering
Quang Hung Do (University of Transport Technology, Vietnam)
Engineering Science Reference • © 2021 • 275pp • H/C (ISBN: 9781799832386) • US $245.00

Multimedia and Sensory Input for Augmented, Mixed, and Virtual Reality
Amit Kumar Tyagi (Research Division of Advanced Data Science, Vellore Institute of Technolgy, Chennai, India)
Engineering Science Reference • © 2021 • 310pp • H/C (ISBN: 9781799847038) • US $225.00

Handbook of Research on Deep Learning-Based Image Analysis Under Constrained and Unconstrained Environments
Alex Noel Joseph Raj (Shantou University, China) Vijayalakshmi G. V. Mahesh (BMS Institute of Technology and Management, India) and Ruban Nersisson (Vellore Institute of Technology, India)
Engineering Science Reference • © 2021 • 381pp • H/C (ISBN: 9781799866909) • US $295.00

AI Tools and Electronic Virtual Assistants for Improved Business Performance
Christian Graham (University of Maine, USA)
Business Science Reference • © 2021 • 300pp • H/C (ISBN: 9781799838418) • US $245.00

Advanced Concepts, Methods, and Applications in Semantic Computing
Olawande Daramola (Cape Peninsula University of Technology, South Africa) and Thomas Moser (St. Pölten University of Applied Sciences, Austria)
Engineering Science Reference • © 2021 • 305pp • H/C (ISBN: 9781799866978) • US $215.00

Applications of Artificial Intelligence for Smart Technology
P. Swarnalatha (Vellore Institute of Technology, Vellore, India) and S. Prabu (Vellore Institute of Technology, Vellore, India)
Engineering Science Reference • © 2021 • 330pp • H/C (ISBN: 9781799833352) • US $215.00

701 East Chocolate Avenue, Hershey, PA 17033, USA
Tel: 717-533-8845 x100 • Fax: 717-533-8661
E-Mail: cust@igi-global.com • www.igi-global.com

Table of Contents

Detailed Table of Contents

Chapter 1

Sandhya Devi R. S., Kumaraguru College of Technology, India
Vijaykumar V. R., Anna University, Coimbatore, India
Sivakumar P., PSG College of Technology, India
Neeraja Lakshmi A., PSG College of Technology, India
Vinoth Kumar B., PSG College of Technology, India

The enormous growth of the internet of things (IoT) and cloud-based services have paved the way for edge computing, the new computing paradigm which processes the data at the edge of the network. Edge computing resolves issues related to response time, latency, battery life limitation, cost savings for bandwidth, as well as data privacy and protection. The architecture brings devices and data back to the consumer. This model of computing as a distributed IT system aims at satisfying end-user demands with faster response times by storing data closer to it. The enormous increase in individuals and locations, connected devices such as appliances, laptops, smartphones, and transport networks that communicate with each other has raised exponentially. Considering these factors in this chapter, edge computing architecture along with the various components that constitute the computing platform are discussed. The chapter also discusses resource management strategies deliberate for edge computing devices and integration of various computing technologies to support efficient IoT architecture.

Chapter 2

Margaret Mary T., Kristu Jayanti College, India
Sangamithra A., Kristu Jayanti College, India
Ramanathan G., Kristu Jayanti College, India

Internet of things (IoT) architecture is an ecosystem of connected physical objects that are accessible through the internet. The 'thing' in IoT could be a person with a heart monitor or an automobile with built-in-sensors (i.e., objects that have been assigned an IP address and have the ability to collect and transfer data over a network without manual assistance or intervention). The embedded technology in the objects helps them to interact with internal states or the external environment, which in turn affects the decisions taken. IoT world where all the devices and appliances are connected to a network and are used collaboratively to achieve complex tasks that require a high degree of intelligence, and IoT is an interaction between the physical and digital words using sensors and actuators. Furthermore, the IoT architecture may combine features and technologies suggested by various methodologies. IoT architecture is designed where the digital and real worlds are integrating and interacting constantly, and various technologies are merged together to form IoT.

Chapter 3
Stephen R., Kristu Jayanti College, India
Ayshwarya B., Kristu Jayanti College, India
R. Shantha Mary Joshitta, Jayaraj Annapackiam College for Women, India
Hubert B. J. Shanthan, Kristu Jayanti College, India

Naturally, IoT network consists of constrained devices with limited power, storage, and processing capabilities. However, IoT has some challenges to face internal and external issues, for instance, security issues, connectivity complex, data management, etc. In such a case, IoT is not supported by a heavyweight protocol suite. So, developing the lightweight protocol suite is the challenge for IoT environment. This chapter also describes such protocols that fulfill the requirements of IoT. In fact, IoT environment consists of a huge amount of devices. The controlling of all the devices is another issue, as well as data analytics among different devices, also considered a major issue. As a constraint, this chapter focuses to design a standard protocol suite for IoT environment.

Chapter 4
Sangamithra A., VIT University, India
Margaret Mary T., Kristu Jayanti College, India
Clinton G., Sambharm Institute of Technology, India

Edge computing is the concept of the distributed paradigm. In order to improve the response time and to save the bandwidth, it brings the computation and the storage of the data closer to the location whenever it is needed. Edge computing is one of the very famous and blooming concept in today's era. It has been used in so many applications for various purposes. Edge computing can be defined as infrastructure of physical compute which is placed between the device and the cloud to support various application and which brings the cloud closer to the end user or end devices. In this chapter, the authors discuss the origin of the edge paradigm, introduction, benefits. These are some of the criteria to be elaborated in the chapter overview of edge paradigm.

Chapter 5

Suresh K., Amrita School of Arts and Sciences, Amrita Vishwa
Vidyapeetham, India

The internet of things indicates a kind of system to interface anything with the internet dependent on stipulated conventions through data detecting hardware to direct data trade and correspondences so as to accomplish acknowledgments, situating, figuring out, checking, and organization. IoT empowers various advances about its engineering, qualities, and applications, but what are the future difficulties for IoT? IoT frameworks enable clients to accomplish further mechanization, investigation, and joining inside a framework. They improve the scope of these regions and their precision. IoT uses existing and developing innovation for detecting, systems administration, and apply autonomy. IoT abuses ongoing advances in programming, falling equipment costs, and current frames of mind towards innovation. Its new and propelled components acquire significant changes the conveyance of items, products, administrations, financial, and political effect of those changes.

Chapter 6

Kavita Srivastava, Institute of Information Technology and
Management, GGSIP University, India

The steep rise in autonomous systems and the internet of things in recent years has influenced the way in which computation has performed. With built-in AI (artificial intelligence) in IoT and cyber-physical systems, the need for high-performance computing has emerged. Cloud computing is no longer sufficient for the sensor-driven systems which continuously keep on collecting data from the environment. The sensor-based systems such as autonomous vehicles require analysis of data and predictions in real-time which is not possible only with the centralized cloud. This scenario has given rise to a new computing paradigm called edge computing. Edge computing requires the storage of data, analysis, and prediction performed on the network edge as opposed to a cloud server thereby enabling quick response and less storage overhead. The intelligence at the edge can be obtained through deep learning. This chapter contains information about various deep learning frameworks, hardware, and systems for edge computing and examples of deep neural network training using the Caffe 2 framework.

Chapter 7

Soumya K., Kristu Jayanti College, India
Margaret Mary T., Kristu Jayanti College, India
Clinton G., Sambhram Institute of Technology, India

Edge analytics is an approach to data collection and analysis in which an automated analytical computation is performed on data at a sensor, network switch, or other device instead of waiting for the data to be sent back to a centralized data store. Cloud computing has revolutionized how people store and use their data; however, there are some areas where cloud is limited; latency, bandwidth, security, and a lack of offline access can be problematic. To solve this problem, users need robust, secure, and intelligent on-premise infrastructure for edge computing. When data is physically located closer to the users who connected to it, information can be shared quickly, securely, and without latency. In financial services, gaming, healthcare, and retail, low levels of latency are vital for a great digital customer experience. To improve reliability and faster response times, combing cloud with edge infrastructure from APC by Schneider electrical is proposed.

Chapter 8

Sunita Panda, GITAM School of Technology, GITAM University
(Deemed) (Bengaluru Campus), India
Padma Charan Sahu, Godavari Institute of Engineering and
Technology, India
Kamalanathan Chandran, GITAM School of Technology, GITAM
University (Deemed) (Bengaluru Campus), India

Edge computing (EC) is a rising innovation that has made it conceivable to deal with the huge volume of information generated by terminal devices connected with the internet. Here the authors represent the issues of EC. The reconciliation of EC in those settings would suggest an improvement of the cycles that are ordinarily executed in a distributed computing condition, bringing impressive favorable circumstances. Before they are sent to the cloud or central server, the primary commitment of EC is a superior preprocessing of the information gathered through gadgets.

Chapter 9

Chinnasamy P., Sri Shakthi Institute of Engineering and Technology, India

Rojaramani D., Sethu Institute of Technology, India

Praveena V., Dr. N. G. P. Institute of Technology, India

Annlin Jeba S. V., Sree Buddha College of Engineering, India

Bensujin B., University of Technology and Applied Sciences, Nizwa, Oman

Several researchers analyzed the information security problems in edge computing, though not all studied the criteria for security and confidentiality in detail. This chapter intends to extensively evaluate the edge computing protection and confidentiality standards and the different technical approaches utilized by the technologies often used mitigate the risks. This study describes the latest research and emphasizes the following: (1) the definition of edge computing protection and confidentiality criteria, (2) state-of-the-art strategies used to mitigate protection and privacy risks, (3) developments in technical approaches, (4) measures used to measure the efficiency of interventions, (5) the categorization of threats on the edge device and the related technical pattern used to mitigate the attackers, and (6) research directions for potential professionals in the field of edge devices privacy and security.

Chapter 10

Manoranjini J., Swami Vivekananda Institute of Technology, India

Anbuchelian S., Anna University, India

The rapid massive growth of IoT and the explosive increase in the data used and created in the edge networks led to several complications in the cloud technology. Edge computing is an emerging technology which is ensuring itself as a promising technology. The authors mainly focus on the security and privacy issues and their solutions. There are a lot of important features which make edge computing the most promising technology. In this chapter, they emphasize the security and privacy issues. They also discuss various architectures that enable us to ensure safe technologies and also provide an analysis on various designs that enable strong security models. Next, they make a detailed study on different cryptographic techniques and trust management systems. This study helps us to identify the pros and cons that led us to promising implementations of edge computing in the current scenario. At the end of the chapter, the authors discuss on various open research areas which could be the thrust areas for the next era.

The whole world is changing quickly into a mechanical world. One of the most encouraging innovations is the smart sensor innovation which is presently accessible all over the place. Nowadays the utilization of internet is exaggerated in our lives everywhere so that most of the things we use in our day-to-day lives are dependent on internet, which leads to a new era of internet of everything (IoE). The internet of everything (IoE) has different applications in medication, from far off seeing to smart sensors and clinical appliances. It can ensure and screen patients and improve the degree of care. This technology shows improvements in different sectors, specifically in critical sectors which lead everything in the world to be very smart.

Chapter 12

The evolution in computing strategies has shown wonders in reducing the reachability issue among different end devices. After centralized approaches, decentralized approaches started to take action, but with the latency in data pre-processing, computing very simple requests was the same as for the larger computations. Now it's time to have a simple decentralized environment called edge that is created very near to the end device. This makes edge location friendly and time friendly to different kinds of devices like smart, sensor, grid, etc. In this chapter, some of the serious and non-discussed security issues and privacy issues available on edge are explained neatly, and for a few of the problems, some solutions are also recommended. At last, a separate case study of edge computing challenges in healthcare is also explored, and solutions to those issues concerning that domain are shown.

Chapter 13

Kumar R., Kristu Jayanti College, India
Ayshwarya B., Kristu Jayanti College, India
Muruganantham A., Kristu Jayanti College, India
Velmurugan R., Kristu Jayanti College, India

Dynamic observation of blood sugar levels is essential for patients diagnosed with diabetes mellitus in order to control the glycaemia. Inevitably, they must accomplish a capillary test three times per day and laboratory test once or twice per month. These regular methods make patients uncomfortable because patients have to prick their finger every time in order to measure the glucose concentration. Modern health monitoring systems rely on IoT. However, the number of advanced IoT-based continuous glucose monitoring systems is small and has several limitations. Here the authors study feasibility of invasive and continuous glucose monitoring system utilizing IoT-based approach. They designed an IoT-based system architecture from a sensor device to a back-end system for presenting real-time data in various forms to end-users. The results show that the system is able to achieve continuous glucose monitoring remotely in real time, and a high level of energy efficiency can be achieved by applying the nRF compound, power management, and energy harvesting unit altogether in the sensor units.

Preface

The need of edge computing emerged with the success of IoT and cloud services that allows data processing happens at the network edge. Recently, many firms have begun to have a simplified administration and flexibility of cloud computing architectures to distributed infrastructures that span across multiple working units and networks. At the initial stage, Edge computing first emerged by virtualizing network services over WAN networks, taking a step away from the data center. Use cases were driven by a desire to leverage a platform that delivered the flexibility and simple tools that cloud computing users have become accustomed to. In the recent days, As new edge computing capabilities emerge, we see a changing paradigm for computing—one that is no longer necessarily bound by the need to build centralized data centers. Thus, edge computing is reshaping IT and business computing. Take a comprehensive look at what edge computing is, how it works, the influence of the cloud, edge use cases, tradeoffs and implementation.

In Edge computing environment, it system generates continuous data which help in building real-time context as well as patterns that can be observed over a period of time. Industrial enterprises have recognized that they must store, process and analyze as much, if not all, data that is available to them in order to survive and thrive in the digital economy. This includes data produced by the myriad of sensors, embedded computers, industrial controllers and connected devices such as vehicles, wearable computing devices, robots and drones that make up the emerging Internet of Things (IoT).

This book facilitates and features the Edge Computing with respect to Mobile, IoT and IIoT technologies. This book comprises of 13 chapters which covers from evolution, architecture, implementation and role of Edge computing with use cases. I hope the book will provide clarity about Edge Computing, architectures, issues, applications and use-case scenarios.

Chapter 1 highlights the introduction to the Edge computing and the technologies and elaborates the challenges and solutions in edge computing. Technologies like mobile edge computing, Fog Computing, cloudlets, Multi-access Edge Computing,

Micro Data Centers, Cloud of Things were also discussed. Added to that, applications and key benefits were also elaborated in this chapter.

Chapter 2 discusses various layers of edge architecture. Challenges with respect to security, data extraction, data mining, data storage in an edge computing environment are also explained in this chapter.

Chapter 3 describes the various standard protocols based on IoT layers, protocols and their appropriate applications. Also, this chapter lists out various issues and challenges of the IoT protocol suite with real-time scenarios. A case study on health care management system is also elucidated in this chapter.

Chapter 4 discuss about the origin of the edge paradigm along with its benefits. Technologies involved in edge, benefits and applications are also presented in this chapter.

Chapter 5 depicts the recent trends in IoT which plays a vital role in edge computing. Various scenarios with respect to IoT technologies are also discussed in this chapter.

Chapter 6 gives insight on a very important technique for imparting intelligence at the network edge – the Deep Learning technique. This chapter describes several aspects of Deep Learning which are applicable for Edge Computing. This chapter starts with an introduction to Edge Computing and Deep Learning. How the Deep Learning can leverage Intelligent Edge Applications is also explained. Several Deep Learning Frameworks are also explained in this chapter. Various real-life applications of the usage of Deep Learning with Edge Computing and future research directions are also presented.

Chapter 7 focuses on innovative techniques and the use cases for Edge based Data Analytics for IoT. Edge computing Vs Cloud Computing technologies were discussed along with modern use cases. This chapter provides insights about data analytics in the edge computing. The impact of IIOT (Industrial Internet of Things) in the field of Edge based data analytics is discussed in this chapter.

Chapter 8 speaks about the origin of the edge in the era of computers and its emergence. Later, the chapter expands the types of edge computing, phases and various applications with the types. The impact of business methods without edge and with edge computing and drawbacks are also discussed.

Chapter 9 presents about the edge computing, elements of edge, applications of edge. Issues pertaining to security and privacy in edge are elaborated in this chapter. Security of core infrastructure, edge servers, edge networks and edge devices are also discussed.

Chapter 10 discuss on various architecture that enables to ensure safe technologies and also provide an analysis on various designs that enable strong security models. In this chapter a detailed study on different cryptographic techniques and trust management systems. This study helps us to identify the pros and cons that led us to promising implementations of edge computing in the current scenario. And also discuss on various open research areas which could be the thrust areas for the next era.

Chapter 11 covers late advancements in remote human services frameworks to give a knowledge of the mechanical arrangements, spread models, correspondence of clinical web of things and remote human services frameworks.

Chapter 12 explains about the security architecture and generic issues in edge. Various security threats and attacks are also discussed in this chapter. Solutions and techniques to enforce security is also presented. Finally, this chapter concludes with the use case scenario and applications.

Chapter 13 presents feasibility of invasive and continuous glucose monitoring system utilizing IoT based approach. In this chapter an IoT-based system architecture from a sensor device to a back-end system for presenting real time data in various forms to end-users also designed.

Chapter 1
Edge Architecture Integration of Technologies

Sandhya Devi R. S.
https://orcid.org/0000-0001-7021-845X
Kumaraguru College of Technology, India

Vijaykumar V. R.
Anna University, Coimbatore, India

Sivakumar P.
https://orcid.org/0000-0002-8469-6492
PSG College of Technology, India

Neeraja Lakshmi A.
PSG College of Technology, India

Vinoth Kumar B.
PSG College of Technology, India

EXECUTIVE SUMMARY

The enormous growth of the internet of things (IoT) and cloud-based services have paved the way for edge computing, the new computing paradigm which processes the data at the edge of the network. Edge computing resolves issues related to response time, latency, battery life limitation, cost savings for bandwidth, as well as data privacy and protection. The architecture brings devices and data back to the consumer. This model of computing as a distributed IT system aims at satisfying end-user demands with faster response times by storing data closer to it. The enormous increase in individuals and locations, connected devices such as appliances, laptops,

DOI: 10.4018/978-1-7998-4873-8.ch001

smartphones, and transport networks that communicate with each other has raised exponentially. Considering these factors in this chapter, edge computing architecture along with the various components that constitute the computing platform are discussed. The chapter also discusses resource management strategies deliberate for edge computing devices and integration of various computing technologies to support efficient IoT architecture.

INTRODUCTION

The IoT is a fusion of the technologies of infrastructure, applications, and networking. Data is an important aspect of an IoT device, which must be analyzed immediately. Based on the specific IoT devices that are installed under the network, an IoT framework will produce unlimited data within a second as per business needs. The data generated from IoT devices or sources are limitless and will easily absorb network bandwidth, resulting in excess data storage requirements. Aggregating and digitizing the data at the edge of the network is important, and can then be transmitted to back-end applications (Gubbi et al., 2013). Edge computing takes control of this burden and aims to reduce or automate the IT infrastructure. Such edge computing systems are positioned next to the IoT devices/data sources and therefore implement the necessary security. Edge computing has a significant benefit in reducing the response and maximizing the usage of network resources. This also aims to reduce bottlenecks in the bandwidth and the network.

Thus, IoT systems and infrastructure must be capable of serving heterogeneous devices producing vast quantities of data and events. Taking such ideas into consideration, Edge Computing improves IoT efficiency through its clustered structure where network traffic may therefore be substantially reduced and latency between the cloud's edge node and end-users may be improved. Thus, this makes IoT applications' real-time responsiveness relative to cloud and fog computing (Premsankar et al., 2018). Edge computing provides cloud services such as processing, storage, and networking closer to software, computers, and consumers. It achieves this by utilizing tiny power cell stations to facilitate high-speed transport of data without needing to drive large distances to a server or data center. The innovation of edge computing is to introduce artificial intelligence, machine learning, data analytics through the Internet of Things (IoT), the ability to operate containers, and also the ability to run entire virtual machines directly through a wide variety of computers and devices. Such devices may be as compact as a smartphone, or as large for sophisticated processing as complete computing racks. Regardless of the device's size and capacities, the information on certain computers is still connected to the cloud.

IoT-enabled systems have made cutting edge computing technologies a market requirement. Data density, speed, and new capabilities have rendered cloud computing increasingly unrealistic for devices requiring millisecond data processing. Latency is just too high (Ganz et al., 2015). Complex event processing occurs in the device or a network near to the device with edge computing architecture, which removes round-trip issues and allows activities to occur faster. For instance, vehicles with autonomous driving capability need the brakes immediately applied or will lead to the risk of crashing. With cloud computing services, the round-trip time to the cloud is too slow for this task to accommodate. If the Edge computing capabilities are equipped in a vehicle, the critical decision to stop the car will exist solely on the device of the vehicle avoiding an accident. Following this incident, the data will then be transferred to the cloud for further vehicle tracking and maintenance. Thus, edge computing is a new platform that aims to have a decrease in delays owing to its "proximity" to end-users or applications with the necessary processing and storage facilities.

The main objective of this paper is to discuss Edge computing architecture and its components. It also focusses on efficient resource management in edge computing and the Integration of various technologies to provide a flexible IoT paradigm.

BACKGROUND

Shi et al. (2016) offer a detailed overview of edge computing, with the argument that computation will occur close data sources. It lists many instances where edge computing might flourish from offloading cloud to a smart ecosystem like home and area. It also implements interactive edge, as the edge can physically and theoretically connect end-user and cloud, and not only is the traditional cloud computing model still supported, but it can also bring long-distance networks together for data exchange and coordination due to device closeness. Lastly, it overviews the problems and opportunities worth focusing on, including programmability, naming, aggregation of data, service management, privacy, and protection, as well as metrics for optimization.

The research given proposed by Sittón-Candanedo et al. (2019) is a state-of-the-art edge computing analysis and is a transformative technology powered by the growth of the Internet of Things and the environment's sensors that are constantly attached to the web. IoT applications produce the data continuously and in real-time. The huge number of sensors, connected devices, regional mobility for data storage, real-time requests responses have contributed to Edge Computing. It also improves the efficiency of IoT applications by minimizing network latency and convergence of Blockchain sequence technologies. The authors suggest the construction of an edge computing reference architecture for IoT scenarios as potential lines of study.

In the work of Asim et al. (2020), the authors analyzed the strategies of four critical Cloud (CC) and Edge (EC) computing problems: resource allocation, task offloading, joint issues, and job scheduling. The paper introduces the basic CC and EC principles along with essential problems and measurements and then concentrates on five types of Computational Intelligence (CI) methods used in CC and EC: Evolutionary Algorithms, Swarm Intelligence Algorithms, Fuzzy System, Learning-based Systems, and Edge computing. It is found Learning-Based System being used intensively in CC and EC followed by Evolutionary Algorithms and Swarm Intelligence Algorithms. The authors also highlighted some challenges and future trends in CI, CC, and EC research.

Ai et al. (2017) discuss and analyze state-of-the-art edge computing technologies. The entire paper is broadly divided into cloudlet, desktop edge computing, and fog computing to learn more intricacies of the core technologies. It provides a comprehensive overview of the theory, device design, specifications, and implementations for each of these areas. Nonetheless, despite the field's relative infancy, there are already still a variety of unresolved problems that need to be more explored from the viewpoint of core approaches and innovative solutions. In fact, with the advent of sophisticated big data mining and network slicing, the emergence of varying degrees of freedom along with the related limitations further beckons the creation and testing of the initial models in the light of edge computing.

In this survey paper proposed by Hong et al. (2019), the authors acknowledged that the technical difficulties of handling the minimal fog or edge computing tools have been tackled to a large degree. Nonetheless, there are still a few obstacles ahead to enhance resource utilization in terms of fog or edge computing technologies and efficiency. Fog and edge computing platforms also hire resource-limited machines such as WiFi APs and set-top boxes which are not ideal for operating heavyweight data analysis resources like Apache Spark and deep learning libraries. In fog or edge computing, accelerator scheduling algorithms that consider real-time characteristics are needed to reduce latency in the time-constrained workloads.

Baktir et al. (2018) discuss the computational resources required for implementing Edge computing platforms. The traditionally clustered services in Cloud data centers are being suggested to be available through Edge computing architectures at the edge of the network. Edge services should be internationally dispersed and federated with a globally open Edge layer that will meet demands from all data centers and consumer devices. This paper illustrates some of the problems facing the federating geographically dispersed Edge layer that will need to be tackled. It also deliberates the additional resource and simulation problems for a federated Edge. There is a range of relevant technical problems in networking, management, infrastructure, and modeling that need to be solved to implement innovative approaches and render the federated edge computing a reality.

The work done by Jha et al. (2019) suggests novel approaches and strategies that must be checked before the applications being introduced to the consumers. The implementation of the IoT application methods and techniques in the real environment is a complex, time-consuming process and not cost-effective, either. The application needs significant data collection and processing on autonomous end devices that require careful validation before implementation in the real world. There is a need to check the scalability of modern technologies and techniques and usability. To integrate all these unique features, the paper suggests a novel IoTSim, an Edge simulator that models various features like de-vice heterogeneity, task structure, variety of IoT connectivity protocols, system movement and agility, and battery functions. It also discusses the bottlenecks, test methods, and strategies, and their efficiency at no expense that will help to improve the reliability and performance of their proposed techniques.

MAIN FOCUS OF THE CHAPTER

Issues and Challenges in Cloud Computing:

Cloud computing (CC) is a computing technology paradigm that provides its customers with services on demand. Cloud computing's motive is to dynamically deliver processing, storage, and network services in distributed environments, connected to data centers, backhaul networks, and core networks (Zhang et al., 2010). It is an architecture that enables access to a common pool of configurable services correctly, pervasively, and on request. A large number of resources available in the central cloud can then be leveraged to deliver resource-constrained end devices with elastic computing capacity and storage capability. It has driven the rapid growth of many Internet enterprises (Bojanova & Samba, 2011). While cloud computing offers a large range of services, easy backup, and recovery, high usability as well as an environmentally safe ecosystem for consumers, it will not be able to fulfill the criteria of low latency and high-efficiency real-time applications because the central cloud is far from consumers. Some of the difficulties traditional cloud computing technology (Moghaddam et al., 2015) suffer from are,

1. **Bandwidth:** Through transferring vast volumes of data produced through edge devices to the cloud in real-time, the network bandwidth would be put under tremendous pressure. For example, a typical aircraft produces more than 5 GB

per second of data, but there's inadequate bandwidth between an aircraft and satellites to sustain real-time transmission.

2. **Latency:** In the case of IoT, innovative systems have high requirements in real-time. Applications send data to the data center in the conventional cloud computing model and elicit a response, which decreases device latency. For starters, autonomous high-speed driving vehicles require milliseconds of response time. Serious effects will arise if latency in the device crosses expectations due to network problems.

3. **Security and Privacy:** Security has a major impact on communication systems. Data on thousands of household devices are directly related to the lives of people. Data protection and privacy issues have become more relevant for cloud computing providers with the implementation of the EU General Data Protection Regulation (GDPR).

4. **Energy:** A lot of energy consumption is used in data centers. Due to the increase in numbers of machines and communications, energy usage may become an obstacle to the growth of cloud computing centers.

5. **Availability**: Since Internet systems are gradually being built on the cloud, the provision of these services has become an important part of daily life. Smartphone owners, for example, who are used to voice-based systems may be annoyed if the app is inaccessible for a limited period. So, keeping the 24x7 promise is a big challenge for cloud service providers.

Cloud computing is not adequate when low latency is necessary for devices running the Internet of Things (IoT). High network loads, traffic congestion, and cloud-based data processing will contribute to suffering from response times. For IoT applications, edge computing can solve cloud computing challenges. Edge computing increases the performance of the IoT environment by the delivery of low latency, low energy resources.

SOLUTIONS AND RECOMMENDATIONS

Edge Computing

Edge computing refers to enabling technologies to perform computing on the edge of the network, on the cloud-based downstream data, and the upstream IoT services. Thus, Edge can be described as any device and network services along the path between data sources and data centers in the cloud. A smartphone, for instance, is the edge between body things and the cloud, a portal in a smart home is the edge between home things and the cloud, a micro data center and a server (Liu et al.,

2019) is the edge between a mobile computer and server. The simple explanation for edge computing is that processing will take place close to the origins of data. Sometimes, edge computing can be interchanged with fog computing, but edge computing concentrates more on the dimension, whereas fog computing concentrates more on infrastructure. Figure 1 depicts how the data gets processed in the Edge computing platform.

Figure 1. Data processing in Edge computing

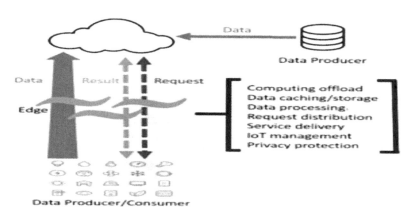

Edge Computing Architecture

Figure 2 shows the overview of general Edge computing architecture. The overall edge computing architecture consists of various nodes which makes them an important component.

1. **Device Edge** The devices at the edge, such as monitors, sensors, and other physical objects, capture or connect with edge data. They collect or send data, or both, through single edge tools. The more complex edge systems can conduct more tasks. In each case, the applications on these edge devices need to be deployed and managed (Liu et al., 2019). Different video processing, profound learning AI frameworks and basic real-time apps are examples of such technologies.

2. **Local Edge**: They are the systems running at the edge of the network or on the premises. The edge network layer and edge cluster or server may either be independent physical or virtual nodes or be merged in a hyper-converged device. This design framework comprises two main sublayers. There are all

elements of the structures required for such applications to be handled in certain levels of design and equipment on the edge of computers.

3. **Cloud** It is an infrastructure commonly named as the cloud that may be run on-site or in the public domain. This design layer includes workloads which are computing tasks that cannot be managed at the other edge nodes and the management levels. Workloads require server and network workloads and use the correct orchestration levels for running them at the different edge nodes.

Figure 2. General Architecture of Edge Computing platform

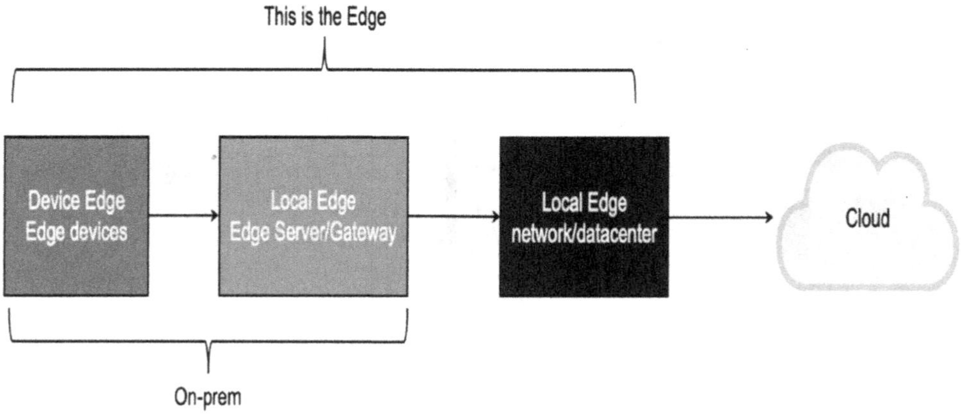

Detailed View of Edge Computing:

Figure 3 shows the components within each edge node which are significant. The key components are

1. **Edge cluster/server:** An edge cluster or server is a general-purpose IT machine situated in remote operating facilities such as a warehouse, store, hotel, or bank. An edge cluster or server is usually designed with a factor in the form of an industrial PC or a racked computer. Edge servers with 8, 16, or more cores of computing capacity, 16 GB of memory, and hundreds of GBs of local storage are commonly found. The edge cluster or server is usually used to perform workloads and shared resources for business applications.

2. **Edge gateway:** The Edge Gateway is usually an Edge Cluster or Server that offers services to perform network functions such as protocol transfer, network termination, tunneling, firewall protection, or wireless connection, in addition to application workloads and common services. While some edge devices can

act as a limited gateway or host network functions, edge gateways are most commonly isolated from the edge devices.

3. **Edge Devices:** Edge computing device is meant to perform particular functions and is fitted with the programmes needed to execute these activities. One example is the use of sensors to track temperature at the unit. In this case, a sensor that can fit into the palm of your hands gathers computer temperature data and transfers the data to a data centre or an IoT server. Businesses use edge devices in various capacities. Their uses are well known in industrial processes, but their applications reach beyond the production and service provision. The use of edge computing systems in rescue efforts is an example of that. A rescue robot is a edge computing device here that can be relocated and visual data gathered autonomously in locations that are hard to access. The data collected will then be moved to a wider visual screen for decision-making purposes.

4. **Edge Software:** The Edge software increases the portability of software on edge platforms and facilitates growth and operating progress process. Sensor connections, edge hardware, and cloud connection are abstracted to provide a common API, which enables application development on the edge without the awareness of hardware resources. The applications created using the API can be implemented on different sensors and edge devices to improve applications' portability. Figure 4 shows the hardware abstraction by Edge software.

Figure 3. Edge Computing components

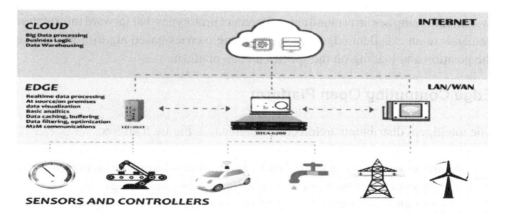

Figure 4. Hardware abstraction by Edge Software

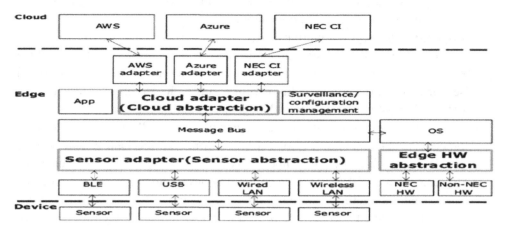

Content Caching at the Edge

Reducing backhaul, latency and growing performance consistency (QoS) are strong reasons to drive web aggregation and network security. A caching system may be as basic as a fundamental reverse-proxy or as complicated as an entire software stack that not only caches content but provides additional features, such as video transcoding using the client profile of user equipment (UE), position, and bandwidth accessible. Edge networks will use the proximity and the device load, as well as other parameters for deciding which edge data center can hold payloads to the ends. Caching networks will be used in edge settings (Tang et al., 2019). Smart caching systems are using a central cloud agent for recent prototypes that forward information demands to an excellent edge data center using metrics-based algorithms, such as the position and loading on the specified edge platform.

Edge Computing Open Platform

The intelligent distributed architecture as shown in Figure 5 allows:

1. **Smart assets:** provide flexibility and teamwork through the incorporation of ICT technologies, such as network, computation, and storage.
2. **Smart gateways:** connect the physical and digital realms with functions like network connections and transfer protocols, provide fast communication control, data processing in real-time, and device management.
3. **Smart networks**: they are based on multiple mobile gateways or cloud partnerships and have an elastic network, processing, and storage capability.

4.   **Smart Services:** include the technology service structure and the management and operational service framework, based on a single model service architecture with a range of roles including the network and maintenance staff, corporate decision-makers, systemic integrators, and program developers.

Figure 5. Intelligent Distributed Architecture based on Edge computing platform

INTEGRATION OF IoT TECHNOLOGIES

IoT includes data collection along with the cloud technology Cloud providers are typically implemented throughout the main network throughout broad data centers. With a modest response time, the Core Cloud provides a strong processing capability, which satisfies the needs of distributed and intermittent providers. However, it is not a flexible long-term approach, in particular, because IoT system volume and data are supposed to burst, to collect information, and place it in a central cloud network (Mao et al., 2017). The IoT analytics deployment between the core cloud and the edge of the network (Ex first analyses on the edge of the cloud and big data processing on the core cloud) is a robust and effective solution both at the network and application level. To order to deliver IoT analytics effectively and leverage network resources, transport network controls must be built into the dispersed edge and cloud infrastructure, so that complex, effective IoT applications can be implemented.

Figure 6 demonstrates the Software-Defined Networking (SDN) and cloud infrastructure for multi-layer, IoT-aware transport. It comprises multiple packets and optical transport domains, which provide links to core-DCs as well as micro and small-DCs (on the edge of the network called edge nodes). IoT Flow Monitors (IoT-FM) are implemented on the edge of packet network domains. IoT-FMs are in charge of tracking aggregate IoT traffic's maximum bandwidth.

Figure 6. Integration of various networks

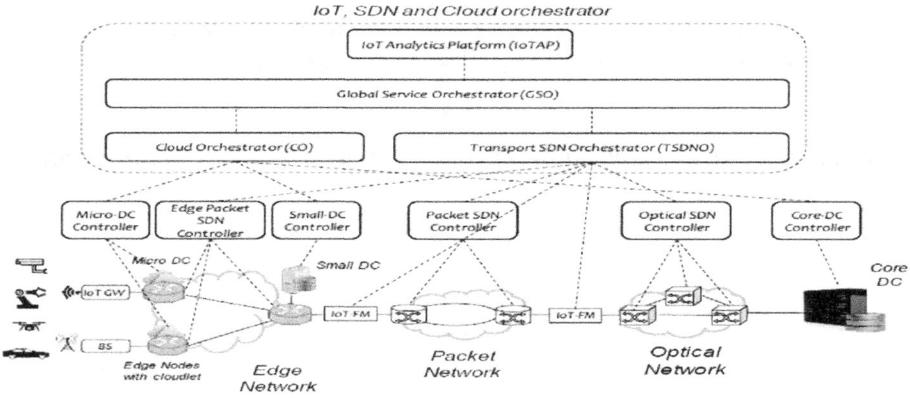

Edge Computing Technologies

There are few edge computing technologies in the IoT, such as Mobile Edge Computing (MEC), Fog computing, Cloudlets, Mobile Edge computing, Microdata centers, and a new concept called Cloud of Things.

1.   Mobile Edge Computing

MEC incorporates information management and Cloud computing functionality within a mobile access network, which has become a standard. MEC is a modern network model. In its 2014 proposal to standardize MEC, European Telecommunications Standards Institute (ETSI) suggested that MEC provide a new ecosystem and value chain, which can use MEC to move the Mobile unit to nearby nodes for intensive calculation tasks. As the MEC is within the Radio Access Network (RAN) and similar to Mobile Users (the RAN), it has the capacity to increase service quality (QoS) and quality of experience (QoE) by lower latency. The MEC also has additional bandwidth. MEC is also a major 5G development technology (Mao et al., 2017) that contributes to meeting high 5G delay, programming, and scalability standards.

MEC can not only reduce the congestion but also effectively respond to user requests by integrating services and caching on the outskirts of the network. Edge computing (EC) is the term that is most similar to MEC. The EC refers to a modern processing mode at the edge of the network. Cloud services are represented by the edge data in the EC and interconnection service is the upstream data. The edge of the EC applies to any network measurement and boundary from the data source into the CC hub. The MEC emphasizes that the Edge Server (ES) between the Cloud computing center and the edge device is responsible for calculating MU data on the ESs, but that the MU is not computing able in the main. The Mobile User (MU) has a high computational potential in the EC model, by comparison. The MEC should therefore be considered as part of the EC scheme. The key cases in the MEC, i.e. device uploading, were checked by the customer. In specific, three sub-issues were discussed in the device offloading study: decision-making, allocating capital, and control of mobility.

Figure 7. Mobile Edge Computing Architecture

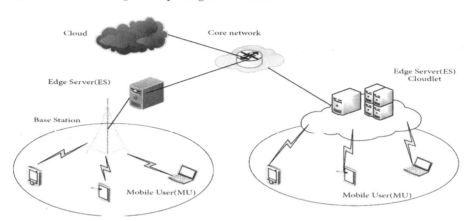

The MEC architecture as illustrated in Figure 7 can be seen as the mid-range between MUs and cloud that is closer to MUs and provides services for MUs. Therefore, it is an autonomous system with two layers made up of MUs and ESs. MU applies commonly to handheld computers, phones, laptops, etc. ES often typically applies to the base station in conjunction with the server or cloudlet. MUs offload ES computing tasks, which allow MUs not only to run apps effectively but also to reduce latency due to public cloud access.

2.   Fog Computing

Fog computing is a term used to describe a decentralized computing infrastructure or just a "fogging." This extends cloud infrastructure to the edge of a network while at the same time putting the most rational and productive files, processing, storage, and applications. This location takes place between the cloud and the source of the data, often called "out in the fog". The edge devices are connected to the cloud as seen in Figure 8 below called "fog nodes." Such nodes are fog computing systems

Figure 8. Fog computing architecture

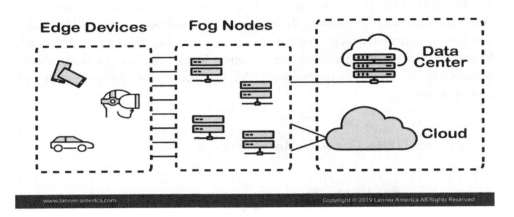

that have the capability for processing and sensing. The purpose of fog computing is to extend both cloud computing and network-level service and to reduce the data transported to the cloud for processing, analysis, and storage (Naha et al., 2018).

As shown in Figure 8, Fog computing fills the distance between the server and end-users, i.e. the IoT nodes, by enabler of network nodes near IoT devices processors, storage, network, and data processing. As a consequence, not just in the cloud, but also in the IoT-to-Cloud route is processing, saving, networking, evaluating, and handling data while moving over to the cloud (preferably closer IoT). In Intelligent Transport Systems (ITS), for example, GPS data can be compressed at the edge before being transmitted to the cloud. OpenFog Consortium (2017) describes Fog Computing as "the device level horizontal architecture delivering computation, storage, control and networking to the user in a cloud-to-all spectrum." Fog computing functions are spread across networks and industry by the "horizontal" model in the field of Fog Computing, while the vertical model supports Siloes.

A vertical framework can offer good support of one application category (silo), but may not take the user of device contact with other vertically oriented applications with consideration. Fog computation offers a scalable medium to satisfy the data-driven needs of operators and consumers, as well as enabling horizontal architecture. Fog computing is planned for the Internet of Things to be embraced firmly. In cloud computing, computational services are accessible at a fairly large energy usage while in fog computing, computing resources are available at a modest amount with small energy consumption (Jalali et al., 2016). The cloud uses huge storage facilities, while the fog uses tiny computers, switches, gateways, set-top boxes, or connection points. Cloud infrastructure usually requires tiny data centers. Since fog computing hardware has far fewer room than cloud computing hardware, it is more user friendly.

Connected devices from the network's edge to the network center will use Fog computing, while the network center needs cloud computing. In fact, continuing Internet access is not necessary for the operation of fog networks. This implies, programs can operate individually with minimal to no Internet access and, if the link is accessible, they can submit required notifications to the cloud. On the other hand, cloud-based computing requires the connection of devices in advance of the cloud service. Fog assists devices in the measurement, monitoring, processing, analysis, and reaction, and distributing IoT device computation, communication, storage, monitoring, and decision-making (Fatemeh et al., 2016). To their benefits, several companies may exploit fog: electricity, manufacturing, transport, education, intelligent cities, to name a few.

3.   Cloudlets

Cloudlets are tiny cloud data centers at the edge of a network that are strengthened by versatility (Satyanarayanan et al., 2009). These form the second level of the hierarchy with three levels as shown in Figure 8: the IoT or edge network, Cloudlet, and Edge. Cloudlets are intended to boost smartphone applications that are resource-intensive and responsive, by offering more powerful computational services with less delay close to mobile devices. Thus, the latency delays commonly associated with WAN cloud computing can be avoided. Cloudlets will offer the required assistance to 5G networks upon their launch. To achieve the highest possible level in the network coverage, they also need to be decentralized and broadly dispersed, thus helping to leverage resources from close mobile computers. Cloudlet architecture is shown in Figure 9.

Figure 9. Cloudlet Architecture

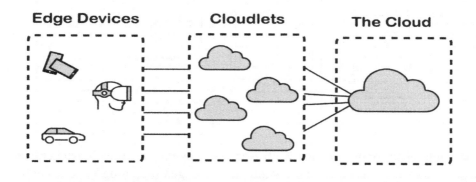

Network service owners (e.g. AT&T, Nokia, etc.) may authorize virtualized databases to be similar to their Personal devices with fewer equipment compared with large cloud data centers. The limited scale of the clouds results in less storage, resulting also lower latency and energy usage than in cloud computing. The aim of Cloudlet computing is to support local devices. Even like Mobile Adhoc Cloud Computing (MACC) varies greatly from cloud computing, it often varies drastically from desktop storage. Cloudlet requires virtualization technology in VM, while such architecture is not a prerequisite for MACC (Yousefpour et al., 2018).

4.   Multi-Access Edge Computing

Multi-Access Edge Computing is a networking architecture that allows the placement of Radio Access Network (RAN) computing and storage resources. The Multi-Access Edge Computing increases network performance and provides consumers with content (Taleb et al., 2017). To this end, it can be adjusted to the radio load to increase network performance and reduce the need for backhauling over long distances. The enhanced location, augmented reality, and the Internet of Things capabilities could be supported by mobile edge computing too. It offers these businesses a lead time until 5G networks continue to grow and respond to new technology (Mach & Becvar, 2017).

Figure 10. Multi-Access Edge Computing reference architecture

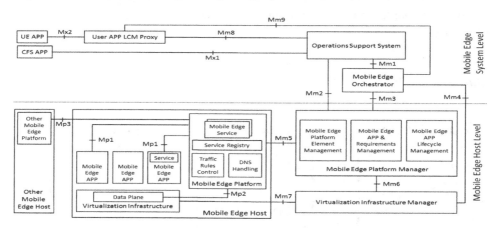

The reference architecture for Multi-Access Computing Edge is shown in Figure 10, provides a clear overview of the Multi-Access Edge Computing System features and interfaces (Taleb et al., 2017). The Reference Architecture for Multi-Access

Edge Computing focuses on the level of mobile edge systems and the level of mobile edge house excluding networks. The host stage for the mobile edges is the network operator, the manager of the mobile edge framework, and the manager of the virtualization infrastructure. The Mobile Edge Host supports applications (APPs), which offer an infrastructure of virtualization that offers computing, storage, and network resources and a set of fundamental functions (mobile edge services) that are needed for mobile edge platform APPs. The mobile edge network helps apps to find, publicize, and access edge resources and provides a set of guidelines for forwarding aircraft to the virtualization system. Such communication law is focused on suggestions provided by the managers of network edge and cell networks. The mobile edge platform configures the local DSS management system that enables user traffic to access the desired mobile edge app and communicates with other peer platforms via the Mp3 interface.

Multi-access edge computing expands edge computing by connecting close low energy, low-resource handheld devices with computers, and storage space. RAN operators may connect edge computing capabilities to established base stations with a Multi-Access Edge Computing device. Small-scale virtualization power data centers may also be similarly found in multi-access cloud computing as edge computing (Taleb et al., 2017). The computing resources are moderate compared to cloud computing because of the hardware underlying MEC and edge computing.

Nevertheless, multi-access edge computing offers connectivity through WAN, DHCP, and cellular networks, while edge computing may typically decide any type of communication. MCC analysis often focuses primarily on the partnerships between Internet customers (on mobile devices) and cloud service providers, while Multi-Access Edge Computing research focuses on (RAN-based) connectivity providers. In MCC, multi-access edge computing focuses on network technology. The upcoming 5 G platform is expected to greatly benefit MEC. 5G is similarly used as an enabler for multi-access tops since it provides reduced latency and greater network app capacity and a wide variety of finest granular connected applications. MEC facilitates the use of edge computing for a wide spectrum of latency, connected computers, and more effective data core networks. MEC often requires mobile network applications that are prone to crucial delays.

5.   MicroData Centers

With the rise of the Internet of Things already encouraging the production of new smart devices and IoT sensors, a business study predicts that within the next two and half years the Microdata center solution sector could be worth an astounding 32 billion dollars. Microdata centers are expected to be more useful for small to medium-sized enterprises that do not have their own data centers, since big businesses tend to have more capital and do not require these solutions. The Microdata centers have all the core components of a conventional data center. For some edge computing applications, micro data centers, although usually much smaller for scale, are far more suited than large data centers. The size means that both within and outside conditions the microdata center can be deployed. This makes them perfect for edge computers as they can be locally distributed where the database is located and can be customized to the needs of those who wish to implement it.

6.   Cloud of Things

In a Cloud of Things (CoT), the extreme edge, the final user, takes away all processing power. While the computing power of IoT devices is still small, many modern mobiles have a high potential (Wang et al., 2018). It may be coordinated to run a cloud service on the edge. For example, a car might send warning signals to others and attempt to rearrange other routes without the user's feedback. Cloud infrastructure may be delivered at the very edge using mobile devices or IoT systems. A term related to fog computing is The Cloud of Things. A CoT is a virtualized cloud network that is used in all IoT devices.

Cloud of Things, though, is measured using the cloud created by pooled IoT sources. Edge nodes are used for identifying, virtualizing, and creating an IoT Tools (CoT) application network as near agents on the ground. Its network is an architecture that has been dispersed globally and application agents continuously discover IoT system services and pool them as server tools. CoT enables remote sensing and centralized data collection inside the network. The CoT framework can be scale-based to IoT networks, enables IoT device heterogeneity and edge computing nodes to be used, and offers a foundation for fog sensing.

Like CoT, there is a concept of PClouds (Jang et al., 2014), which are distributed as networks, both locally / personally and remotely / publicly and in machines. If remote cloud services are unavailable or hard to reach due to poor network coverage PCloud will support end-users. Cloudrone, the concept of utilizing low-cost aircraft, single-board machines, and light-weight OS systems to install ad-hoc micro-cloud infrastructures in the sky is another innovative idea, close in design to Cloud of stuff and MACCs. The drones create a cloud storage cluster in the sky that delivers the cloud resources close to the customer, often without terrestrial web connectivity networks.

Femtoclouds were also introduced to use the calculative capabilities and overall ness of under-utilized cell apps, analogous to the idea of Cloud of Things. Clusters of devices tend to be located in places such as schools, public transport, or centers, are utilized by Femtoclouds. In (Habak et al., 2017) for the control of resources and activities in Femtoclouds, a hybrid edge-cloud architecture is introduced, which will allow a low latency.

Resource Management in Edge Computing

Network services are installed on distributed cloud servers to enhance network consistency (Service quality, QoS) and gain unlimited capital. These servers will often also host data centers situated in various locations for service distribution. In the next 2020, though, the expected network interface volume would be 25 billion in the future. The networking infrastructure for the mobile network is progressed by growing the number of internet subscribers and rising the use of cellular broadband. This involves video sharing applications and software connected to computer gaming. When the Internet of Things arises, the program gathers and transfers a ton of data to the cloud. Such heavy traffic burdens the core network and QoS would impact the delivery of enhanced transmission services by the service suppliers.

Despite the rising competition in the future, telecoms service providers also face the task of providing customer access faster and growing network delivery delays. Edge Computing is a way to decentralize certain processing power into a leading network and discharge the network into the edge network so that it can spread the load on the server. Although IT companies have various edge computing concepts, edge computing may be embedded in the cloud environment. The edge network will be responsible for managing loads of data pre-processing to enable the quickest infrastructure and the application that demands a significant number of computational power or the remote storage has to be managed by the cloud. The fusion of cloud and boundary has become a phenomenon owing to the challenges of cloud computing and the benefits of edge computing. However, edge computing is less powerful than the server. Consequently, edge network resource control is a significant problem (López et al., 2015).

Three problems should be addressed. First, how edge nodes can be used for tasks (Richard & Dimitrios, 2017). The technology is commonly known as a virtual machine (VM) in the cloud computing, but the usage of a virtual computer and software upgrades is a concern for late-sensing edge networks. Second, how many cloud resources the edge node needs. It is possible to install such broad network networks with a ton of computing resources in the cloud, but a big network infrastructure with high bandwidth may be challenging at the end of the network. The extension of the infrastructure is a fatal blow to the limited-resource network. Thirdly, how edge node resources are managed. The usage of resources in the edge node is dynamically updated. The edge band node is likely to use constraints on size because of its restricted resources relative to the cloud with infinite resources.

Each service has an importance and is often taken into consideration through the allocation of resources to prioritize the service.

Key Benefits of Edge Computing

Many new IoT technologies may depend on cutting edge computing, such as autonomous cars, drones, or smart grids Some of the benefits found by IoT edge computing include (Shi et al., 2016):

1. **Low latency:** The edge of the IoT system is by its definition closer to the heart of the server. This ensures a faster round trip to meet local computing capacity which accelerates network transmission which data collection dramatically.
2. **Resilience**: The edge has more connectivity possibilities than a clustered layout. The stability of data transmission is ensured by this delivery. In case of an interruption at the bottom, appropriate tools to ensure continuous service are available.
3. **Longer battery life for IoT devices:** By being able to use better latency to access communication networks for shorter periods, battery life of driven IoT devices may be enhanced. Distributed ledger or a modified open-source ledger execution such as BigchainDB may be used for gaining from a distributed ledger that offers functionality from the MongoDB NoSQL database on which it is centered.
4. **Scalability:** As communication with the edge model is decentralized, less load can be applied to the network in the end. In particular, when the application and control airplane is situated on the edge next to the results, scaling IoT devices will have less resource effect on the network
5. **Access to data analytics and AI:** The capacity of edge computing, data collection, and analysis and AIs, which allow very fast response times to handle massive 'real-time' data sets that can't be submitted to centralized networks, can all be integrated.
6. **Efficient data management:** The edge data processing enhances easy control of data content, such as extraction and prioritization. When the data storage is performed at the bottom, simpler data sets may be provided for more review for cloud-based computing.

Use Cases of Edge Computing in IoT

1. Device Management:

There are several system characteristics and settings that can be managed at the edge, with many application management systems expanding their capabilities to handle devices connecting to edge networks (Li et al., 2018). Below are descriptions of four specific characteristics that system control at the edge would need to support:

a. Device configuration updates: Edge systems must be set up locally when networks improve. When networks shift. This can be controlled remotely from the ground.

b. Distributed firmware updates: the usage of the edge gateway to locally deliver software changes, through the edge node control application, relative to the method that usually deals with the delivery of a firmware update centrally.

c. Edge node or gateway management: device management systems may be used to handle the operator 's edge network as well as the IoT system.

d. Diagnostics of devices: Using edge analytics, deep learning, or pattern detection may aid in detecting particular issues with field tools.

   2.   Security:

The IoT itself is a centralized, dynamic computer network. For successful IoT service, edge computing brings most of the logic and data storage closer to end-users and the edge deployment of protection systems often presents the ability to expand security capacities, as well as to provide native security for modern applications with low latency.

In data protection, the edge has a big role to play. Many specialized tools and strategies can be deployed to make sure the edge contributes to the overall IoT delivery efficiency (Ni et al., 2017). The IoT edge protection will be handled in the same manner as every other protected setting, but modern technologies are available which can guarantee security at different edge and system rates. For example, with good ID management for devices on the edge, the security becomes simpler and the concept of edge processes rigorously to ensure that they stay protected.

3.   Priority Messaging:

Most of the IoT data is low in importance – irregular status changes and low priority data. However, other details would be very critical and attention will be provided to ensuring that action is taken rapidly. The essential data is possibly quite small but is the most significant percentage of the overall volume generated. To facilitate a cascade of acts through multiple platforms and computers, the reach of the priority messages extends beyond just specific applications (Grewe et al., 2017). The edge helps the production, storage, processing, and execution of high-value data rather than transferring the data to the cloud.

As part of the overall architecture of IoT devices, networks, and data processing facilities, priority communications would need to be addressed. Various forms of priority communication are open. Priority communications, for example, a fire alarm, are mainly in the established format as a contribution from a known procedure. Often, the message cannot be recognized by the system as a high priority, but it may also be detected through processing at the bottom. For example, voltage variations in a smart grid that allow data collection from multiple devices to prioritize. IoT edge is allowed for high-priority communications and more behavior. Faster answers can only be ensured by interacting with local IoT windows, clouds, and preserving the effect of local priority messages.

For more distribution and decision-making, details that have a greater influence outside the local region will, for instance, be uploaded to the central cloud for feeding into bigger databases for computational purposes, instantly or after addressing local scenarios. For fast transmission of high-priority messages, data processing is needed in near-real-time. As tagged data is obtained, if the appropriate classifications are established inside edge gateway programs, then it can quickly be detected and prioritized. Further, sorting may be used for the detection of data from many applications and computers to allow for the same priority. The program on the edge of the gateway or node will determine automatedly what to do about a high-priority message. It could well be necessary for established data types from known applications or devices to start a pre-defined procedure.

4.   Data Aggregation:

Related data will overload a network if transmitted at once, e.g. if each intelligent meter sends a message concurrently with a power failure. In such situations, the function of the application running on top is to recognize and aggregate a few related messages (Lu et al., 2017). This can be achieved in a variety of ways:

a.   Aggregated data generation: If a new edge node receives several messages within a brief period of time, such messages may be inserted and the original messages replaced. If several messages are sent, the edge does not submit any messages or info. There is also a new dataset that analyses the obtained results. It will provide a summary of all incoming communications, likely daily alerts until a shift in status happens.

b.   Sampling: A second choice is to perform sampling of systems. If a significant number of identical messages are sent, the edge may opt to only track a handful of affected units, rather than the entire fleet before the status of these shifts. When vehicles enter traffic queues, data can only be taken from each tenth car before they start moving again instead of getting status reports from an automobile in the crowd.

5.   Cloud Enablement:

It is anticipated that the edge would be desirable for cloud companies as it provides them with the opportunity to efficiently manage data loading and computing capacity to help low-latency applications, increase the efficiency of infrastructure and minimize the burden at their current data centers (Yousefpour et al., 2018). There will be a mutually profitable partnership between cloud providers and mobile operators where operators provide local ability to encourage cloud providers to use IoT edges, and cloud providers provide networks to deliver a wide spectrum of services on the operator's leading network. Some IoT consumers, whether factories or smart cities, may also insist on local storage and management of their results.

IoT edge systems never run entirely independently from a business point of view. For power, tracking, and upgrading purposes at the very least, a link to a centralized server is always important, and hence the relationship between edges and servers is complex. The great thing for both realms is a mixed edge and cloud design.

APPLICATION OF EDGE COMPUTING IN SMART AGRICULTURE

Edge computing has now started to label a number of sectors around the world. There seem to be few areas in which the presence of any sort of edge computing can't be sensed from processing and logistics to healthcare and retail. Farming and Agriculture are one of the fields in which edge computing continues to change the landscape (Li et al., 2020).

1.   **Environmental Monitoring:**

The ability to track various facets of agricultural activities from a farmer is one of the main benefits of Edge computing on agriculture and farming in the last couple of years. Sensor networks that range from several intermittent sensors to thousands of integrated instruments measuring soil, wind, humidity and temperature conditions and acidity and pH levels. Edge computing makes it possible to produce and capture data nearer to source in order to provide these applications while still allowing some data processing operations in the edge devices themselves to be carried out.

2.   **Automation:**

In the fourth industrial revolution, the use of virtualization, robotics, and big data have become main factors and robotics is therefore no longer playing a growing role in so many intelligent farming and agricultural enterprises. As stated, autonomous robot systems can all be used with the use of edge computing and automation systems as well as injections of soil, heaters and lighting. Automation will become a valuable tool for farmers in combination with numerous remote-control apps and tools now provided to smart farms and farmers.

3.   **Vertical Farming:**

Vertical Farming requires the use of data from an IoT sensor and computer network to maximise food and plant production without cultivating soils. In vertical farms, for example, a network of sensors tracks humidity levels continuously around the plant (O'Grady et al., 2019). Most of the analysis of data involved in such tasks, using edge computing, can be performed on the edge devices without needing to be sent to the cloud and thereby contribute more to the importance of such systems in the agricultural environment.

4.   **Robotics:**

Robotics has been an integral part of many industries for decades now, but automotive production, for instance, is also steadily gaining momentum elsewhere. This is no longer the case with the help of edge computing and IoT computer networks. Within agriculture, the introduction of smart farming technologies has enabled the use of sophisticated edge computing devices and the Internet of Things (IoT) programmes. These devices may be planned for automatic tasks such as plant picking and spraying plants and seeds, and further implementations are under development.

CHALLENGES IN EDGE COMPUTING

1.   **Accessibility and Resource constraints:** Sometimes, Edge technologies face technical challenges to handle human IT resources and do not permit large user costs. In order to track and manage any Edge spot, businesses should provide the dedicated admin. This operator constraints – due to size, system scale, geographical connectivity and other costs/ROI requirements, Edge implementations are obliged to be very low not only on the machine footprint but also in terms of overhead technological IT. They must be "plug & play" from the perspective of installation and continued operation (Shi et al., 2016).

2. **Compute and hardware constraints:** From the point of view of technical computing, many edge environments are limited. For example, it is difficult accommodate as much hardware as a full-scale data center in the case of embedded devices.

3. **Connectivity:** The infrastructure provider's capacity to cope with latency and jitter problems of all kinds is also important.

4. **Remote management:** Skilled workers cannot routinely install and maintain the system in certain settings. An unqualified operator can have to make easy deployments for plugs and play. This covers stable edge technology upgrades, debug-ability for bugs and extra system implementation (Shi et al., 2016). Edge systems need to be extremely specialised and should provide a variety of capabilities to provide: network cache with missing links, data stream processing, appropriate data analysis, event-based message broking, system control, fault tolerance, etc.

5. **Security:** This is a critical problem. This involves protected communication between the data centre and Edge to protect data protection, whether in rest or in movement – anonymization of Edge-specified confidential consumer data. Other specifications for safety include mutual trust between the central data center and Edge devices, the ability to find and avoid rogue devices while attacking and secure communication via the WAN.

6. **Support for Air-gapped deployments**: A crucial advantage of edge computing is the ability to handle distant, air-locked devices of compute-controlled locations without the need for manual interference (Shi et al., 2016). Strong cloud latency can lead to delays and can interfere with the application's service. This also implies that expectations from the "Standard operating mode" of networking in data centers frequently tend to be valid in edge environments.

DISCUSSION

Since cloud, fog, and edge computing are designed and each is established to transcend those limits in the preceding paradigm, some of its properties are identical. The variations and needs, however, identify each model and promote the resources and applications that are expected. The design differs, but they both have the same goal of supplying devices and data. Any non-functional specifications accomplish the features of these paradigms. In terms of model protection, this can be extended in cloud computing to the service provider or framework created The first is the application creator, like configuration and control of the device, from the viewpoint of a SaaS vendor, is a manufacturer, is subject to protection controls of providers such as the network separation protocols or physical infrastructure access policies. This means that the contractor is liable for designing the software that monitors the utilization and frequency of the program. On the other side, fog computing privacy is maintained by minimizing data transmission across the network and managing data locally, thus decreasing protection vulnerabilities and growing data privacy.

Data was stored globally but closer to the device for the edge network than fog computing, to help ensure privacy. The bandwidth and reaction time metrics have proved their leading both in terms of efficiency and in terms of fog paradigms. To obtain smaller data parts that enable the achievement of low end-to-end latency, large bandwidth, and low jitter operation, Edge computing nodes have to be near to the end devices (Yousefpour et al., 2018). In comparison, fewer data in the fog computing network are transported to the data centers: local data pre-processing, and direct communication with wired computer queries that minimize the bandwidth required. Although latency is even better in cloud storage, data is still sent to the cloud and the cloud addiction is very high. But customers demand a fast operating system for cloud storage with SaaS applications. The theoretical performance constraint during design must also be taken into account and projects that utilize principles such as distributed execution, the architecture of microsystems, the functionality of multi-data, and more must be incorporated. Besides, flexibility is highly essential as SaaS models manage vital business solutions. Unforeseen downtime can lead to losses of SaaS clients, so the plan doesn't go wrong. Factors contributing to the Recovery Tune Objective (RTO) and the Recovery Point Objective (RPO) need to be taken into account.

Some other popular aspects of fog and edge computing endorse complexity as the nodes may be multiple types without a defined norm. This is extremely relevant as numerous products from different manufacturers and vendors should be associated with the recent production of IoT. Their storage and measuring output vary from the end devices and the fog or edge nodes. In contrast with cloud networks, the edge and fog nodes are significantly less computable and maintained. In addition, terminal machines and fog nodes can dynamically switch and connect to promote IoT system computing functionality. Location perception in fog-based models is another key aspect because end devices need sensing and positioning capacity to decide where the data needs to be processed. In fact, it will allow it easy to pre-process, search, and store in multiple ways, and often helps minimize latency. The existence of the design restricts this property in cloud computing (Yuyi Mao et al., 2017).

CONCLUSION

The IoT is a combination of infrastructure, applications, and networking capabilities. The development of IoT implementations both in customers and industrial use cases would result in innovations and IoT products. For an efficient and integrated IoT approach, edge computing is necessary. In the IoT domain, there are various open-source platforms. Cloud service providers provide very rich IoT and edge computing capabilities. IoT software requirements include loosely linked flexible, platform-independent, and open standards-based guidance. This paper focusses on the general architecture for the Edge computing paradigm and various components involved in the platform. The integration of various Edge technologies to provide an efficient IoT system is also discussed. Now that many businesses and development providers shifting towards the Edge environment, new architectures, a different ecosystem, and a different kind of latency constraint may emerge as a need for distributed applications.

REFERENCES

Ai, Y., Peng, M., & Zhang, K. (2017). Edge cloud computing technologies for Internet of things: A primer. *Digital Communications and Networks*, *4*(2), 77–86. doi:10.1016/j.dcan.2017.07.001

Asim, M., Wang, Y., Wang, K., & Huang, P. (2020). *A Review on Computational Intelligence Techniques in Cloud and Edge Computing.* ArXiv, abs/2007.14215.

Baktir, A. C., Sonmez, C., Ersoy, C., Ozgovde, A., & Varghese, B. (2019). *Addressing the Challenges in Federating Edge Resources.* Fog and Edge Computing. doi:10.1002/9781119525080.ch2

Bojanova, I., & Samba, A. (2011). Analysis of Cloud Computing Delivery Architecture Models. *2011 IEEE Workshops of International Conference on Advanced Information Networking and Applications*, 453-458.

Cziva, R., & Pezaros, D. P. (2017, June). Container Network Functions: Bringing NFV to the Network Edge. *IEEE Communications Magazine*, *55*(6), 24–31. doi:10.1109/MCOM.2017.1601039

Fatemeh, T., Samdanis, K., Mada, B., Flinck, H., Dutta, S., & Sabella, D. (2017). On Multi-Access Edge Computing: A Survey of the Emerging 5G Network Edge Cloud Architecture and Orchestration. *IEEE Communications Surveys and Tutorials*, *19*(3), 1657–1681. doi:10.1109/COMST.2017.2705720

Ganz, F., Puschmann, D., Barnaghi, P. M., & Carrez, F. (2015). A Practical Evaluation of Information Processing and Abstraction Techniques for the Internet of Things. *IEEE Internet of Things Journal*, 2(4), 340–354. doi:10.1109/JIOT.2015.2411227

Grewe, D., Wagner, M., Arumaithurai, M., Psaras, I., & Kutscher, D. (2017). Information-Centric Mobile Edge Computing for Connected Vehicle Environments: Challenges and Research Directions. *Proceedings of the Workshop on Mobile Edge Communication*, 7-12. 10.1145/3098208.3098210

Gubbi, J., Buyya, R., Marusic, S., & Palaniswami, M. (2013). Internet of Things (IoT): A vision, architectural elements, and future directions. *Future Generation Computer Systems*, 29(7), 1645–1660. doi:10.1016/j.future.2013.01.010

Habak, K., Zegura, E., Ammar, M., & Harras, K. A. (2017). Workload management for dynamic mobile device clusters in edge Femtoclouds. *Proceedings of the Second ACM/IEEE Symposium on Edge Computing*, 1-14. 10.1145/3132211.3134455

Hong, C., & Varghese, B. (2019). Resource Management in Fog/Edge Computing: A Survey on Architectures, Infrastructure, and Algorithms. *ACM Comput. Surv.*, 52, 97:1-97:37.

Jalali, F., Hinton, K., Ayre, R., Alpcan, T., & Tucker, R. (2016). Fog Computing May Help to Save Energy in Cloud Computing. *IEEE Journal on Selected Areas in Communications*, 34(5), 1728–1739. doi:10.1109/JSAC.2016.2545559

Jang, M., Schwan, K., Bhardwaj, K., Gavrilovska, A., & Avasthi, A. (2014). Personal clouds: Sharing and integrating networked resources to enhance end-user experiences. *IEEE INFOCOM 2014 - IEEE Conference on Computer Communications*, 2220-2228.

Jha, D. N., Alwasel, K., Alshoshan, A., Huang, X., Naha, R. K., Battula, S. K., Garg, S., Puthal, D., James, P., Zomaya, A. Y., Dustdar, S., & Ranjan, R. (2020). IoTSim-Edge: A simulation framework for modeling the behavior of Internet of Things and edge computing environments. *Software, Practice & Experience*, 50(6), 844–867. doi:10.1002pe.2787

Li, C., Xue, Y., Wang, J., Zhang, W., & Li, T. (2018, April). Edge-oriented computing paradigms: A survey on architecture design and system management. *ACM Computing Surveys*, 51(2), 1–34. doi:10.1145/3154815

Li, X., Zhu, L., Chu, X., & Fu, H. (2020). Edge Computing-Enabled Wireless Sensor Networks for Multiple Data Collection Tasks in Smart Agriculture. *J. Sensors, 2020*, 4398061:1-4398061:9.

López, P., Montresor, A., Epema, D., Datta, A., Higashino, T., Iamnitchi, A., Barcellos, M. P., Felber, P., & Rivière, E. (2015). Edge-centric Computing: Vision and Challenges. *Computer Communication Review*, *45*(5), 37–42. doi:10.1145/2831347.2831354

Lu, R., Heung, K., Lashkari, A., & Ghorbani, A. (2017). A Lightweight Privacy-Preserving Data Aggregation Scheme for Fog Computing-Enhanced IoT. *IEEE Access: Practical Innovations, Open Solutions*, *5*, 3302–3312. doi:10.1109/ACCESS.2017.2677520

Mach, P., & Becvar, Z. (2017). Mobile Edge Computing: A Survey on Architecture and Computation Offloading. *IEEE Communications Surveys and Tutorials*, *19*(3), 1628–1656. doi:10.1109/COMST.2017.2682318

Mao, Y., You, C., Zhang, J., Huang, K., & Letaief, K. (2017). A Survey on Mobile Edge Computing: The Communication Perspective. *IEEE Communications Surveys and Tutorials*, *19*(4), 2322–2358. doi:10.1109/COMST.2017.2745201

Mirkhanzadeh, B., Shakeri, A., Shao, C., Razo, M., Tacca, M., Galimberti, G., Martinelli, G., Cardani, M., & Fumagalli, A. (2018). An SDN-enabled multi-layer protection and restoration mechanism. *Optical Switching and Networking*, *30*, 23–32. doi:10.1016/j.osn.2018.05.005

Moghaddam, F. F., Ahmadi, M., Sarvari, S., Eslami, M., & Golkar, A. (2015). Cloud computing challenges and opportunities: A survey. *2015 1st International Conference on Telematics and Future Generation Networks (TAFGEN)*, 34-38.

Naha, R. K., Garg, S., Georgakopoulos, D., Jayaraman, P., Gao, L., Xiang, Y., & Ranjan, R. (2018). Fog computing: Survey of trends, architectures, requirements, and research directions. *IEEE Access: Practical Innovations, Open Solutions*, *6*(47), 980–009. doi:10.1109/ACCESS.2018.2866491

Ni, J., Zhang, A., Lin, X., & Shen, X. (2017). Security, Privacy, and Fairness in Fog-Based Vehicular Crowdsensing. *IEEE Communications Magazine*, *55*(6), 146–152. doi:10.1109/MCOM.2017.1600679

O'Grady, M., Langton, D., & O'Hare, G. (2019). *Edge computing: A tractable model for smart agriculture?* Academic Press.

OpenFogConsortium. (2017). *Openfog reference architecture for fog computing*. https://www.openfogconsortium.org/ra/

Premsankar, G., Francesco, M. D., & Taleb, T. (2018). Edge Computing for the Internet of Things: A Case Study. *IEEE Internet of Things Journal*, *5*(2), 1275–1284. doi:10.1109/JIOT.2018.2805263

Satyanarayanan, M., Bahl, P., Cáceres, R., & Davies, N. (2009). The Case for VM-Based Cloudlets in Mobile Computing. *IEEE Pervasive Computing*, *8*(4), 14–23. doi:10.1109/MPRV.2009.82

Shi, F., Tang, G., Li, Y., Cai, Z., Zhang, X., & Zhou, T. (2019). A Survey on Edge Computing Systems and Tools. *Proceedings of the IEEE*, *107*(8), 1537–1562. doi:10.1109/JPROC.2019.2920341

Shi, W., Cao, J., Zhang, Q., Li, Y., & Xu, L. (2016). Edge Computing: Vision and Challenges. *IEEE Internet of Things Journal*, *3*(5), 637–646. doi:10.1109/JIOT.2016.2579198

Sittón-Candanedo, I. & Corchado Rodríguez, J. (2019). An Edge Computing Tutorial. *Oriental Journal of Computer Science and Technology*, *12*, 34-38. . doi:10.13005/ojcst12.02.02

Tang, L., Tang, B., Kang, L., & Zhang, L. (2019). A Novel Task Caching and Migration Strategy in Multi-Access Edge Computing Based on the Genetic Algorithm. *Future Internet*, *11*(8), 1–14. doi:10.3390/fi11080181

Wang, J., Pan, J., Esposito, F., Calyam, P., Yang, Z., & Mohapatra, P. (2018). *Edge Cloud Offloading Algorithms: Issues, Methods, and Perspectives*. Networking and Internet Architecture.

Yousefpour, A., Fung, C., Nguyen, T., Kadiyala, K.P., Jalali, F., Niakanlahiji, A., Kong, J., & Jue, J. (2019). *All One Needs to Know about Fog Computing and Related Edge Computing Paradigms: A Complete Survey*. ArXiv, abs/1808.05283.

Zhang, Q., Cheng, L., & Boutaba, R. (2010). Cloud computing: State-of-the-art and research challenges. *Journal of Internet Services and Applications*, *1*(1), 7–18. doi:10.100713174-010-0007-6

Chapter 2

Architecture of IoT and Challenges

Margaret Mary T.
https://orcid.org/0000-0001-5756-266X
Kristu Jayanti College, India

Sangamithra A.
Kristu Jayanti College, India

Ramanathan G.
Kristu Jayanti College, India

EXECUTIVE SUMMARY

Internet of things (IoT) architecture is an ecosystem of connected physical objects that are accessible through the internet. The 'thing' in IoT could be a person with a heart monitor or an automobile with built-in-sensors (i.e., objects that have been assigned an IP address and have the ability to collect and transfer data over a network without manual assistance or intervention). The embedded technology in the objects helps them to interact with internal states or the external environment, which in turn affects the decisions taken. IoT world where all the devices and appliances are connected to a network and are used collaboratively to achieve complex tasks that require a high degree of intelligence, and IoT is an interaction between the physical and digital words using sensors and actuators. Furthermore, the IoT architecture may combine features and technologies suggested by various methodologies. IoT architecture is designed where the digital and real worlds are integrating and interacting constantly, and various technologies are merged together to form IoT.

DOI: 10.4018/978-1-7998-4873-8.ch002

ARCHITECTURE OF IOT AND CHALLENGES

World of IoT (Internet of Things) is a place where devices and appliances are correlated to a network and are used collaboratively to obtain complicated tasks that require a high degree of intelligence. It act as an interplay between the physical and digital phrases using sensors and actuators. Like Remote help supplications, communication networks, and setting mindful processing of events are some of the building blocks of IoT. IoT attempts to picture as a combined network of smart objects and human beings accountable for operating them who are successful of collectively and universally communicating with one other. It's a genuine model in a dispensed environment, making an interconnectivity among objects as a serious constraint. A faultless activity of its components to interface the physical and virtual domains together a comprehensive system design of IoT is needed. Additionally a crucial part of IoT systems with the great use of smartphones(little change in the statement), state-of-the-art architectures need to have a sure level of adaptableness to suitably handle dynamic communications within the complete ecosystem due to the fact of mobility and dynamic trade of vicinity. In fact, some distance from being a mere buzzword, it stands for many more. Indeed, just as the IoT has the strength to alternate and improve our everyday lives along with the method in which we function as a society, it can also radically changes the way business run and ultimately the way we become aware of every issue of our world. There is no single harmony on architecture for IoT which is approved comprehensively. Various architectures have been projected by means of distinct researchers. And also Government encouraged, to support the environment, standard living and increasing more smart IOT applications to play the vital roles in the market. (Er.Pooja yadav and Ankur mittal,2018)

Three- and Five-Layer Architectures

IoT ecosystem there is no solitary harmony on architecture for IoT, which is approved universally. The most fundamental architecture is a three -layer architecture as shown in Figure 1 to be in initial stages of IoT. The architecture has three layers, i.e., perception, network, application layers.

The perception layer also known as a physical layer, is use to sense physical parameters or finds different smart substances in the environment, the data which is sensed in perception layer can be transferred via networks like 3G, LAN, radio frequency identification RFID, (Zhang, D, Yang, L.T. Chen, M & Zhao S,2016) Bluetooth, near field communication (NFC) (Nagashree, R.N & Rao,2014) and wireless devices. The network layer is mainly used to connect the smart devices. The application layer is liable for taking care of the particular application services of the handler. It characterizes an assorted variety of applications wherein the IoT can be sorted out, like smart health, homes and cities.

The main aim of IoT is described at three –layer of architecture, but researches are focused on superior phases of IoT. Thus three –layer architecture is not sufficient and compatible to keen wellbeing, homes and urban communities. The principle point of IoT is portrayed according to required advance technologies, so from the three-layer architecture much more layered has been proposed. Which is the five-layer architecture, additionally includes the processing and business layer. The five layers are namely, perception, transport, processing, application, and business layers (see Figure 1). The activity of the perception and application layers is the proportionate as the plan with three layers, as a structure attribute of the end three layers. The transport layer moves the sensor data from the perception layer to the processing layer and other route around through frameworks, for instance systems, for example, network, 3G, LAN, Bluetooth, RFID, and NFC. The processing layer is besides perceived as the inside item layer. It stores, analyzes, and methods huge quantities of information that drive from the transport layer. It can control and allow a various set of services to the bottom most layers. It utilizes numerous advances for example databases, cloud computing, and big data processing modules. The business layer manages the entire IoT framework, comprehensive of applications, business profit models, and client's protection.

Each and every IoT device is different, the basis for every IoT architecture as well as its popular data manner go with the flow is roughly the same. Most importantly, it comprises of the things habitually connected with Internet. By method for their implanted sensors and actuators can detect the surroundings around them and assemble data then surpassed on to IoT entryway. The following next stage comprises of IoT data securing systems and entryways that accumulate the top rate mass of unprocessed information, convert it into digital streams, filter and pre-process it so that it is ready for analysis. The third layer is represented with the aid of edge devices which are accountable for similarly processing and improve analysis of data. This layer is also the place for visualization and machine learning technologies might also step in. After that, the data is transferred to data centers which can be either cloud-based or mounted locally. This is where the data is stored, managed and analyzed in depth for actionable insights.

Perception Layer

Perception layer is also referred as a recognition layer and also called as physical layer which has sensors for sensing and collecting data about the referred location. This layer identifies smart objects in the location. It is also the bottom layer of the IoT architecture. In IoT we can receive the information through the things, but the things can be identified with the aid of this perception layer. (Pallavi Sethi & Smruthi R. Sarangi,2017) .The main role of this layer is to identify the things and collect the information and transform them in a digital setup.

So sensors like RFID, 2-D barcode, ESN and many more sensor is attached to the object to collect the information. Based on the application requirements the sensors are chose to collect the information. There more chances of attackers to attack the sensors.

Figure 1. Architecture of IoT (A: three layers) (B: five layers).

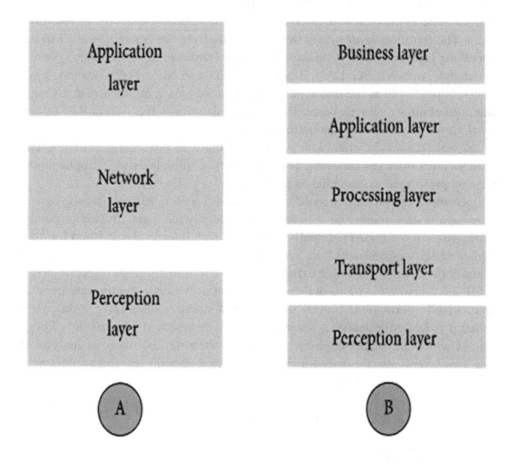

For every IoT system, as a foundation linked devices are accountable for presenting the parameters in the outside or inside world of the object itself. This foundation linked is known as telemetry data principle of the IoT. Let's think about a smart watering system with all the critical sensors in place. The framework inspects the circumstance progressively and instructs the actuators to open chosen water valves situated in places dependent on the information provided by utilizing the sensors where soil dampness is under the set value. These valves are stored open until the sensors report that the qualities are reestablished to default. Clearly, the entirety of this happen other than a solitary human intervention.

Transport Layer

This layer is the genius of conventional IoT architecture. The layer's impenetrable data broadcast between the perception and application layer of IoT architecture is the main responsibility, then gathers facts and supplies to the perception layer in the course of various purpose and servers. Ultimately, this layer is a merging of internet and communication-based webs. According to present day researcher that the network layer is the giant layer of traditional IoT architecture on several communications based technologies.

Figure 2. Perception

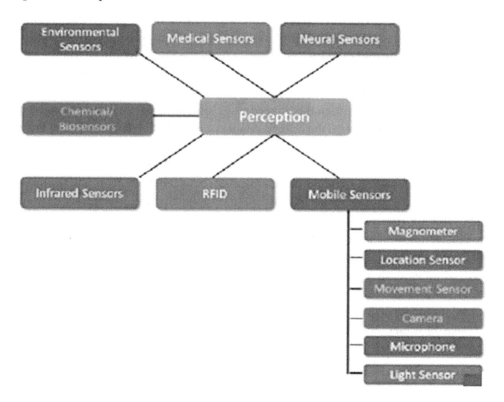

It is the core layer (network layer) of IoT that is performed of advancing the information for relevant procedures. The data processing eccentric responsibilities treated to IoT management, that additional ensures unique addressing and routing facilities to the unified integration of limitless devices in a single cooperative network done by this layer. Various types of technologies are contributed for this phenomenon such as wired, wireless and satellite. The implementation of 6LoWPAN protocol towards IPV6 for unique addressing of devices IETF demonstrates a high degree of effort involved. (Pallavi Sethi & Smruthi R. Sarangi, 2017)

Processing Layer

The other name for the processing layer is a middleware layer. The processing layer is used to collect the information that is sent from the transport layer. The processing is done by this layer to the information which is collected, while processing the collected information, this layer has the restraint to extract only the useful information, and discard all the unnecessary information. In big data IoT, the large amount of information is been stored, these types of problem can be recovered by the processing layer.

Despite the fact that this layer by the capacities in closeness with sensors and actuators on given devices. It is basic to reveal as a different IoT design and organize as a fundamental for the methodologies of data assortment, separating and move to edge infrastructure and cloud-based stages. Given the huge amount of information yield that million-device organizations might also generate competencies for the total assurance and transportation of information in the spotlight.

As intermediaries between the linked things, cloud, analytics gateways and data acquisition structure furnish the critical connection point that ties the closing layers together.

Processing layer resides at the edge of the worlds of Operation Technology and Information Technology, and the communication between the sensors and the rest of the system by transforming the sensor data into setups that are effortlessly movable and usable for the other system components down the line.

This can also be able to control, filter and select data to minimize the quantity of information that wishes to be progressed to the cloud, which positively affects network transmission costs and response times. The place for a local preprocessing of sensor data provided by gateway which is squeezed into beneficial bundles is geared up for further processing.

(Martin Bauer, Nicola Bui, Jourik De Loof & Walewski W. Joachim, 2013)

Figure 3. processing layer

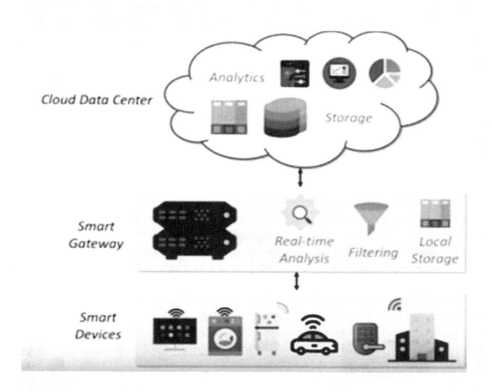

Application Layer

The application layer is regarded as a pinnacle layer of conventional IoT architecture. This layer makes available the personalized primarily based services according to user relevant needs. The layer's foremost accountability is to link the essential gap between the users and applications. Application layer combines the industry to obtain the high-level smart applications type options such as the disaster monitoring, fitness monitoring, transposition, fortune, medical, ecological environment, and treated world administration application to wise kind application. All functions that utilize the IoT technology or in which IoT has deployed can be defined by the application layer.

The applications of IoT can be animal tracking, smart homes, cities, health etc. There are many issues in the application layer in which security is the key issue. When we construct the smart home with the help of IoT, there is the more number of chances of threats and vulnerabilities be raised from outside or inside. To put in a force robust safety in an IoT based smart homes one of the main troubles is that the devices used in smart homes have susceptible computational power and a low amount of storage such as ZigBee. ZigBee is a standard based on the IEEE 802.15.4 standard for wireless individual networks. This standard takes into account the formation of lost expense and low force networks - these applications run for a long time rather than months. These networks are made from sensors and actuators and would wireless be able to control numerous electrical items, for example, controllers, clinical, modern, and security sensors. (Drew Gislason, 2008, ISBN: 9780750685979)

Figure 4. Application

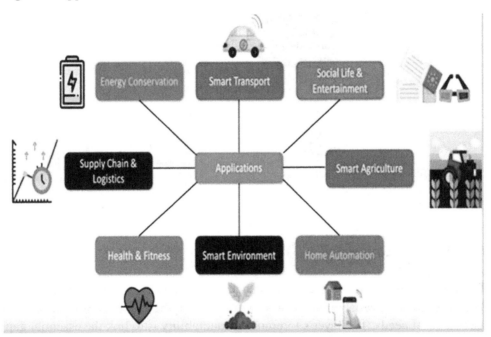

Business Layer

The business layer is also known as a planned behavior of an application and acts like a director of the whole system. Business layer manages the user privacy part. The main role of this layer is to manage and control the business, profit models, applications. This layer determines how the information can be created stored and changed. By avoiding business logic, the attackers can misuse an application.

Business Logic Attack is a common issue of the layer occurs due to the error in programming leads to advantage and control, thus manage the information exchange between the supporting application database and the user. Some of the common errors are also exists in business layer like immature coding by the programmer, validation problem like password recovery, input validation and encryption techniques. Other issues like Zero-Day Attack which is like a problem in an application or security hole. The attacker takes the control without the understanding of the user by breaking the security hole. The security needs are driven by the idea of the resources in every environment. In an IT domain, the most basic component and the objective of attacks has been data. In an IOT domain, the basic resources are the process members, workers and hardware. Security needs separate dependent on those distinctions. (David Hanes Gonzalo Salguerio, Robert Barton & Jerome Henry, 2017)

CHALLENGES OF SECURITY

Lack of Testing and Updating

In worldwide there are over 24 billion IoT connected devices. The number of IoT devices around us can increase further more year by year. The problem in the tech company providing this type of devices is lack of security. There are no enough updates in some of the Iot devices and some will not get the updates at all. These types of devices are eventually prone to hackers and other security issues. IoT devices are manufactured, produced and delivered with high speed but not without giving too much of security.

In order to protect the customer who bought the Iot device against attacks, before each device has launched into the role it should be tested and update properly in order to avoid these types of attacks. If the device is launched to public without any testing and updating it will be bad for both the companies as well as the customers.

Brute Force and the Issue of Default Passwords

When we talk about the brute force the common is dos attack which will come in the hipping devices. The devices which all shipped have come with the default password, which will not be changed immediately as soon as the customer receives the device. When the device enabled with default password, there are 99% chance of hackers can hack the password and can be handle the device without the knowledge of the customer. The safety and security are vital design and effective requirements for IoT systems. The blend of computational and physical system requires safe system design and secure computer system design. (Dimitrios Serpanos & Marilyn Wolf, 2018)

Untrustworthy Communication

IoT devices mostly send message to the network without any encryption. This is one of the major security challenges in IoT systems. So, whenever the data is transferred through the IoT devices via network, encryption is mandatory that most of the vulnerable can be avoided when the data is transformed. In order to avoid this, we have to use transport encryption and standard like TLS.

Privacy Challenges in IOT

Due to Large number of connecting devices, services and common communication sharing privacy plays a key role in IoT. The major privacy issue in IoT environment is to secure the user data. The privacy challenge of IoT includes

Too Much Data

Currently, the usage of IoT device is more and its keep on increasing with the peoples. When so many peoples are using the IoT devices, the data also will be too high. The amount of data the IoT devices overwhelming will be more. In the analysis of federal trade commission report that 10000 household can generate 150 million data every day. This creates way for the hackers to hack the devices.

Eavesdropping

Spying Manufacturers or programmers could utilize an associated device to for all intents and purposes attack an individual's home. German analysts achieved this by capturing decoded data from a smart meter device to figure out what network show when somebody was viewing right then and there. Eavesdropping it is an attack where the digital device can be intended by the person who is not intended. The hackers can easily take the control through the television if the television is IoT device. Through the vision of television, they can monitor and control.

Consumer Confidence

Because of these issues, the IoT devices lack the confidence from the consumer. Because of the less customer confidence, the Iot device will not go high in the market or to the customers.

Data Extraction Using IoT

The web of things (IoT) has been touted as the next challenge for enterprises to adopt and exploit.

But what precisely is IoT and how can it influence stockpiling and the manner in which we deal with our information? IoT alludes to an expansive system of physical devices that incorporate sensors, vehicles, mobile devices and even home appliances that create and share data.

The breadth of choices for IoT implies that almost any device outside the data center that creates helpful data could be a piece of an IoT solution. Naturally, IoT gadgets are viewed as individuals remotely oversaw and embedded appliances, for example, cameras. However this isn't generally the situation. Numerous organizations have appropriated situations that run at least one servers at branch areas to screen building access, ecological controls or different tasks that relate straightforwardly to the business itself. Accordingly, IoT is a work of gadgets that could make, store and procedure content crosswise over numerous physical locations.

Probably the most obvious statement here is that the information created is outside the data center. We are progressively observing the term "edge" used to portray processing and information the executive undertakings performed outside data center. Despite the fact that edge processing has existed for a long time, the present development in IoT and edge registering is prominent for the sheer volume of information made in non-core data center areas. This carries one of a kind difficulty to IT divisions that must guarantee, this information is satisfactorily verified, ordered and prepared.

Most IT associations are accustomed to knowing precisely where their data resides. With IoT, the test of putting arms around the entirety of the substance claimed by a business is a lot more prominent, with clear ramifications on client security and guidelines, for example, the General Data Protection Regulation (GDPR). Information is going in to the camera and information going will be called as raw information and maximum granularity of data. Data can be processed using edge for taking backup of cloud data and improve performance using algorithms batch basis.

IoT data mining processes are broken up into multiple stages, as follows: Data is integrated according to different data sources. Data is cleaned, so it can be easily extracted and processed. Some parts of data are extracted and prepared for future processing. So, in this, IoT analytics introduces to the analysis of information from numerous IoT data sources, including sensors, actuators, smart devices and other internet associated objects (Moncef Gabbouj & Thanos Stouraitis). Sophisticated algorithms are used to identify patterns. Data is restructured and presented to the users in a coherent way. Complex calculations are utilized to recognize designs. Information is rebuilt and exhibited to the clients in a sound manner.

Figure 5. Data Extraction of IoT

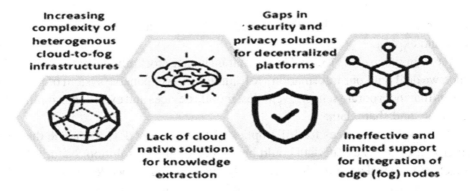

DATA MINING CHALLENGES WITH IOT

Increasingly Huge Volume of Facts

As new applications become increasingly complex, developers are facing greater pressure to process much larger data sets. Some applications require data scientists to extract and analyze multiple petabytes of data.

Data Sets Aren't Homogenous

The IoT has introduced a new layer of complexity for data analysis. Data is curated from many different sources in multiple formats, such as web documents, CSV sheets, and SQL tables.

Before big data analytics tools can process it, they must clean the data and convert it into a single structure.

Integrity of Different Sources

Since data is curated from various sources, it may be difficult to make balls-to-balls comparisons between data sets. Each system may use its own methodology to develop data, which will always introduce some level of ambiguity.

Need for Real Time Analysis

Some applications expect information to be removed and prepared continuously. This can be a challenge while breaking down informational indexes that are terabytes or petabytes in size.

Solutions to These Challenges

While various enormous information mining issues have surfaced with the IoT, new arrangements have been created to address them. Fast and effective data mining approaches for huge data corpus to read and write. Need to develop efficient and well-defined data mining framework which considers data security, data privacy, big data, and data sharing of prime importance (Deepti Sehrawat & Nasib Singh Gill, 2018). Hadoop and other big data extraction tools have helped make it easier than ever to extract large data sets.

Hadoop is not big data, it's big-data knowledge. One can separate the storehouses however Hadoop is additionally a structure for preparing the data. Hadoop is the primary facts operational structure for data mining process to extract large volume of data in IoT technology.

Most of the IoT challenges in data extraction can be solved with the assistance of renowned algorithms:

- Decision Tree
- Random Forest Association
- Rule Mining
- K Means Clustering

IoT challenges in data extraction were involved in finding unexpected value from a complex data and generally find some intelligent decision making across a large scale or at a high velocity (Andrew Minteer, 2017, ISBN: 9781787120730).

The overall inquiry while beginning the advancement of the IOT item is whether the gadget is or will be IP-empowered. In such manner, the dominating systems administration stack is an IP stack which incorporates an application library to open or close associations with remote devices and can send and get information between the remote devices.

Need quicker and high-volume information storage frameworks IoT information is created by sensors from a differing set of devices inside a particular system. The vast majority of the IoT information (organized or unstructured) will get saved and perform examination capacities to create bits of knowledge.

Figure 6. Data Science

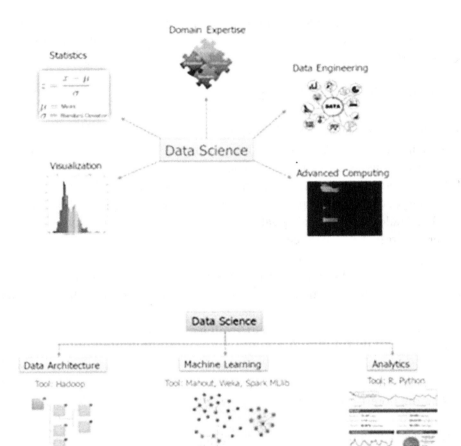

The dissected outcomes must be pushed back to a central terminal. This triggers a prerequisite for high-capacity storage, high-speed storage, and memory handling advancements like NVMe over textures, Intel's 3D xpoint, and Magnetic RAM (MRAM). IoT information records are commonly little documents, yet because of this reality, it can rapidly include petabytes of information.

Object storage is prescribed for the capacity of IoT as it can oblige an expanding number of information records into storage devices. The greater part of the cloud specialist co-ops decide on object storage because of this component, which makes cloud-integrated storage or distributed storage perfect for IoT precise data.

Need Adaptable and Agile System With High Data Transfer Capacity and low Latency

Aside from capacity, the system foundation is a basic angle for IoT information to get devoured by data center while additionally pushing broke down outcomes to target devices.

A system needs to have ultra-low latency and high transfer speed for enormous scale IoT applications like modern IoT, medicinal services, and transport. Move of information should be close to continuous. As a significant level of IoT applications request the preparing of crucial information, any system disappointment results may majorly affect tasks.

The rise of 5G is a help for IoT as it offers a coordinated and adaptable system that takes into consideration the system cutting technique where organize transmission capacity is separated and distributed to various applications.

Secure Storage and System Network

A sensitive data transfers storage to a data center, the security of information turns into a conspicuous worry for associations engaged with IoT organization. Because of the different advances included, an IoT framework gets mind boggling and powerless for aggressors to break into storage or sniff into a system for performing breakdowns. Due to cyber security difficulties, system and capacity framework must plan them and limit the hazard by testing frameworks before sending. They ought to likewise have the option to identify and report malicious activities at each level of IoT infrastructure.

As of now, storage and system foundation have difficulties giving 100 percent execution to IoT devices, yet late headways away and organize innovations keep the expectation alive for IoT smart cities. The available energy additionally restricts the IoT execution regarding, for example, the quantity of estimations, information examination, and information correspondence. The energy cost for unit tasks, for example, information examining, calculation and correspondence and the harvesting and capacity limit of various advancements at that point become significant (Walter De Gruyter, 2017).

Storage Challenges in IoT

IoT data will be mostly time series data. The data can be both sensor data and platform data moreover information must be convenient, precise and actionable.

Data integrity is very important with query efficiency, data visualization and anomaly detection. The majority of the information's are co-related. E.g., Temperature data how they related to environment and how that relates to some of the failure. Here both the data points in particular time, if the data moves across the fixed time boundary and not able to co-relate it is meaningless.

The amount of jitter is coming out and it should be minimal or it's very difficult to translate the information and what value can bring by co-relating the data. Coherence need to be captured in the data. Good visualization of data helps in obtaining pattern out in the data and the way systems are working, visualization is important aspects of this entire data analysis. Data may be structured and unstructured; data is used for trouble shooting for forensics purpose.

Figure 7. Storage Process

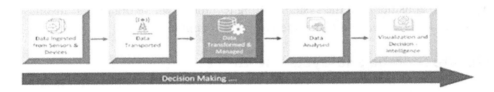

How Data is Processed?

Data that can be processing immediately close where the information originates, edge computing comes in. For edge level we required some kind of storage, some kind of computing ability to take care of everything about to process the data and taking some action immediately.

For long term retention like data analysis and bringing some planning activities will be done in cloud.

How Data is Stored?

Edge computing for local processing of data, decision making ability and write intensive. Data required storage at the edge level which is fast (SSD) and with low latency.

Challenges: Nature of Data in IoT

A large portion of the information will be multi model and heterogeneous. The volume of information with so many sensors out there the heterogeneity of data itself is a problem. Coherence of data unless and until co-relate the data with two discrete point and to itself may not give any information. Only when co-relate it bode well to process the data.

Challenges: Flexibility and Agility of Data

Flexibility and agility to handle the data comes across, edge fine amount of storage so rapid provisioning of data and continuous innovation to process the data is required by enabling free flow of data to and from through sensors without clogging to improve the efficiency of data by means of on-demand analytics with hybrid cloud and multi cloud deployments and mainly distributed storage solutions is required in order to manage huge volume of information to be created.

Figure 8. Data Processing

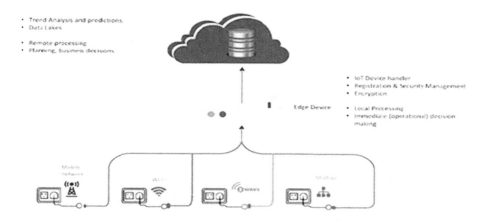

Figure 9. Storage of Data

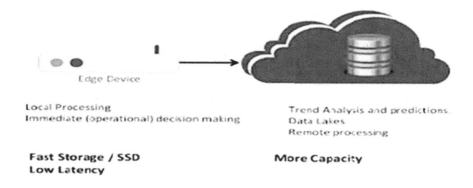

Figure 10. Data Nature in IoT

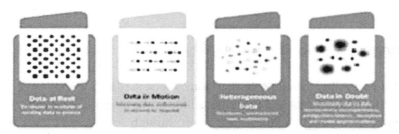

Energy Efficient challenges in IoT

Energy sparing is straightforwardly identified with cash sparing, and in any modern areas, operational expenses vigorously impact significant choices about assembling, generation, and upkeep forms. Since energy utilization significantly adds to huge working costs, organizations must group round to use advances that help upgrade energy.

IoT can basically be characterized as a system of smart devices associated over the Internet with access to a much bigger system including sensors, smart phones, data management, report frameworks, and then some. For example, wearable devices, health monitoring groups use sensors to gauge your vitals and show on a user interface likewise matching up with its advanced smart phone application. The devices associated with IoT incorporate appliances, vehicles, telephones, and display frameworks.

In an assembling plant, administrators get alarms from the equipment introduced and convey the live data on errors, glitches, or deviations. These IoT applications are called mechanical IoT. Here, associated devices support tasks and maintenance forms and are controlled from a remote PC or smart phone application.

Effect of IoT on Energy Utilization

IoT applications can decidedly influence plan execution and vitality proficiency with improved following and observing knowledge. As information is conveyed constant on a single central dashboard interface, administrators can have ideal accommodation for arranging and separating them. The energy productivity experienced during communications among equipment and devices develop better, which brings about growing further developed operational profiles.

Automation gets conceivable and very achievable as amazing IoT associated sensors get sufficiently brilliant to utilize control just when they require and expend less energy in its quiescent mode.

IoT improved visibility in energy efficiency connected with Big Data that structures a significant part in breaking down and gathering unstructured information. IoT applications can offer helpful perceivable and sorted out understanding into notable information needed to achieve fair energy saving. The huge development of the Internet of Things (IoT) technologies enables easy access and control of a variety forms of information and data, and leads original applications such as smart home, smart factory, etc. Although due to the small sizes and different operating environments of the IoT devices, it is hard to directly power the sensors from the grid and batteries are usually employed to power the sensors. Hence, sensor charging and efficient energy utilization become key challenges. A substantial amount of works considers the energy gathering communication models, where the wireless sensor devices can harvest energy from an peripheral source in their natural environment. (Zhong, S., & Wang, X., 2018)

It is a result of this most extreme perceivability and clarity of information that producers can track energy execution by methods for incredible sensors and monitor leaks and predicaments active in current situations. To make things dynamic and energy effective in a running place, we may examine the accompanying IoT-empowered assets: basic sensors, (for example, temperature or power assessment) Complex great sensors (vitality reserve funds, issue identification, and so on). Actuators Computerization board for mechanical structure or activity room circuit breakers, apparatuses, and switches.

IoT applications can set up a synchronized and upgraded correspondence among various systems administration devices extending from basic temperature controller to increasingly complex robotization of energy calculation or it can be building appliances that need on-and-off switching to secure optimal environment inside the rooms.

Connected with the Internet, IoT-empowered devices, for example, sensors and actuators enable conventional to build the board framework that works with programmable rationale controllers to send sensor-specific signals to actuators. With IoT innovation set up, each control framework in an operational structure goes continuous as it interfaces with a central structure control application.

APPLICATIONS OF IOT

1)Smart Cities

IoT plays a very important role in order to improve the smartness of cities, there are so many applications invented to monitor the parking place, vehicle monitoring, sound monitoring, diversion according to climate in order to avoid accidents, smart roads etc. There are so many applications related to iot has introduced for making our city as a smart city.

Figure 11. Smart Cities

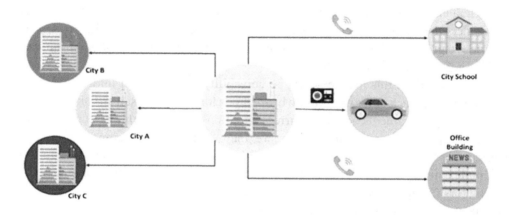

2)Smart Agriculture and Smart Water

To control and maintain the amount of vitamins in agriculture products, to control the climate condition to maximize the production and strengthen the agriculture work by monitoring with the help of IoT. Even the study of the weather condition can also be monitored, so that they can cultivate the crop according to the situation of the weather condition. To study the sustainability of the water in the river and sea for agriculture use can be detected with the help of the IoT. In order to implement this smart agriculture and smart water it uses the single sensor and wireless sensor network and the bandwidth range as medium.

Figure 12. Smart Agriculture

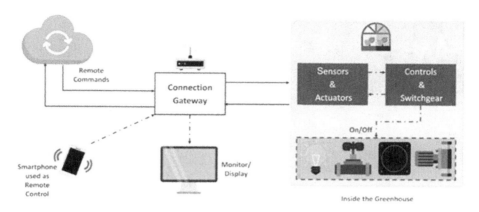

3)Health Care

There are so many devices they have introduced in the health care domain of Iot, Which is very much helpful in the health care system. Because health care is one of the major things in the world, with the help of Iot we can easily monitor so many things related to the health issues easily. The one thing tracking of object, staff and patients, identification of the people, we can identify the person or the object in motion. Applications include different devices in order to monitor the patients conditions, even so many applications like wearable devices also they have introduced. One of the main wearable device is the glucometer, where it will keep track of the glucose level, blood pressure of the patients. Likewise so many handed devices are introduced with the help of the Iot. Some of the devices like where the data from the wearable device will get transferred to the doctor automatically, so it is easy for the doctor to maintain the record of the patient, and when the patient visit the doctor they can see the record from the data where they have collected through the IoT device, and easy for the doctor to suggest a medication for the patients.

4)Industrial Automation

This is one of the fields where both faster developments, as well as the quality of products, are the critical factors for a higher Return on Investment. One could re-engineer products and to deliver better performance with cost and customer experience IoT applications are used.

Figure 13. Health Care system

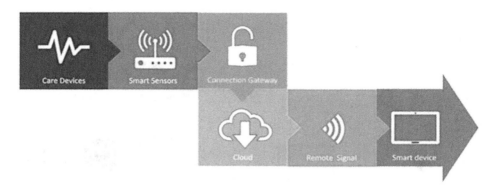

Figure 14. Industry Automation

Conclusion of IoT Architecture:

As stated previously, IoT architecture may also differ from solution to solution, however its core consists of the five constructing blocks that are key in imparting the imperative aspects that make a sustainable IoT ecosystem: functionality, scalability, accessibility, maintainability and cost-effectiveness. In an IoT ecosystem there will be millions and trillions of devices that are associated and collaborating with each other using some form of wireless technology. Energy gathering technologies refer to the use of power generating essentials such as solar cells, piezoelectric elements, and thermoelectric elements, in order to convert various types of energy such as light, vibration, and heat energy into electricity (Pethuru Raj & Anupama C. Raman, 2017).

What is fundamental right here is presently not to leave one alone overpowered with help of the apparent intricacy of the IoT design and not to dismiss the conceivable outcomes for forcing eye-getting and future-evidence of IoT ventures. It is significant that a creating center point around the improvement of a hearty IoT design decided among numerous primary business players from different industry areas which has driven them to achievement in pressing more business esteem from their information to supply them an aggressive part and help to beat their rivals.

While it is actual that there are nonetheless tons of work to be accomplished in phrases of overcoming. IoT technology know how fragmentation upon searching back, is pretty evident that lots effort has been carried out to date to integrate the great vary of applied sciences and standards embraced by IoT and there is hope for a greater unified and standardized future.

However, before this will become reality, the key to making the promise of IoT show up doesn't always lie in acquiring a single rule-them-all IoT technology, but as a substitute inserting all the technologies in line so that they are environment friendly in the collection, management, analysis, and exploitation of the data by way of building a strong, future-proof, scalable and tightly closed IoT architecture.

REFERENCES

Gabbouj & Stouraitis. (n.d.). Building Blocks for IoT Analytics. *River Publishers.*

Gislason. (2008). *Zigbee Wireless Networking* (1ˢᵗ ed.). Zigbee Alliance.

Minteer. (2017). *Analytics for the Internet of Things (IoT).* Academic Press.

Nagashree, R. N., Rao, V., & Aswini, N. (2014). Near field communication. *Int. J. Wirel. Microw. Technol., 2014*(4), 20.

Raj & Raman. (2017). *The Internet of Things.* Enabling Technologies, Platforms, and Use Cases.

Salguerio, Barton, & Henry. (2017). *IoT Fundamentals: Networking Technologies, Protocols, and Use Cases for the Internet of Things.* Cisco.

Sehrawat & Gill. (2018). Data Mining in IoT and its Challenges. *International Journal of Computer Sciences and Engineering, 289 – 293*, 2347 – 2693.

Serpanos & Wolf. (2018). *Internet-of-Things (IoT) Systems Architectures, Algorithms, Methodologies.* Springer.

Sethi, P., & Sarangi, S. R. (2017). Internet of Things: Architectures, Protocols, and Applications. *Journal of Electrical and Computer Engineering, 1-4.* doi:10.1155/2017/9324035

Walter De Gruyter. (2017). *IoT Energy Storage – A Forecast.* Author.

Yadav & Mittal. (2018). *IoT, Challenges and issues in Indian Perspective.* Cornell University Library.

Zhang, D., Yang, L. T., Chen, M., Zhao, S., Guo, M., & Zhang, Y. (2016). Real-time locating systems using active RFID for Internet of Things. *IEEE Systems Journal, 10*(3), 1226–1235. doi:10.1109/JSYST.2014.2346625

Zhong, S., & Wang, X. (2018). Energy Allocation and Utilization for Wirelessly Powered IoT Networks. *IEEE Internet of Things Journal, 5*(4), 2781–2792.

Chapter 3
Internet of Things (IoT):
The Standard Protocol Suite for Communication Networks

Stephen R.
https://orcid.org/0000-0001-7123-4371
Kristu Jayanti College, India

Ayshwarya B.
Kristu Jayanti College, India

R. Shantha Mary Joshitta
Jayaraj Annapackiam College for Women, India

Hubert B. J. Shanthan
Kristu Jayanti College, India

EXECUTIVE SUMMARY

Naturally, IoT network consists of constrained devices with limited power, storage, and processing capabilities. However, IoT has some challenges to face internal and external issues, for instance, security issues, connectivity complex, data management, etc. In such a case, IoT is not supported by a heavyweight protocol suite. So, developing the lightweight protocol suite is the challenge for IoT environment. This chapter also describes such protocols that fulfill the requirements of IoT. In fact, IoT environment consists of a huge amount of devices. The controlling of all the devices is another issue, as well as data analytics among different devices, also considered a major issue. As a constraint, this chapter focuses to design a standard protocol suite for IoT environment.

DOI: 10.4018/978-1-7998-4873-8.ch003

1. INTRODUCTION

Internet of Things (IoT) is an innovative paradigm which comprises billions of things communicating intelligently. In recent years, IoT has become an emerging technology in different application domains. The term IoT is defined as the future of internet or next generation of the internet in which billions of things or objects are communicating together. The connected things in IoT environment are called as "Smart things". The devices in the IoT network are wirelessly connected through the communication technologies such as WiFi, Bluetooth, etc. Generally, IoT has five layers, each layer consists of appropriate protocol suite (Raheem Ali et al.,2014). The constrained devices are connected by a set of IoT protocols that allow devices to communicate together. The IoT protocols like 6LoWPAN, RPL, COAP, IPv6, MQTT, TCP/IP used as standard protocols in IoT environment. These protocols making the network as an intelligent communication.

Naturally, IoT network consists of constrained devices with the limited power, storage and processing capabilities. However, IoT has some challenges to face internal and external issues. For instance, security issues, connectivity complex, data management etc. In such case, IoT is not supported for heavy-weight protocol suite. So, developing the light-weight protocol suite is the challenge for IoT environment. This chapter also describes such protocols which are fulfill the requirements of IoT. In fact, IoT environment consists of huge amount of devices, the controlling of all the devices is another issue as well as data analytics among different devices also considered as major issue. As a constrained, this chapter focuses to design of standard protocol suite for IoT environment.

The following are the key features of this chapter:

- Describes the various standard protocols based on IoT layers
- Provides the IoT protocols and their appropriate applications
- List the issues and challenges of IoT protocol suite
- Designing the real time scenarios (Case Study)

1.1 Various Standard Protocols Based on IoT Layers

There is no single consent on architecture for IoT, which is agreed universally. Different architectures have been proposed by different researchers. Generally, the basic architecture has three layers such as perception layer, network layer and application layer as shown in figure 1 (a).

(Pongle Pavan et al.,2015), This three-layer architecture was introduced in early stage of IoT research area. The three-layered architecture defines the basic idea of the IoT. But, it is not sufficient for IoT research, because it focuses on magnificent aspects of the IoT. Hence, architecture with additional layers are proposed in the literature. The five-layer architecture which includes perception, transportation, processing, application and business layers as shown in figure 1 (b).

Figure 1. IoT architecture (a) Three Layers (b) Five Layers (Borgia Eleonora et al.,2014)

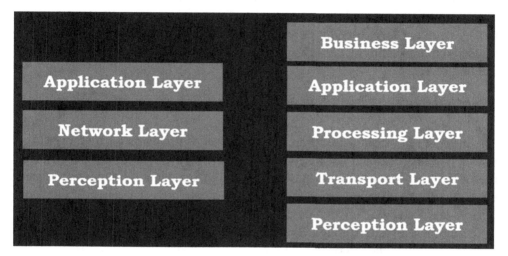

Perception Layer: This layer is also known as physical layer, which contains sensors for sensing and gathering information about environment. It senses some physical parameters and identifies objects in the environment. This layer uses the RFID, actuator, Web camera etc.

Network Layer: The major work of this layer is to perform host addressing and packet routing. This layer routes the information gathered by the perception layer. IPv6 is adopted for device addressing and identification of the host is done using the IP address which is mostly used in hierarchical manner.

Transport Layer: The end to end message is transported in this network. This layer transfers the sensor data from perception layer to the processing layer via Wi-Fi, Bluetooth, NFC etc. The major functions of this transport layer are error control, flow control and segmentation.

Processing Layer: The processing layer is also known as the middleware layer. It stores, analyzes, and processes huge amounts of sensor data that comes from the transport layer. It can manage and provide a varied set of services to the lower layers. It employs many technologies such as database, cloud computing and big data processing modules.

Application Layer: This layer defines the interfaces to communicate with low layer protocol through which the data flows over the networks. The data are encoded in the application protocol and encapsulated by the transport layer. This is achieved using process to process connections using ports. This layer is responsible for delivering application specific services to the user (Rehman Abdul et al.,2016). It defines various applications in which the Internet of Things can be deployed.

Business Layer: This layer manages the whole IoT system, including applications, business and profit models and users' privacy. Business layer is all about making money from the service being provided. Data received at the application layer is molded into a meaningful service and then further services are created from those existing services.

1.2 6LoWPAN

The Internet Engineering Task Force defined a set of standards for IPv6 over Low Power Wireless Personal Area Networks (6LoWPAN) which enables the efficient use of IPv6 on simple embedded devices through an adaptation layer and related protocol. The devices connected to the IoT are of two types namely Full Function devices and Reduced Function devices. The Full Function devices are connected to the internet directly through IP stack. But, the Reduced Function devices are connected through the full function devices. Device to device and device to gateway are the types of connectivity used in 6LoWPAN as shown in figure 1.2.

The two types of routing protocols such as proactive and reactive are used in IoT applications. RPL is a proactive routing protocol and LOADng is a reactive protocol (Althubaity Areej et al.,2017). RPL performs better compared with LOADng protocol. Some of the literatures are reviewed to ensure that RPL is suitable for IoT applications.

1.3 RPL

RPL is a distance vector routing protocol that is designed to operate on 6LoWPAN network. It supports three types of network traffics such as Point-to-Point (P2P), Point-to-Multipoint (P2MP) and Multipoint-to-Point (MP2P). RPL targets collection based networks where the connected nodes periodically send the sensed data to a central device (gateway). (Pongle Pavan et al.,2015) RPL gives a specific routing solution for LLN which has very limited resources in terms of energy, computation and memory size. Hence, RPL has been specifically designed to meet the requirements of resource constrained nodes.

Figure 2. 6LoWPAN Network (Abomhara M et al.,2014)

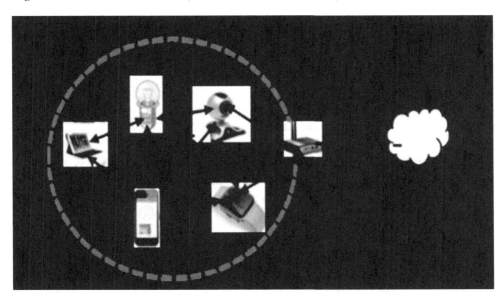

2. IOT PROTOCOLS AND THEIR APPLICATIONS

Some of the literatures are reviewed that RPL is suitable for IoT applications. The role of routing protocol in IoT application is depicted in table 1.

Table 1. Role of Routing Protocols

Application	N/W size	Energy	Routing protocol
Smart home	Small	Re-chargeable battery	LOAD, AODV,RPL
Smart city	Medium	Re-chargeable battery / Energy harvesting	LOAD, AODV, RPL
Smart agriculture	Medium/ Large	Energy harvesting	LOAD, RPL
Smart transport	Large	Re-chargeable battery / Energy harvesting	LOAD
Smart Health	Small	Battery / Re-chargeable battery	LOAD, RPL
Smart Grid	Large	Direct / Re-chargeable battery	LOAD, RPL

3. THE ISSUES AND CHALLENGES OF IOT PROTOCOL SUITE

IoT devices are basically resource-constrained and therefore, the direct use of traditional security mechanisms in the smart equipment is not straightforward. IoT applications have the following major security constraints:

Hardware-based restrictions:

- **Computing and energy limitation:**

Battery-driven IoT systems are often used and low clock-rate CPUs are used. However, compute intensive cryptographic protocols–algorithms using quick computation–cannot be directed to such low-powered devices (Gamundani Attlee M et al.2015).

- **Memory restriction:**

IoT devices are designed with minimal RAM and Flash memory in contrast with the conventionally available digital devices using Real Time Operating System (RTOS) or a lightweight variant of the GPOS. We also operate legacy systems and products. Safety schemes should therefore be effective in memory (Matharu Gurpreet Singh et al.,2014). Nevertheless, current protection algorithms are not specifically designed to memory performance as the conventional digital system requires a large RAM and hard disk. These security systems cannot have ample processing power after the operating system and firmware are booted. Conventional protection algorithms therefore cannot be used to protect IoT devices directly.

- **Surface mounted packaging:**

IoT devices could be deployed and left unsupervised in remote regions. An invader could tamper with IoT devices by catching devices. (Rehman Abdul et al.,2016) later, the cryptographic mysteries can be deleted, programs changed, or malicious nodes replaced. Tamperproof packaging is one way to protect against such attacks.

Software-based restrictions:

- **In-built software limitation:**

IoT operating systems, which are inserted with the IoT gadgets, have dainty organize convention stacks and may need enough security modules. In this manner, the security module intended for the convention stack ought to be slender, yet vigorous and shortcoming tolerant.

- **Active security reinforcement:**

Introducing a powerful security fix on the IoT gadgets and alleviating the potential vulnerabilities is certainly not a clear undertaking. Remote reconstructing probably won't be workable for the IoT gadgets, as the operating framework or convention stack probably won't have the capacity getting and coordinating new code or library.

Network-based Limitations:

- **Portability:**

Versatility is one of the noticeable properties of the IoT gadgets, where the gadgets join a proximal system without earlier arrangement. This versatility nature raises the need to create portability strong security calculations for the IoT gadgets (Alqassem Israa et al.,2014)

- **Adaptability:**

The quantity of IoT gadgets is developing regular and more gadgets are getting associated with the worldwide data arrange (Shafagh Hossein et al.,2014). Current security plans absence of the adaptability property; along these lines, such plans are not reasonable for IoT gadgets.

- **Variety of gadgets:**

Assorted variety of the IoT gadgets inside the IoT organize ranges from the undeniable PCs to low-end RFID labels. In this manner, it is elusive a solitary security plot that oblige even the least complex of gadgets.

- **Assortment of correspondence medium:**

IoT gadgets interface with the neighborhood and open system by means of a wide scope of remote connections (Althubaity Areej et al.,2017). In this way, it is hard to discover an extensive security convention considering both the wired and remote medium properties.

- **Multi-Convention Systems administration:**

IoT gadgets may utilize a exclusive system convention (e.g., non IP convention) for correspondence in proximal systems (Raheem Ali et al., 2014). Simultaneously, it might speak with an IoT specialist co-op over the IP organizing. These multi convention correspondence qualities make conventional security plans inadmissible for IoT gadgets.

- **Powerful system topology:**

IoT gadgets may join or then again leave a system at whenever from anyplace. The fleeting furthermore, spatial gadget including and leaving trademark make a system topology dynamic. Existing security model for the advanced systems doesn't adapt to this sort of abrupt system topological changes. Thus, such a model doesn't fit with the shrewd gadget's security.

3.1 IoT Security Design and Related Issues

Figure 3. IoT Security Design and related issues (Arin Dey, 2019)

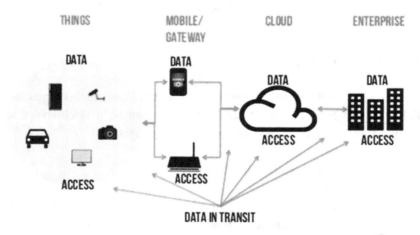

3.2 IoT Security Architecture and Related Issues

Security architecture layering hasn't stopped threats from damaging the network. Each layer was correlated with their own related problem.

Perception Layer (Atzori Luigi et al.,2010) This layer deals with gathering all system-related information. Sometimes called the layer of Recognition. This layer's security issues are:

Physical capture: An attacker tries to damage the physical components associated with network configuration.

Cloning Attack: Scammers try to enter the networking ecosystem by developing malware nodes close to those in the service.

Figure 4. IoT Security Architecture and related issues (Arin Dey, 2019)

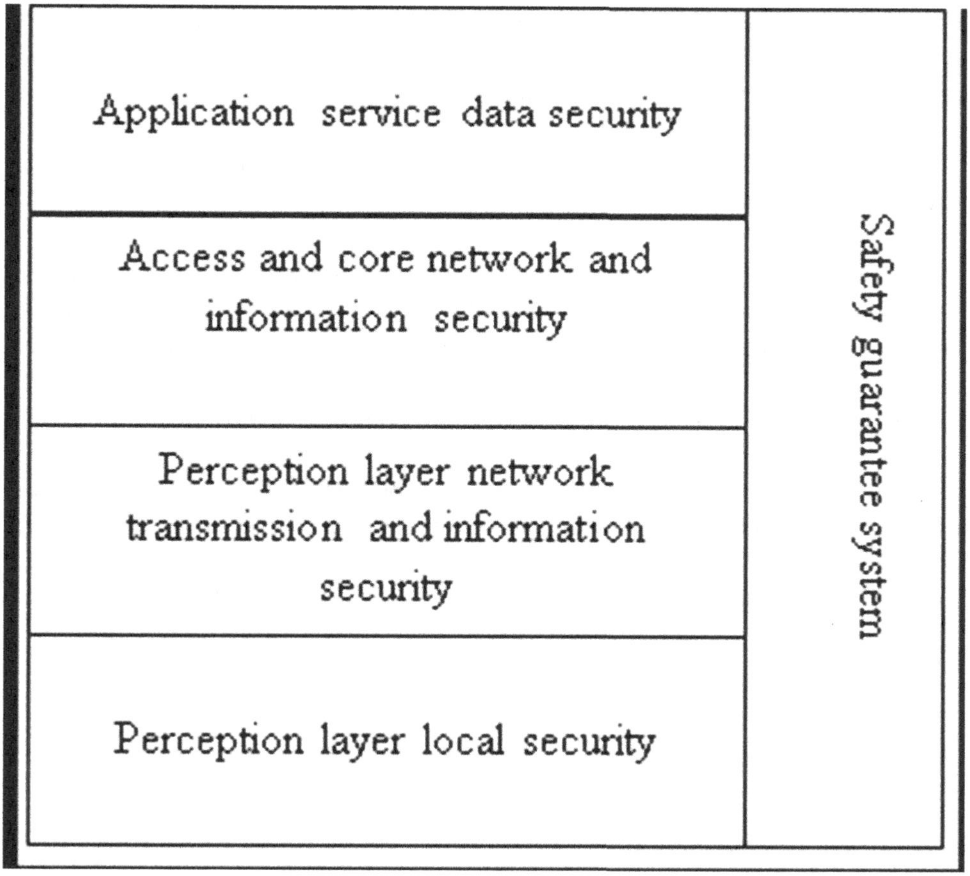

Routing Attack: Spoof attacks, alteration or replay, black hole and selective forwarding attacks, sinkhole attacks, Sybil attacks, wormhole attacks, HELLO flood attacks, and acknowledgement spoofing.

Brute Force Attack: Brute force is a method used by external threats to decrypt encrypted sensitive data such as passwords, etc. by considerable intervention rather than manual techniques.

DoS Attack: This attack disables any network by crashing and performing request messages.

Middleware Layer: (Atzori Luigi et al.,2010)

Middleware Layer is responsible for providing stable application layer framework across various Web Services and Interfaces services.

Unauthorized access: Any attacker attempting to access the network by destroying all security barriers.

Session Attack: Session hijacking, is sometimes called a session key to exploit a valid computer session to gain unsanctioned access to data or utilities in a computer system.

Application Layer: (Atzori Luigi et al.,2010)

These layers will accept users requested services and provide them with actual service

Malicious code: Application layer activities entail high risk when an attacker attempts to penetrate the user interface by sending malicious files with malicious code.

Social Engineering: The term used for a wide range of vindictive tasks performed by human communication (Raheem Ali et al.,2014). It uses mental control to trick clients into making security errors or endlessly delicate data.

The IoT system also has similar weaknesses in popular networking environments such as Insecure Web Interface, Insufficient Authentication / Authorization, Insecure Network Services, Transport Encryption, Privacy Concerns, Insecure Cloud Interface, Insecure Mobile Interface, Insufficient Security Setup, Insecure Software / Firmware.

4. DESIGNING THE REAL TIME SCENARIOS (CASE STUDY)

4. 1 Home care Health Monitoring for Elderly peoples

This section proposes a real time application for the health monitoring of the elderly people at home situation using mobile phones. It elobroates the need for the home care health monitoring and its benefits. Architecture of the Home care Elderly Health Monitoring System (HCEHMS) and its Methodology also explained clearly (Wallgren Linus, et al.,2013). A real time implementation of the HCEHMS with exprimental analysis also presented in this section.

Need for Home Care Health Monitoring

Today, nursing homes and hospitals are facing severe challanges like lack of skilled workforces and cost explosion. On the other hand, global elderly population is keep increasing which demands caretaking. As the healthcare cost is increasing exponentially now-a-days, there comes the home based health monitoring of the elderly persons using smart phones. Moreover, there are growing concerns about cost, agility and growth, the medical care must be constructed in a integrated fashion so that savings can be made incrementally and changes can be made non-disruptively (Hossain Md Mahmud et al.,2015). Thus, there is a great need to assist and nursing them effectively and efficiently around the clock and the proposed system has to provide high availability of medical care, universal health data access, high performance and robust security of the health information.

4.2 Home care Elderly Health Monitoring System (HCEHMS)

Home care elderly health monitoring will be done in three phases. They are healthcare data collection phase, healthcare data storage phase, healthcare data usage phase. Health parameters such as Body temperature, Pulse rate and SpO2 are collected in the healthcare data collection phase and send to the doctors and health personals. Low cost components like ARM7 (LPC2148) processer are used to collect the healthcare data and transmits the collected health data using wireless communication to the physician for monitoring and diagnosis (Keoh Sye Loong et al.,2014),. All the collected healthcare data are stored in the cloud based storage for further references. The proposed system makes the patients care at low cost irespective of the patient's location. More over, this system builds a centralized pool of elderly people health data and brings all the unstructured elderly patients' data under one roof, eliminating the data fragmentation that hampers care cycles and unlocking valuable insights for doctors.

4.3 Architecture of the Home care Elderly Health Monitoring System

The architecture of the Home care Elderly Health Monitoring System is presented in Figure 5.

Figure 5. Architecture of the HCEHMS

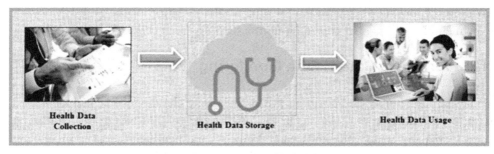

Architecture of the HCEHMS

4.4 Implementation of the HCEHMS

The proposed HCEHMS implementation scenario is explained with the test bed prepared in figure 2. RCE Wh10 is a Smart fitness Band Tracker Smart watch, used to measure the blood pressure, blood oxygen and heart rate[1] of the elderly persons. It has Pedometer for IOS and Android operating Systems. The collected health data are transferred to the gateway. The health team which has access to these healthcare data can view these data by proving their authenticity(Basu Subho Shankar et al., 2015). The health data collection test bed for HCEHMS is presented in Figure 6.

Figure 6. Test bed for HCEHMS Implementation

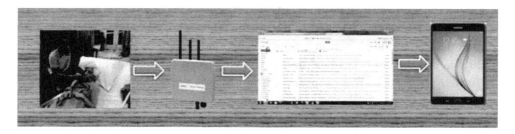

Hardware Details

Hardware details of the Test bed is presented in Table 2.

Table 2 Hardware Details of the Test Bed

S.No	Device Name	Specifications	Quantity
	RCE - Wh10 - Smart fitness Band Tracker – Smart watch with Pedometer	NRF51822 (CORTEX M0 16MHZ) chipset, Built-in 80mah Lithium-ion polymer rechargeable battery, Inbuild NFC Compatibility, Supports Bluetooth 4.0 smart bracelet, Android 4.3 / iOS 7.1	3
	Lenovo ThinkPad X250	5th Generation Core i processors, Windows 8 Pro, SSD 1 terabyte HDD, DDR3L-1600 PC3-12800 1600 MHz, 500GB HDD, 5400 rpm	1
	Cloud Storage – Google Drive	Google Drive Storage Space	15 GB
	Moto G5s Plus	4GB RAM, 64GB Internal memory, Android v7.1 with 2.0GHz Snapdragon 625 octa-core processor	1
	BSNL DSL W200 Modem	Four Ethernet ports (10/ 100 Mbps) for PC connectivity, down-link speed up to 24 Mbit/s and an up-link speed up to 1 Mbit/s, WLAN access as WLAN router, IEEE 802.11b/g/n specifications (Speed up to 150 Mbps), WEP, WPA and WPA2 security specifications **LAN Configuration:** IP Address: 192.168.1.11 Subnet Mask: 255.255.255.0 Default Gateway: 192.168.1.1	1

Details of the Data Collected

The details of the data collected by the ANNA framework are presented in Table 3 and used for implementation by HCEHMS.

Data Collection Team Details

The detailed account of the data collection team is presented in Table 4.

Table 3. Details of the Data Collected

S.No.	Data Collected	Details of the Data
	CID	Patient Aadhaar Number
	Name	Name of the Patient
	Age	Age of the Patient
	Sex	Sex of the Patient
	Date	Date of the Health Data Collected (DD-MM-YY)
	Time	Time of the Health Data Collected (Hr-mm-ss)
	BP	Blood Pressure of the Patient at a particular time (mmhg)
	SpO$_2$	Blood Oxygen of the Patient at a particular time (%)
	HR	Heart Rate of the Patient at a particular time (bpm)

Table 4. Details of the Data Collection Team

S.No.	Details	No. of Persons Involved
	No. of Patients	3
	Health Professionals	Professional Doctor – 1, Staff Nurse – 1 Health Vendor – 1
	Computer Professionals	2

Sample Data

a. Patients' Information

The information of the patients whose health data are collected for the research is presented in Table 5.

Table 5. Patients' Information

S.No	Name	CID	Age	Sex
1	P$_1$	9274 5110 9863	73	Female
2	P$_2$	5591 7371 5963	81	Female
3	P$_3$	9790 0129 0212	63	Female

b. Health Team's Information

Table 6 presents the general information of the medical team.

Table 6. Details of the Medical Team

S.No.	Name	Role	CID	Email	Mobile number
1	MT_1	Doctor	3797 5461 5830	cleetus.jose@gmail.com	9976992411
2	MT_2	Nurse	6830 3191 8784	sr.sheelasat@gmail.com	9489092730
4	MT_3	Health Vendor	8486 5454 7218	annaimedicals@gmail.com	9443156642

c. Health History of the Patients

The health history of the patient will help the viewer to understand the need for continues monitoring of the patient. Patient 1, whose CID is 9274 5110 9863 have very low pressure level with high diabetic. This Patient is under continues monitoring of physician. Patient 2 has CID as 5591 7371 5963. The CID of the Patient 3 is 9790 0129 0212. As diagnosed of having high blood pressure, Patient P_2 has been advised to have BP tablets for last 15 years.

d. Methodology of the Data Collection

The proposed Home care Elderly Health Monitoring System is experimented in a Senior Citizens Care Home where the elderly persons of age more than 60 are selected for analysis (Aazam Mohammad et al.,2014). An experimental set up is created using RCE - Wh10 - Smart fitness Band Tracker a Smart watch with Pedometer, Lenovo ThinkPad X250, Moto G5s Plus and a BSNL DSL W200 Modem. Patients are asked to wear the smart watch for a period of six months from December 2017 to May 2018. Blood Pressure (BP), Blood Oxygen level (spO_2) and heart rate are collected daily twice and collected data are stored in a Laptop. The health data are collected daily between 9 am to 6 pm, to keep them under continuous health surveillance. The health staff carefully observed them by viewing the patients' health data in his mobile. If any change is found then immediate action will be carried out by the doctor as per his instruction.

e. Sample Health Data

The sample health data are tabulated in Table 7.

Table 7. Sample Health Data

S.No.	CID	Date (DD-MM-YY)	Time (Hr-mm-ss)	BP (mmHg)	spO$_2$ (%)	HR (bpm/min)
	83001061	10-12-2017	10-11-31	120/80	99	84
	15432451	10-12-2017	10-40-19	120/80	99	84
	93147888	10-12-2017	10-27-52	140/90	98	70
	83001061	10-12-2017	17-07-29	130/70	99	80
	15432451	10-12-2017	17-28-47	130/70	99	84
	93147888	10-12-2017	18-14-23	130/80	97	80
	83001061	11-12-2017	10-10-50	130/70	99	80
	15432451	11-12-2017	10-49-27	130/70	99	80
	93147888	11-12-2017	11-20-31	120/90	99	82
	83001061	11-12-2017	10-57-29	120/70	98	80
	15432451	11-12-2017	11-34-10	120/70	98	80
	93147888	11-12-2017	16-04-46	130/90	97	84
	83001061	12-12-2017	16-11-29	120/80	98	82
	15432451	12-12-2017	16-28-15	120/80	98	82
	93147888	12-12-2017	09-47-51	140/70	98	82
	83001061	12-12-2017	10-14-41	110/70	99	78
	15432451	12-12-2017	11-40-16	110/70	99	78
	93147888	14-12-2017	18-05-31	140/70	98	82
	83001061	14-12-2017	18-24-59	130/80	99	80
	15432451	14-12-2017	19-57-04	130/80	99	80

Chapter Summary

This chapter describes the various standard protocols based on IoT layers and provides the IoT protocols and their appropriate applications. Also, this chapter list out various issues and challenges of IoT protocol suite. Finally, designing the real time scenarios.

REFERENCES

Abdul, R., Khan, M. M., Lodhi, M. A., & Hussain, F. B. (2016). Rank attack using objective function in RPL for low power and lossy networks. *International Conference on Industrial Informatics and Computer Systems (CIICS)*, 1-5.

Abomhara, M., & Koien, G. M. (2014). Security and privacy in the Internet of Things: Current status and open issues. *Privacy and Security in Mobile Systems (PRISMS), 2014 International Conference on IEEE*, 1-8. 10.1109/PRISMS.2014.6970594

Ali, R., Lasebae, A., & Loo, J. (2014). A secure authentication protocol for IP-based wireless sensor communications using the Location/ID Split Protocol (LISP). *Trust, security and privacy in computing and communications (TrustCom), 2014 IEEE 13th international conference on IEEE*, 840-845.

Areej, A., Ji, H., Gong, T., Nixon, M., Ammar, R., & Han, S. (2017). ARM: A hybrid specification-based intrusion detection system for rank attacks in 6TiSCH networks. *Emerging Technologies and Factory Automation (ETFA), 22nd IEEE International Conference on IEEE*, 1-8.

Dey, A. (2019). *Internet Of Things (IoT), Security, privacy, application and trends*. Retrieved 5 Nov 2020 from https://medium.com/@arindey/internet-of-things-iot-security-privacy-applications-trends-3708953c6200

Eleonora, B. (2014). The Internet of Things vision: Key features, applications and open issues. *Computer Communications*, *54*, 1–31. doi:10.1016/j.comcom.2014.09.008

Gamundani Attlee, M. (2015). An impact review on internet of things attacks. *Emerging Trends in Networks and Computer Communications (ETNCC), 2015 International Conference on, IEEE*, 114-118. 10.1109/ETNCC.2015.7184819

Hossein, S., & Hithnawi, A. (2014). Security comes first, a public-key cryptography framework for the internet of things. *Distributed Computing in Sensor Systems (DCOSS), 2014 IEEE International Conference on IEEE*, 135-136.

Israa, A., & Svetinovic, D. (2014). A taxonomy of security and privacy requirements for the Internet of Things (IoT). *Industrial Engineering and Engineering Management (IEEM), 2014 IEEE International Conference on IEEE*, 1244-1248.

Linus, W., Raza, S., & Voigt, T. (2013). Routing Attacks and Countermeasures in the RPL-based Internet of Things. *International Journal of Distributed Sensor Networks*.

Loong, K. S., Kumar, S. S., & Tschofenig, H. (2014). Securing the internet of things: A standardization perspective. *IEEE Internet of Things Journal*, *1*(3), 265–275. doi:10.1109/JIOT.2014.2323395

Luigi, A., Iera, A., & Morabito, G. (2010). The internet of things: A survey. *Computer Networks*, *54*(15), 2787–2805.

Mahmud, H. M., Fotouhi, M., & Hasan, R. (2015). Towards an analysis of security issues, challenges, and open problems in the internet of things. *Services (SERVICES), 2015 IEEE World Congress on IEEE*, 21-28.

Manish. (2020). *IoT Analytics – 3 Major Uses Cases of Internet of Things Analytics.* Retrieved, 2 Nov 2020 from https://data-flair.training/blogs/iot-analytics

Mohammad, A., Khan, I., Alsaffar, A. A., & Huh, E.-N. (2014). Cloud of Things: Integrating Internet of Things and cloud computing and the issues involved. *Applied Sciences and Technology (IBCAST), 11th International Bhurban Conference on IEEE*, 414-419.

Pavan, P., & Chavan, G. (2015). A survey: Attacks on RPL and 6LoWPAN in IoT. In *Pervasive Computing (ICPC), 2015 International Conference on*. IEEE.

Shankar, B. S., Tripathy, S., & Chowdhury, A. R. (2015). Design challenges and security issues in the Internet of Things. *Region 10 Symposium (TENSYMP), 2015 IEEE*, 90-93.

Singh, M. G., Upadhyay, P., & Chaudhary, L. (2014). The internet of things: Challenges and security issues. *Emerging Technologies (ICET), 2014 International Conference on IEEE*, 54-59.

ENDNOTE

[1]   https://www.nordicsemi.com/eng/Products/Bluetooth-low-energy/nRF51822

Chapter 4
Overview of Edge Computing and Its Exploring Characteristics

Sangamithra A.
VIT University, India

Margaret Mary T.
Kristu Jayanti College, India

Clinton G.
Sambharm Institute of Technology, India

EXECUTIVE SUMMARY

Edge computing is the concept of the distributed paradigm. In order to improve the response time and to save the bandwidth, it brings the computation and the storage of the data closer to the location whenever it is needed. Edge computing is one of the very famous and blooming concept in today's era. It has been used in so many applications for various purposes. Edge computing can be defined as infrastructure of physical compute which is placed between the device and the cloud to support various application and which brings the cloud closer to the end user or end devices. In this chapter, the authors discuss the origin of the edge paradigm, introduction, benefits. These are some of the criteria to be elaborated in the chapter overview of edge paradigm.

DOI: 10.4018/978-1-7998-4873-8.ch004

ORIGIN/HISTORY OF EDGE COMPUTING

Edge computing is one of the most popularity concepts in the IoT platform. This edge computing forms the foundation for the next generation of digital business as one of the top most technology trends.

Figure 1. Era of Edge Computing

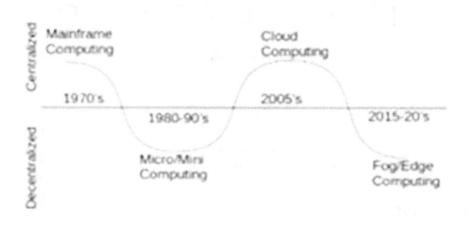

Because of this drastic growth of the edge computing, we were wondering how this edge computing started and how it has become more popular. Within a few decades the entire it has changed to the edge computing, which started from the mainframe, client/server to the cloud and at last to the edge computing. The edge computing platform allows edge nodes to respond to reducing bandwidth consumption, network latency and service demand. (Wei Yu Fan Liang & William Grant Hatcher (2017) In what way these all evolutions are interconnected. Everything is discussed detail in the below paragraph.

DECENTRALIZED COMPUTING:

The edge computing origin can be tracked in the year 1990, when the Akamai has introduced the content delivery network. It is one of the large distributing platforms to serve the web traffic. The primary goal of the CDN is to speed up the delivery of the web content .Where the nodes will be located geographically closest to the user in order to deliver the content which is cached such as images videos documents etc..

In 1997 when nobetetol has demonstrated this agile application on different web servers, which offload the certain task in surrogates. Their surrogates fix the goal to relieve the computing resource load and also to improve the battery life of the mobile devices. In 2001, Satyanarayanan has taken this approach and generalised in the paper of the pervasive computing. (Gheorghe et.al., 2019)

Decentralized and scalable applications were used in 2001 to propose different peer to peer networks. The fault tolerant routing, object location and load balancing has enabled with these self organising overlay networks. The latency of applications is also improved with the peer to peer network. Edge Computing is a paradigm that proposes data processing and storage at the edge of the network. For the Mobile Edge Computing, the edge is represented by pervasive Radio Access Networks. Edge computing addresses a variety of applications and use cases. For instance, edge model can be used in Smart Cities, Cyber-physical infrastructures, Wireless Sensors and Actuators Networks (Gheorghe et.al., 2019)

Figure 2. Origin of Edge computing

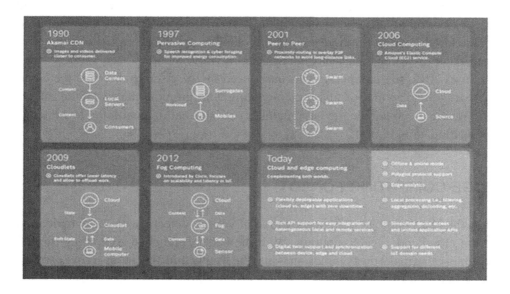

CLOUD COMPUTING

Cloud computing is one of the powerful link to the history of the edge computing, and it has the special mention also. This cloud computing came into the market with attractive attention in the year 2006, this is the year the amazon has introduced the elastic compute cloud (Lizhe Wang & Gregor von Laszewski (2010). Which open the new opportunities in the terms of visualization, computation and capacity of the storage. Even though the cloud computing is not the solution for all the use cases. At the current stage, the Cloud computing is still evolving and there exists no widely accepted definition. Based on our experience, we propose an early definition of Cloud computing as follows: "A computing Cloud is a set of network enabled services, providing scalable, QoS guaranteed, normally personalized, inexpensive computing infrastructures on demand, which could be accessed in a simple and pervasive way" . (Lizhe Wang & Gregor von Laszewski (2010)

FOG AND CLOUDLET COMPUTING

Satyanarayanan has introduced the cloudlet in one of the paper named the case of VM based cloudlets in mobile computing in the year of 2009. In this he has focused major in the latency which is proposed with two tier architecture. Basically among the two tier the first tier indicates for the higher latency and the second indicated for the lower latency. Butmore movers this cloudlet can store only the soft state like cached copies of the data. (Satyanarayanan, M,2009)

So in 2012, fog computing was introduced by the cisco to dispread the cloud infrastructure The aim of this fog computing is to promote the scalability of the IoT. Where it can handle the large number data for real time with the low latency application.

EDGE COMPUTING FOR IOT

Now the IT technology has got a solution of various defects, with the combination of the cloud and edge computing. With the help of the edge computing the IoT generalise can make the complex ones into the simple thing in other way, we can find the solutions for the complex IoT. In any organization needs a storage, computing power to execute the various applications and visualizing the data from the different locations, at that time the cloud computing enters into the play. And in the same way when the need the low latency, with reduced backend traffic and low autonomous action for the confidential data, edge computing enters into the play(Wei Yu Fan

Liang & William Grant Hatcher,2017) With the help of the combination of the cloud and edge computing so many solutions can be found for the complex IoT techniques.

With the rapid development of the technology, there are lot of IoT devices are in use in recent years. There is a chance of increase in the number of usage of IoT devices in future, because in the year 2019, there are more than 6 billion IoT devices are in use. The rise in the usage of the devices it is because there is increase in the data generation. Because of the generation of large amount of data there might be the problem to process the data; this is one of the challenging task to do that.

Figure 3. Edge Computing

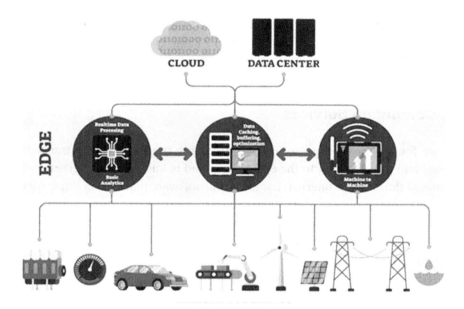

The data which is stored in the cloud can be generated with the IoTdevices, these type of data needs a faster processing and response. Because of the latency transmission increase due to the distance between the cloud and IoT, the IoT devices face some problems in the performance.

At this time the edge computing concept has been came into the play, in order to sort out this problems. Eventhough the edge computing concept similar to the content delivery network, the data generated by the IoT devices is processed by the edge server in edge computing instead of the centralized cloud. This edge server which is serve as a bridge between the user and the cloud in order to decrease the transmission latency to provide a speedy performances of the devices. Because in some area which requires the minimal transmission latency video streaming, smart devices, gaming in cloud etc. Incase if there is any delay in the data transmission, these areas will become more dangerous. Thus, the edge computing can be able to reduce the transmission latency when there is a huge data to be transmitted. (Shi W Cao, J Zhang, Q Li, Y & Xu, L. 2016).

The real time data processing without any transmission latency can be done with the help of edge computing and the network bandwidth also reduced. Edge which refers to the computing infrastructure appears closer to the data's. The edge computing is nesscessary to push from cloud service, pull from IoT and Change from data consumer to producer. So it play very significant role. It is also known as a distributed framework, where the data is processed closest to the origin. Edge computing which connects to the internet for receiving information from the cloud and to deliver back to the cloud. Which requires a effective use of resource that may not be connected to the network (Shi W Cao, J Zhang, Q Li, Y & Xu, L. 2016). The wide range of technologies like wireless sensor network, peer to peer networking cloud/fog computing can be covered with the help of the edge computing.

Edge Computing Services

There are four types of edge computing, like how the data will be transmitted, processed and transfer back to the end user. Cloud is known as the servers, which are accessed through the internet, database and software that run on those servers. Which is located in the data centres for all over the world. Without managing the physical servers or run software applications on the machines manually can be done with the help of the cloud servers.

There are most three main categories of the cloud computing services.

- SaaS – Software as a Service

It is a cloud base service abbreviated as a Software as a Service. It is a method of delivering a software and licensing where the software can be accessed through the subscription than buying and installing in the personal compuers. Some of the example of SaaS are GooleApps, Dropbox, Zendesk, Mailchimp etc. (gudwriter,2018)

- PaaS – Platform as a Service

PaaS stands for Platform as a Service, it is also a cloud based services . According to the name it provides a platform, which includes a programming language, database, operating system etc. Some of the examples of PaaS are Heroku, Force. com, Apache, Openshift etc.

- IaaS – Infrastructure as a Service

It is a instant computing infrastructure which is termed as a Infrastructure as a Service. It is a form of a cloud based services which delivers a fundamental computing networks. Complexity of buying and managing the own physical devices and decentralized network can be avoided with the help of the IaaS. Some of the example of IaaS is Amazon Web Services, Microsoft Azure, Google Compute engine etc. (gudwriter,2018)

Figure 4. SimpleCloudComputing

The cloud works through the internet service connection by enabling the acess of the user and downloading the data from any chosen devices, like smart phones,laptop, tablet etc. With the help of this cloud storage the document can be edited simultaneously along with the other user even when they are away from the working place.

Advantages And Disadvantages

We knew that edge computing is used in many IoT devices for their advantages and it has some disadvantages too, in this content will just describe the advantages and disadvantages of edge computing.

Advantages

- Speed
- Security
- Cost
- Reliability
- Scalability

Speed

In all Company each and every seconds of a business is very much important. Because of latency issue most of the company will be cost 1000 of dollars which will make the company stock growth goes low. This edge computing which has a power like by reducing the latency it will increase the network speed. It will process the data closer to the information part so that travelling distance will b get reduced. Because of this concept of edge computing the latency can be measured in microseconds from milliseconds. Due to this the quality, speed and overall services can be increased.

Security (searchcio.techtarget)

Increasing in the technology, hacking part of the hacker also increased to steal the confidential data to hack and so on. So here whatever the information is present on the cloud, may be has the chances of getting hacked by the hacker easily. So here the edge computing plays a role, which sends only the applicable information or data to the cloud, so the hacking at the cloud can be prevented. Because sometimes the edge computing does not require a network connection. In case if the hackers manage attempt to penetrate the cloud , they cannot fetch all the information. Due to this we cannot assume that edge computing is overall free from hacking, but we can analyze that comparatively edge computing has lower risks than the cloud

Cost

IoT is one of the trending concept in today's world, because of the top trending network bandwidth, data storage and computational power the IoT devices are costly. With the help of edge computing the dta storage and bandwidth can be reduced so automatically the cost of the IoT devices also will get reduced, which is affordable to most of the users in the world. And not all the information's will sent to the cloud, only the needed data will be sent to the cloud. So obviously the infrastructure cost of IoT devices will get reduced to the affordable cost.

Reliability

Reliability part can be handled very well by the edge computing. The uninterruotible services can be given by edge computing because most of the time the edge computing will not depend on the network connections, so the user no need to worry about the internet connection interrupt or slow internet connection etc. A reliable connection is assured for the IoT devices because the data process and storage can be done locally by edge computing in microdata centres. In any remote location if there is no reliable network also the usage of edge computing is recommended.

Scalability

When we process the data in the cloud computing, the data needs to be forwarded to the centralized datacenter. Because of centralized datacenter, if any one wish to modify or expand this datacenter it will be more costly. Our own IoT network can be scaled without worrying about the storage requirements with the help of the edge,

Disadvantages

- Security
- Incomplete Data
- More Storage Space
- Investment Cost
- Maintenance

Security

Security is the main issue in all the IT technology, here also in edge distributed environment security is the challenging task. There might be risk of identity theft and security breaches in edge computing due to the concept of processing data outside of the edge network. Whenever any new IoT devices are added, there might be increase in the opportunity of the attacker to penetrate the device.

Incomplete Data

In edge computing whatever the data only the partial sets of data is analyzed, other than this data other set of data's are discarded. Because of this partial analyze most of the company has chances of losing the valuable information's. The organisation must decide what type of information they are willing to loose before using the edge computing.

More Storage Space

Comparatively edge computing takes a more storage space on any device. In order to implement the process with the hep of edge computing, we need to remember it will take more storage capacity to process the data. (searchcio.techtarget)

Investment Cost

Implementing the edge infrastructure we need additional equipments and resources because of the complexity, so the investment cost is high in edge computing. And the IoT devices also with the edge computing comes with the need of more hardware, so overall it leads to a more efficiency and substantial investment is required.

Maintenance

Edge computing is a distributed system, which means there will be so many network combinations with several nodes. Due to this edge computing requires a higher maintenance cost than any centralized infrastructure. (Gerrit Mur,IEEE)

Top 5 Benefits of Edge Computing

1.   Speed and Latency

When data take much time to process then obviously the relevant of that particular data will be less. In most of the autonomous data, whatever the data it collects and requires, those data will be useless for a couple of seconds, when we take a busy roadway in that milliseconds are also matters especially. In factories milliseconds also matters, because in order to ensure data consistency the system perpetually monitor all aspects of the process manufacturing. In most of the cases there will not be no time to make a round trip of data from and to between the cloud. Latency can be eliminated by confining the data analysis to the edge and also translates into a fastest response time. Because of this the data will become more relevant, actionable and useful. Overall traffic also easily reduced with the help of the edge computing, which improvise the performance of the all enterprise applications and services. (searchcio.techtarget)

2.   Security

The critical business and operating processes which rely on actionable data are highly vulnerable, when all of the data eventually feed in cloud analyzer through a single pipe. At the final result, a single DDoS attack can disturb entire operations for a multinational company. Whenever the tools of data analysis distribute across the enterprises, it will be get distributed with the risk. Because of the argues expansions of the edge computing, as a whole the organisations has been diminishes. And another truth is that when less data are transferred and there will be a less data can be intercepted. The compay issues like local compliance and privacy regulations as well as the issue of data soverginity can overcome with the help of the edge computing.

3.   Cost Savings

When it comes to transporting, managing and securing how one can justify spending the same amount of money on all, since all data is not the same and does not contain the same value. Because some data are critical and some is expendable of the operation. With the help of the edge computing it is easy to categorize the data from a management perspective. With the help of the edge computing we cannot able to eliminate the cloud, it is all about optimizing the flow of the data in order to maximize the operating cost. And it also helps to reduce the redundancy in data,The data that is created at the edge is stored temporarily. Whatever the data that is sent to the cloud it should store again which creates the level of the redundancy, automatically the redundant cost will get reduced if the redundant storage is reduced.

4.   Greater Reliability

When the devices of the edge store and processing the data, it automatically improves the reliability. The micro data centers which are prefabricated are built today to operate any environment. Which means that incase if there is any connection is lost to the cloud, the smart devices will not get impacted with the operation, in all the sites there will be a limitation in order to transfer the data, that is how much data can be transferred at a time. (searchcio.techtarget)

5.   Scalability

Scalability is also one of the advantage of the edge computing, which seen contrary to promoted theory. In cloud computing, whatever the data is transferring, the data will be forwarded to central location datacenter in most of the cases. In that case expanding or any modifying of the data in the centralized datacenter is much expensive. In a single implementation, the IoT devices can be deployed with their processing and data management tools at the edge, instead of waiting on the multiple sites of coordinations.

Figure 5. Benefits of Edge Computing for Business

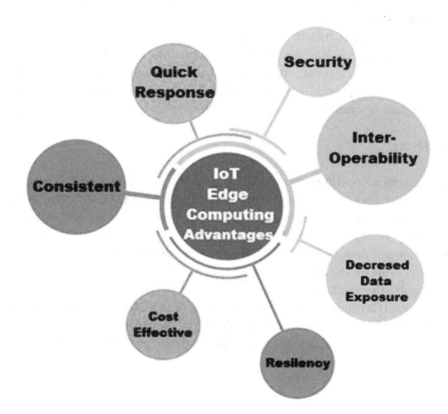

Data processing speed and analysis has increased in business of edge computing. Drastically the Internet of things is expected to grow, in order to reach about $1.6 trillion USD by 2025.(Baotong Chen & Jiafu Wan, 2018)Abundant amount of data that s increased in IoT enabled devices has processed with the help of edge technology.

Immediately the data process storage analyses has informed to the user in order to get into the action, with the help of edge computing, because edge computing process the data at the location itself. One of the major benefit of edge computing compared to cloud is that the data which is analyzed and acted.

Real-Time Data Analysis

Basically the data that is analyzed in order to take a proper action is sent to a central location. Though the edge computing which analyze the data allow to take place in the area near where it is created. With the help of the edge computing the data are kept near to the origin point so that in order to make real time decision is near.

Augmented Reality

Augmented reality can be improved with the help of the edge computing. Even users can gain more realistic and augmented reality experience. By taking this as aadvantage, the technology firms is one of the first thing to provide the upgraded experience to the customer.

Smart Manufacturing

Edge computing has given more improvement in the production of the manufacturing companies. The efficiency and margins are improved with the help of the real time data analysis. The problems are identifying by analyzing the data with the help of edge computing to avoid shutdown. (searchcio.techtarget)

Security Systems

In order to keep their information and business safe the large organization needs a fast and accurate security system. In lower bandwidth operation also the edge computing makes a security system more efficient. Whatever the data processed in security camera is collected and stored in a cloud through the signal. In edge computing which will be having some device in internal computer, with this device transferring the footage to the cloud is possible when it is needed.

In some other companies it is mean for reducing the cost of organizational by using smaller deployments. One of the major key benefits of the edge computing is to meet the company needs in a customized manner. (searchcio.techtarget)

Types of Edge Computing

What exactly edge computing is, seems to be indistinct and vary depending on who you ask. This post focuses on a definition that is started using and breaks down computing into four parts, Cloud, Compute Edge, Device Edge, and Sensor, and everything outside the Cloud is considered Edge Computing.

Cloud: Cloud principally alludes to gigantic server farms worked by cloud suppliers, for example, AWS, Azure, and GCP, however would likewise incorporate VMware Cloud on AWS and other cloud or facilitating suppliers. The primary qualities of the cloud are that it's brought together and work at scale. The advantage is that you have high foundation accessibility, admittance to a great deal of administrations and essentially unbounded measure of assets. The downside is that as these are unified, arrange network to sensors or gadgets at the edge can't be ensured and inactivity will be higher. System traffic to or from the cloud doubtlessly likewise causes an expense.

This is likewise alluded to as a smaller scale DC and is a little datacenter comprising of anything from a couple up to a few racks of workers. These are commonly found close or close to IoT gadgets and may likewise be fundamental for nearby consistence reasons. The key is that these server farms have cooling and so on and contain standard rack-mounted workers, (Weisong Shi & Jie Cao; Quan Zhang, 2016). You can have a considerable amount of assets situated in these server farms, however not similar scope of administrations and limit as in the cloud. An advantage is that idleness to gadgets at the edge ought to be less contrasted with the cloud, and system transmission capacity may be higher and more dependable.

Gadget Edge: This comprises of one or a couple of little workers and is additionally called a nano DC. It would just comprise of one or a couple of little workers and have insignificant figure limit. Workers in this class would likely not be rack mounted and would need to be equipped for running without cooling. They are regularly found in areas for the most part not related with a server farm, for example, in processing plants, wind turbines or vehicles and can be rough to deal with outrageous conditions. The advantage is that they could be found right close to IoT sensors and inertness, transmission capacity or network issues would be insignificant. The disadvantage is such little gadgets would just have the option to give least limit and administrations. (Baktir,et.al.,2017)

Figure 6. Edge computing procedure

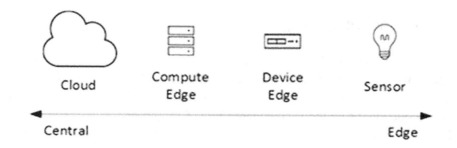

86

What are Edge Computing Applications

While it's not exactly accurate to define programs as specific edge computing applications, there are many ways in which edge computing infrastructure can be deployed to improve network-based services. The key factor involves pushing processing-capable hardware closer to the network edge.

This can take the form of an edge data center, which is often a multi-tenant colocation facility located in or near an emerging market with a rapidly growing consumer base. These markets are often far away from the hyper scale data centers that host the most popular cloud computing applications and streaming media platforms. (Blesson Varghese, 2016). By placing servers in an edge data center, companies can effectively create a relay station of sorts that can process essential data close to end users while passing less urgent data along to a larger facility located elsewhere. Content providers can also cache high-demand media in these data centers to allow local users to access it more easily.

Processing-capable IoT devices can perform in a similar fashion. With enough on-board computing power and storage to handle most tasks, an edge IoT device can collect and analyze local data even when disconnected from a broader network. It may not possess full functionality when running in an "offline" mode, but it can still perform a number of useful tasks. When it does reconnect to the network, it can transmit stored data and access additional processing resources. Even when connected to the network, the IoT device can still use edge computing by handling much of its data processing locally rather than relying on the servers in a cloud data center. This allows it to cut down on latency and provide much greater versatility.

The ability to capture insights from real-time data, without impacts from latency and network-related bottlenecks is changing the way many industries can operate— bringing tangible benefits to consumers and companies alike.

Grid Edge Control and Analytics

Smart Grids, as we now know them, essentially a grid which is evolved from traditional power to smarter grids. It goes on by establishing two-way communication channels between power distribution infrastructure and the recipient consumers (residential households, commercial buildings, etc.) and the efficacy head-end. Wide-area network (WAN) internet protocols plays the backbone. The implausible growth-rate the internet of things is experiencing takes gradually transferred over into the industrial side (IoT), fetching with copious technologies that can flawlessly monitor, manage and control the several functions within the electric grid's distribution infrastructure.

With the quickening development away from petroleum derivatives onto appropriated sustainable power sources (particularly sun based), current force lattices are stressed, presently entrusted with grasping demonstrated shrewd advances that are fit for incorporating and dealing with these dispersed vitality assets into existing matrices, making a blended and practical circulation arrange a brilliant matrix.

Edge grid computing technologies are aiding benefits with innovative real-time monitoring and analytics aptitudes, creating actionable and respected insights on power plant like renewables. This is something SCADA-based systems might not ever do, as they were intended well before the renewable and technological boom.

From private housetop sun oriented to business sun based homesteads, electric vehicles, wind ranches and hydroelectric dams–smart meters are creating gigantic measure of valuable information that can help utilities with investigation on vitality creation, accessibility, prerequisites and pinnacle utilization expectations. This permits utilities to all the more naturally keep away from blackouts and overcompensation lessening generally speaking expenses and vitality squander. Grid Edge Controllers are intelligent servers deployed as an interface between the edge nodes and the utility's core network.

Oil and Gas Remote Monitoring

Ongoing Safety observing is absolutely critical for basic foundation and utilities like oil and gas. In view of this wellbeing and dependability, many forefront IoT checking gadgets are as yet being created so as to shield basic apparatus and frameworks against catastrophe.

Current progressed hardware utilizes Internet of Things tactile gadgets for temperature, dampness, pressure, sound, dampness and radiation. Along with the expansive vision capacities of web convention empowered cameras (IP cameras) and different innovations, this creates a tremendous and persistent measure of information that is then joined and investigated to give key bits of knowledge that can dependably assess the soundness of any running framework.

Registering assets at the edge permit information to be investigated, handled and conveyed to end-clients progressively(Baotong Chen & Jiafu Wan,2018). Empowering control focuses with admittance to the information as it happens, anticipating and forestalling glitches in the most improved opportune way.

This is the most viable arrangement, as time is of the substance in these basic frameworks. This rings most obvious when managing basic foundation, for example, oil, gas and other vitality benefits, any disappointments inside certain will in general be cataclysmic in nature and ought to consistently be kept up with most extreme insurance and security methods.

1.   Edge Video Orchestration

Edge video organization utilizes edge processing assets to actualize an exceptionally improved conveyance strategy for the broadly utilized at this point data transfer capacity substantial asset video. Rather than conveying video from a brought together center system through all the system bounces, it cleverly coordinates, stores and disseminates video records as near the gadget as could be expected under the circumstances. Think o fit as an exceptionally proficient and specific occurrence of a substance download organize (CDN) only for video, directly at the edge for end-clients.

MEC-fueled video arrangement is generally helpful for huge open settings. Sports arenas, Concerts and other restricted occasions depend intensely on live video web based and investigation to make and increment income streams. (lanner-america,2018)

Newly made video cuts and live transfers can rapidly be served to paying clients in settings through rich media preparing applications running on portable edge workers and hotspots. This brings down the administration costs and dodges numerous quality issues emerging from bottleneck circumstances with terabytes of weighty video traffic hitting the versatile systems.

This is something 5G edge figuring is intended to unravel in the coming years. As of now, arrange administrator EE is examining the potential for these sorts of administrations in a joint effort with Wembley Stadium, the public soccer arena of the UK.

2.   Traffic Management

Because of the computationally costly complexities of traffic the board productivity (Read: Traveling sales rep issue), perhaps the most ideal approaches to enhance traffic the executives frameworks is by improving ongoing information. Insightful transportation frameworks utilize edge figuring advancements, particularly for traffic the executives measures

The flood of IoT gadgets and enormous measures of live information require preprocessing and sifting nearer to the gadgets, before these a great many information streams can hit the center/cloud systems.

Utilizing edge figuring the gigabytes of tangible and uncommon information is examined, separated and packed before being communicated on IoT edge Gateways to a few frameworks for additional utilization(lanner-america,2018) This edge preparing saves money on organize costs, stockpiling and working expenses for traffic the board arrangements.

3.   Autonomous Vehicles

While independent vehicles are not yet prepared for the standard, without edge figuring strategies their feasibility would be a lot more years later. With the lull of moore's law and generally advance computational force the installed PCs will currently frame a sizeable cost of self-ruling vehicles.

The hordes of complex tangible innovations associated with independent vehicles require enormous data transfer capacity and continuous equal processing abilities (Weisong Shi & Schahram Dustdar (2016). Edge and conveyed figuring methods increment wellbeing, spatial mindfulness and interoperability with current-age equipment.

With versatile edge processing, vehicles can trade on-going tangible information, substantiate and improve choices with less locally available assets bringing down the developing cost of self-governing AI frameworks.

Making the Edge Computing Business Case

As inventive gadgets like self-governing vehicles and clinical sensors become more normal, edge processing will have an inexorably huge effect on society. With edge figuring system, associations will have the option to broaden organize administrations into zones that were beforehand past the range of customary structures. On account of numerous gadgets, the capacity to improve execution could actually spare lives. Consider, for example, the effect of utilizing clinical gadgets in hard to-arrive at provincial territories with restricted medicinal services choices. Edge processing can likewise improve wellbeing for mechanical assembling by recognizing gear issues before they cause glitches that could harm laborers.

Why Edge Computing Applications
Make Market Expansion Easier

The preparing capability of edge registering innovations additionally makes it simpler for organizations to grow their system administration into new business sectors without making similar framework ventures that were so important before. (Jianli Pan James Mc Elhannon (2018). That is uplifting news for districts with littler urban focuses and for provincial networks that come up short on the high-transmission capacity arranges availability normal to the Tier 1 business sectors found in and around significant urban communities.

Edge server farms are a lot littler and more affordable to fabricate and keep up than the hyper scale offices utilized by numerous endeavors and distributed computing suppliers. Building a vitality proficient edge in a little market is a generally unobtrusive venture that could give organizations a "first mover" advantage that delivers significant profits in both the short and long haul. Small scale server farms give significantly greater adaptability, permitting associations to target end clients with unmatched exactness. While an edge server farm may grow administration into a formerly underserved market, a miniaturized scale could be set in territories with more noteworthy interest to improve arrange execution or in considerably more removed regions to additionally broaden the system edge.

By and large, notwithstanding, IoT gadgets will beat these offices to the edge. Customers in generally detached zones (regarding system access) are now going to cell phones and cell systems to compensate for the absence of direct broadband access. Numerous organizations are as of now exploiting this pattern by introducing smaller scale server farms at the base of cell pinnacles to more readily encourage IoT availability. As these gadgets become more normal, imaginative systems like this will help organizations to arrive at more clients and incredibly grow their market reach.

Edge Computing and IoT

The quantity of IoT gadgets available for use today is now stunning, and there's a lot of information to propose that this figure will increment fundamentally in the coming years. With so numerous IoT gadgets associated with systems around the globe, edge registering is as of now majorly affecting how organizations structure their frameworks (Jianli Pan James Mc Elhannon,2018) The continuous interest for quicker, more proficient administrations and substance conveyance will push associations to improve their current edge systems. Organizations that neglect to put resources into edge figuring today could wind up in the unenviable situation of scrambling to make up for lost time to their rivals in the years ahead.

Gadgets associated with the web produce tremendous measures of information that gives a gigantic chance to organizations, yet in addition a similarly huge test regarding overseeing, examining, and putting away that information. Generally, these cycles were taken care of in an organization's private cloud or server farm, yet the sheer volume of information has stressed these systems to their outright cutoff points.

Edge frameworks ease this weight by pushing information handling endlessly from a unified center and dispersing it among nearby edge server farms and different gadgets closer to the source. Examining information closer to where it's gathered gives tremendous advantages regarding cost and proficiency. By using edge frameworks, organizations can likewise address issues related with low availability and the expense of moving information to a concentrated worker.

Industrial IoT

Industrial organizations remain to profit gigantically from edge processing since it permits them to change produced IoT edge gadgets (particularly modern machines) into expansions of their system foundation. Joined with present day AI and constant examination, information can be assembled, dissected, and applied quicker than at any other time, empowering IoT edge gadgets to self-control and react to changes.

5G Networks

The expansion of 5G systems, which will expand transmission capacity essentially and make it simpler to send high volumes of cell information, opens up various open doors for edge processing applications. Since G will assist with combatting inertness with its disseminated engineering, organizations will have the option to utilize these systems to extend their own system edge and move information unquestionably more effectively. As opposed to directing everything back to an incorporated worker, covering 5G systems will permit them to keep more information on the edge. These edge systems will likewise assist with conquering the inertness inciting "last mile" issue, in which communicated information bottlenecks through a progression of imperfect associations before arriving at its proposed clients. The innovation will likewise observe the development of shrewd city activities. (Gupta et., al., 2015).

Drawbacks of Edge Computing

The preparing capability of edge registering innovations additionally makes it simpler for organizations to grow their system administration into new business sectors without making similar foundation ventures that were so vital previously. That is uplifting news for districts with littler urban focuses and for country networks that come up short on the high-data transfer capacity arrange availability basic to the Tier-1 business sectors found in and around significant urban areas.

Edge server farms are a lot littler and more affordable to manufacture and keep up than the hyper scale offices utilized by numerous undertakings and distributed computing suppliers. Building a vitality effective edge in a little market is a moderately unobtrusive venture that could give organizations a "first mover" advantage that delivers significant profits in both the short and long haul. Smaller scale server farms give considerably greater adaptability, permitting associations to target end clients with unrivaled accuracy. While an edge server farm may grow administration into a formerly underserved market, a miniaturized scale could be set in territories with more prominent interest to improve organize execution or in considerably more inaccessible regions to additionally broaden the system edge.

As a rule, notwithstanding, IoT gadgets will beat these offices to the edge. Purchasers in generally secluded zones (regarding system access) are now going to cell phones and cell systems to compensate for the absence of direct broadband access. Numerous organizations are now exploiting this pattern by introducing smaller scale server farms at the base of cell pinnacles to all the more likely encourage IoT network. As these gadgets become more normal, creative systems like this will help organizations to arrive at more clients and extraordinarily grow their market reach.

The Future of Edge Computing

Moving information handling to the edge of the system can assist organizations with exploiting the developing number of IoT edge gadgets, improve arrange speeds, and upgrade client encounters. The versatile idea of edge figuring additionally makes it an ideal answer for quickly developing, light-footed organizations, particularly in the event that they're as of now utilizing colocation server farms and cloud framework. By exploiting edge figuring, organizations can enhance their systems to offer adaptable and dependable support that will reinforce their image and keep their clients cheerful.

Edge processing offers a few favorable circumstances over conventional types of system design and will doubtlessly keep on assuming a significant job for organizations going ahead. With increasingly more web associated gadgets hitting the market, inventive associations have likely just start to expose what's conceivable with edge processing.

REFERENCES

Baktir, A. C., Ozgovde, A., & Ersoy, C. (2017). How Can Edge Computing Benefit from Software-Defined Networking: A Survey, Use Cases & Future Directions. *IEEE Communications Surveys and Tutorials, 1.* Advance online publication. doi:10.1109/COMST.2017.2717482

Chen & Wan. (2018). Edge Computing in IoT-Based Manufacturing. *IEEE Communications Magazine, 56*(9). Advance online publication. doi:10.1109/MCOM.2018.1701231

Fan Liang, W. Y., He, X., & Hatcher, W. G. (2017). A Survey on the Edge Computing for the Internet of Things. IEEE Access, 6. doi:10.1109/ACCESS.2017.2778504

Gheorghe, A.-G., Crecana, C.-C., Negru, C., Pop, F., & Dobre, C. (2019). Decentralized Storage System for Edge Computing. *2019 18th International Symposium on Parallel and Distributed Computing (ISPDC),* 41–49. doi:10.1109/ISPDC.2019.00009

Gupta, A., & Jha, R. (2015). A Survey of 5G Network: Architecture and Emerging Technologies. *IEEE Access : Practical Innovations, Open Solutions, 1.* Advance online publication. doi:10.1109/access.2015.2461602

Mur. (1994). Edge Elements, their Advantages and their Disadvantages. *IEEE Transactions on Magnetics, 30*(5).

Pan & McElhannon. (2018). Future Edge Cloud and Edge Computing for Internet of Things Applications. *IEEE Internet of Things Journal, 5*(1). Advance online publication. doi:10.1109/JIOT.2017.2767608

Satyanarayanan, M., Bahl, P., Caceres, R., & Davies, N. (2009). The Case for VM-Based Cloudlets in Mobile Computing. *IEEE Pervasive Computing, 8*(4), 14–23. doi:10.1109/MPRV.2009.82

Shi, W., Cao, J., Zhang, Q., Li, Y., & Xu, L. (2016). Edge Computing: Vision and Challenges. *IEEE Internet of Things Journal, 3*(5), 637–646. doi:10.1109/jiot.2016.2579198

Shi & Dustdar. (2016). The Promise of Edge Computing. *Computer, 49*(5). Advance online publication. doi:10.1109/MC.2016.145

Varghese, B., Wang, N., Barbhuiya, S., Kilpatrick, P., & Nikolopoulos, D. S. (2016). Challenges and Opportunities in Edge Computing. *2016 IEEE International Conference on Smart Cloud (SmartCloud).* 10.1109/SmartCloud.2016.18

Wang, von Laszewski, Younge, He, Kunze, Tao, & Fu. (2010). *Cloud Computing: a Perspective Study.* doi:10.100700354-008-0081-5

Yi, L., & Li. (2015). A Survey of Fog Computing: Concepts, Applications and Issues. *Proceedings of Workshop on Mobile Big Data,* 37-42.

Chapter 5
IoT Trends

Suresh K.
Amrita School of Arts and Sciences, Amrita Vishwa Vidyapeetham, India

EXECUTIVE SUMMARY

The internet of things indicates a kind of system to interface anything with the internet dependent on stipulated conventions through data detecting hardware to direct data trade and correspondences so as to accomplish acknowledgments, situating, figuring out, checking, and organization. IoT empowers various advances about its engineering, qualities, and applications, but what are the future difficulties for IoT? IoT frameworks enable clients to accomplish further mechanization, investigation, and joining inside a framework. They improve the scope of these regions and their precision. IoT uses existing and developing innovation for detecting, systems administration, and apply autonomy. IoT abuses ongoing advances in programming, falling equipment costs, and current frames of mind towards innovation. Its new and propelled components acquire significant changes the conveyance of items, products, administrations, financial, and political effect of those changes.

INTRODUCTION

The Internet of things indicates to a kind of system to interface anything with the Internet dependent on stipulated conventions through data detecting hardware to direct data trade and correspondences so as to accomplish acknowledgments, situating, figuring out, checking, and organization. The way IOT empowers various advances, about its engineering, qualities and applications, IOT useful view and what are the future difficulties for IOT.

DOI: 10.4018/978-1-7998-4873-8.ch005

IoT frameworks enable clients to accomplish further mechanization, investigation, and joining inside a framework. They improve the scope of these regions and their precision. IoT uses existing and developing innovation for detecting, systems administration, and apply autonomy. IoT abuses ongoing advances in programming, falling equipment costs and current frames of mind towards innovation. Its new and propelled components acquire significant changes the conveyance of items, products, administrations, financial and political effect of those changes.

IoT Special Features

The most important features of IoT include artificial intelligence, connectivity, sensors, active engagement, and small device use. A brief review of these features is given below:

- AI –IoT essentially makes virtually anything "smart", meaning it enhances every aspect of life with the power of data collection, artificial intelligence algorithms, and networks. This can mean something as simple as enhancing your refrigerator and cabinets to detect when milk and your favourite cereal run low and to then place an order with your preferred grocer.
- Connectivity –New enabling technologies for networking, and specifically IoT networking, mean networks are no longer exclusively tied to major providers. Networks can exist on a much smaller and cheaper scale while still being practical. IoT creates these small networks between its system devices.
- Sensors –IoT loses its distinction without sensors. They act as defining instruments which transform IoT from a standard passive network of devices into an active system capable of real-world integration.
- Active Engagement –Much of today's interaction with connected technology happens through passive engagement. IoT introduces a new paradigm for active content, product, or service engagement.
- Small Devices–Devices, as predicted, have become smaller, cheaper, and more powerful over time. IoT exploits purpose-built small devices to deliver its precision, scalability, and versatility.

Literature Survey

The innovative smart city will be practice as an important perception to sort it out urban growth difficulties. It accumulates data expansively and evidently, communicate data extensively and securely and development data logically and resourcefully. This is not only to progress city managing and effective, it also advances urban facility stages, but then encourage workable city progress.

In this process, towards to construct a novel system of city development, the city can predetermine wisdom and actual identity result creation, such that the community public can sense the knowledge of the urban providing by intellect facilities and submissions.

Web of Things (IoT) is a system worldview in which physical, advanced, and virtual items are outfitted with proof, identification, systems administration, and handling capacities to impart with one another. Numerous IoT applications are given to bring solace and encourage the human life. The use of IoT innovations in the car industry has offered ascend to the idea of Industrial Internet of Things (IIoT) which encouraged utilizing of Cyber Physic Systems (Embitel, n.d.).

Due to the decent diversity, heterogeneity and huge volume of information produced by these elements, the utilization of customary database the board frameworks are not reasonable when all is said in done. In the structure of IoT information the executive frameworks, numerous distinctive standards have to be considered. These extraordinary standards permitted the proposition of a few methodologies for IoT information the executives. A few middleware or engineering focused arrangements encourage the reconciliation of created information (Motlagh, 2020).

Other accessible arrangements give proficient storing and ordering unstructured information just as the help to the NoSQL language. In this manner, this paper distinguishes the most significant ideas of information the board in IoT, reviews the present arrangements proposed for IoT information the board, talks about the most encouraging arrangements, and distinguishes pertinent open research issues on the theme giving rules to facilitate commitments(Suresh & Praveen, 2020).

Most as of late, another idea called, Internet of Things (IoT), shows up and it is viewed as the primary development to the fourth era of the Internet. IoT doesn't have an unambiguous and adequate definition from clients of the worldwide network. One of the best IoT definition thinks of it as a dynamic and worldwide system framework. Each system hub is viewed as keen with for the most part exceptionally constrained assets, particularly those of capacity, preparing and vitality. This suggests, among different issues, like legitimacy of information, execution, and security(Educba, n.d.).

Throughout the years, with the improvement of RFID innovation, sensors and actuators, remote versatile correspondence, installed frameworks and distributed computing of utilizations that advance around the Internet arrange. These applications are utilized to improve individuals live conditions in numerous zones. The applications are being produced for car industry with the idea of Industrial Internet of Things (IIoT), for example, dispersion frameworks, social insurance, reconnaissance also, security, fabricating industry, and so on (Medium, n.d.).

These IoT applications improve the support of human life, however it is more controls to streamline work standard and individual just as the advantage obtainable to the business. Mechanical IoT considered as a subset of IoT covers the spaces of machine-to-machine (M2M) and modern correspondence advances with robotization applications. In this way, IIoT has permitted a superior comprehension of the assembling procedure for proficient and reasonable creation. Besides, to expand profitability and effectiveness through knowledge and remote administration, utility organizations, agribusiness makers and human services suppliers have embraced the IIoT(SDGlobalTech, n.d.).

Background Study of IoT Trends

The decent variety of gadgets that constantly send information gives a huge volume of topographically scattered and heterogeneous information continuously. Right now, study and plan of databases the board strategies that consider every one of these specificities of IIoT-based applications are along these lines essential. (Motlagh, 2020) Generally, information the board is a wide idea that refers to structures, practices different techniques for dealing with the information lifecycle prerequisites of framework. With regards to IoT, information the executives should go about as a layer between the articles and gadgets where the applications use information for investigation purposes and administrations. Because of the exceptionally enormous measure of information and their particular attributes, the utilization of customary database frameworks would not be a superior arrangement. Without a doubt, the plan of IoT's information the board frameworks depend on a few standards. Depending on these various standards, a few information the executive's approaches have been proposed, for example, middleware-based IoT arranged on information and sources, information stockpiling and IoT information construction reinforce arrangements. The middleware based IoT approaches give a middleware among trainings and information storing ranges. Along these, the middleware encourages information streams directing in real time applications. IoT information can be produced quickly even in the huge volume of information and with a decent diversity of information types. So as to address these possible issues, information stockpiling arrangements propose information related conditions not just empowering effective putting away of enormous IoT information. These frameworks use hash tables with brought together ordering to perform discrete ordering in unique IoT systems. As information volumes are differing, arrangements that characterize adaptable diagram strengthen will guarantee interoperability.

There are some distributed review works that present various parts of the information the board in IoT. For instance, the creators investigate some proposed information the executive's answers for IoT. They give the unmistakable plan natives that ought to be tended to in an IoT information the executive's arrangement, and they present their information the board structure for IoT.

The creators of talk about various parts of information in IoT including the sources of information, information gathering, information handling, and the transmission gadgets. They additionally talk about difficulties brought by the requirements to oversee huge amounts of heterogeneous information across heterogeneous frameworks. The capacity of a colossal amount of created information turns out to be increasingly unpredictable, and developed the cloud IoT worldview. In this manner, the combination of Cloud and IoT talking about their complementarity and specifying what is heading to their reconciliation.

IoT in Networks

The idea of the Internet-of-Things (IoT) is imagined to progress the nature of current life. IoT measures have altogether changed different points of view in numerous structures through various yardsticks. It has connected with different fields including industry, human services, homes, car, game, amusement and others. This is acquired through the huge scale organization of Sensor Nodes (SN) with the capacity of noticing and publicizing data security. Be that as it may, this commitment raises significant issues since a ton of traffic needs to traverse the system. The various classes of system traffic for instance those produced from voice, money related exchange, driverless vehicles, SNs, and need to overcome rapidly or be separated because of security concerns. The prerequisites for different applications in IoT are quickly being expanded that outcome in the interest for progressively precise grouping of system traffic.

System traffic characterization has been a subject of enthusiasm from the beginning period of the Internet. It started by introducing port-based methodologies by which the system traffic is arranged dependent on the pre-owned ports. The advanced measurable and social methodologies where the system traffic is profoundly examined in a fine-grained way by profound learning draws near. Because of the quality of arrangement of system traffic as the initial step to recognize and characterize obscure system classes. It has been the fundamental enthusiasm of Internet Service Providers (ISP) so as to deal with the general execution of their system. In many cases, the most essential parts of the Internet that explicitly profits by the traffic order of system is security. This is on the grounds that the security arrangements can be upheld in the wake of dissecting the system traffic. Because of the significance of security and protection for various gatherings, arrange traffic order has gotten the most considerations in IoT.

In spite of the fact that most of endeavours in organize traffic grouping have been distributed in IP systems and it has more extensive space that gives answers for address different edges of the Internet of Things (IoT). This scope is because of the wide mix of different domains, for example, sensors and hubs that inducement in IoT to manage various issues. Persuaded by the way that IoT traffic is not quite the same as different kinds of system traffic that follows a steady example and an anticipated system conduct.

In the most recent decade, there are a lot of study papers that have been led for evaluating the current arrangements and applications for IoT. There are likewise various survey papers that distinguish new difficulties from alternate points of view. (Liu et al., 2018) For model, presents a far-reaching review of the Internet of Things worldview and empowering advances followed by an inspection of the significant research issues on IoT. It additionally examines ongoing innovations, for example, large information examination and cloud and haze registering identified with IoT. Security dangers and vulnerabilities in IoT were audited. It was trailed by proposing a scientific categorization of the present security dangers in the settings of utilization, design and correspondence in IoT.

Figure 1. IoT in Network

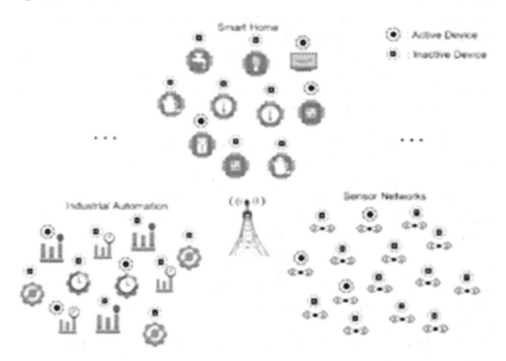

IoT in Smart City Technology.

The fast advancement and profound application of novel ideas and advances carried by the Internet of Things and distributed computing everywhere throughout the world. These advancements have progressively infiltrated into the field of brilliant urban communities. The customary urban framework, the framework that has been passed on since antiquated occasions, has an extremely inefficient and difficult method of activity and the data between the frameworks has not been adequately shared and interconnected. So as to take care of this arrangement of issues, this first investigations the advancement of the Internet of Things are distributed computing related advances and centres around the key advancements of the Internet of Things and cloud registering in the field of structure and application. Framework engineering, application framework structure, application bolster stage, different transmission systems and run of the mill sensors are examined in detail and on various levels. In city frameworks dependent on the Internet of Things, sensor systems are regularly set in inconsistent correspondence situations, and this generally causes the transmission of data to fall flat. Regardless of whether the sensor decides to transmit again after the data transmission is an improved issue. This examination study proposes an information accumulation in Markov chain to take care of the issue of transmitting information. The trial results show that the framework can understand data sharing, trade and combination between different detecting subsystems, comprehend the past data island wonder and meet the genuine needs of keen urban areas.

The procedure of the fast improvement of the city is likewise developing social issues: traffic blockage framework, inefficient urban administration, usual checking frameworks are imperfect, crisis reaction framework are not agreeable. The idea of city development focused on cutting edge advancements, for example, the Internet of Things and distributed computing has gotten another model for future urban advancement. Keen urban communities are the inevitable consequence of the advancement of urban models. The development of smart urban areas can fundamentally unknot the difficulty identified with urban advancement. The new brilliant city can be utilized as a basic way to take care of urban advancement issues. It can gather data exhaustively and straightforwardly, transmit data broadly and securely, and process data cleverly and effectively. (Educba, n.d.) It cannot just improve urban administration and operational proficiency, improve urban assistance levels in advance economical urban improvement. The foundation of fast urbanization and human progress, significant urban areas on the planet are for the most part confronting improvement issues, for example, vitality deficiency, natural contamination and traffic block. Urban figuring is another idea dependent on IoT recognition, with related information innovation and examination innovation as the centre.

Figure 2. IoT in Smart City Technology

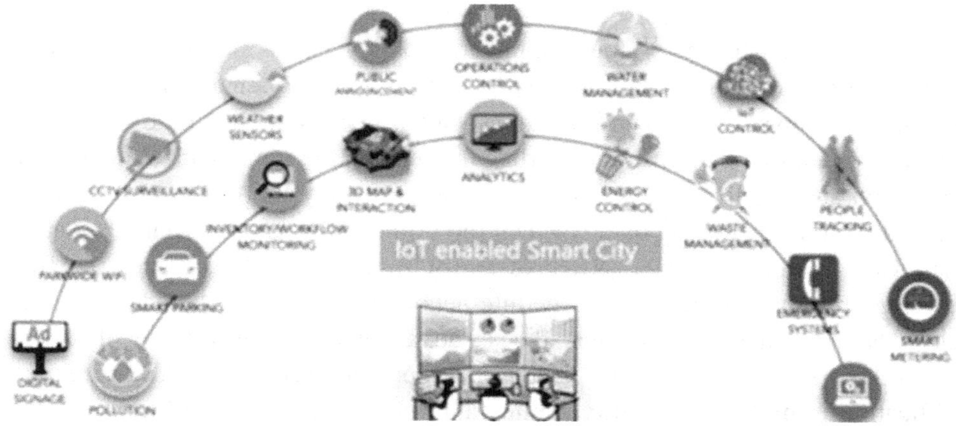

IoT in Supply Chain

In advancement of IoT, it is conceivable to follow the different data through its generation cycle and stored it in network. In today, these advances are as yet used to recognize preoccupations into unlawful markets just as the presentation of fake items. This guarantees the total trustworthiness of the item inventory network. (Suresh & Praveen, 2020) Complete honesty that incorporates the physical respectability and the trustworthiness of the item and all its subcomponents. Sensors are utilized to guarantee that the item is presented to natural conditions without harming any damages. The honesty of the methods for transport can be guaranteed, i.e., the item has never been in a territory where it ought not be. For example, risky process can't be moved to thickly populated or naturally touchy regions given the genuine results of a mishap. The trustworthiness of an item and all its sub-segments as indicated by the methods for generation should likewise be guaranteed. IoT advancements can empower recording of the considerable number of outflows created during the generation and in the vehicle of each sub-part through a staggered of a mind-boggling inventory network. By and large, new innovations are for the most part used to guarantee the full consistence of all the production network members against a lot of concurred rules, inside arrangements, and administration level understandings.

Figure 3. IoT in supply chain

IoT in Energy

The utilization of present-day advances related with the ideas of IoT and Internet of Services (IoS) has headed to a worldview change with new ideas and imaginative applications. The present pattern is to give increasingly unique administrations and market-based foundation where productivity and vitality investment funds can be better tended to through intelligent conveyance systems. One model is the production of Advanced Metering Infrastructure (AMI) in the vitality field. (Suresh & Mohan, 2020) These frameworks allude to frameworks that gather, measure and investigate the utilization of vitality from cutting edge gear, for example, power, gas, and water meters. These gadgets are for the most part alluded to as savvy meters. They are remote sensors that associate with one another, however can likewise help out sensor arranges at home to transmit their information. They have added to an IoT acknowledgment by incorporating genuine items, for example, remote sensor systems, inserted gadgets, and home apparatuses with other Internet content.

Figure 4. IoT in energy

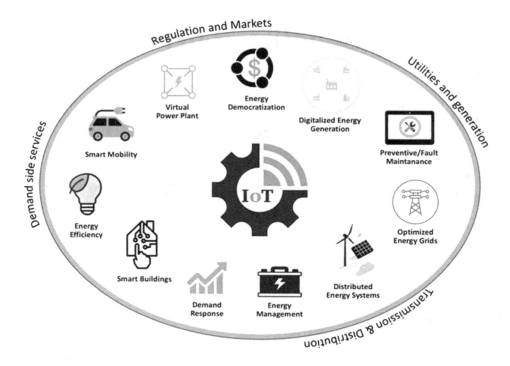

IoT in Healthcare

IoT is proposed to improve the personal satisfaction and prosperity via robotizing the essential errands that people ought to perform. Right now, and basic leadership can be overseen explicitly by machines. One of the primary utilizations of IoT in the restorative space is for helped living situations. Sensors are coordinated into the wellbeing observing gear utilized by patients. Consequently, the data gathered by these sensors is accessible on the Internet for doctors, relatives, and different overseers to improve treatment and responsiveness. (Embitel, n.d.) Moreover, IoT gadgets can be utilized screen patients observing medications and to assess the danger of new medications if there should be an occurrence of unfavourably susceptible responses and negative connections. Right now, creators of proposed the use of IoT in the therapeutic framework, particularly in clinical consideration. So also, at the Jena University Hospital in Germany, RFID innovation and IoT are utilized to advance both calculated procedures and to give better mind, to follow the gear of patients, particularly babies, and medications. This advantage both therapeutic suppliers as investment funds just as for patients since bogus medicines can be evaded. RFID innovation applied to blood the board can viably accomplish persistent distinguishing proof, lessen blood sullying and improve information assortment adequately. Notwithstanding RFID, sensors are sent in persistent rooms to catch quiet information and move it to wellbeing experts or clinic staff

Figure 5. IoT in healthcare

IoT in Transport and Distribution

The vehicle and conveyance part is among the first to receive IIoT. Basic applications created on vehicles permit remote observing and encourage the area and preparing of armadas, trucks, and vans. Logging driver hours, speed and driving conduct can improve security and rearrange consistence. Vehicles like transports and prepares with sensors-prepared streets and rails can give exact data to the driver for better and more secure travel. With the utilization of helped driving, it is conceivable to locate a decent course with data in need on congested roads and episodes. So also, in the new brilliant vehicle leaves, sensors are introduced to recognize appearance and take off of vehicles. This gives broad stopping the executive's arrangements that help drivers to spare time and fuel and to have a decent traffic the board. A noteworthy commitment to clog originates from drivers looking for open parking spots. (Suresh & Kashyap, 2020) Giving precise data about parking spots gives a superior progression of traffic, and it will likewise help reservation of parking spots legitimately from the vehicle. The execution of IoT in retail chain checking has a few focal points: RFID and Near Field Communication (NFC) can be utilized for observing each connection in the inventory network, extending from the subtleties of the item, acquisition of crude materials, generation, transportation and capacity, item deals and after-deals administrations. IoT will follow the stock in the stockroom, so the stock can be reloaded at the perfect time for a constant deal, which will decrease the holding up time of the client bringing about consumer loyalty and expanded deals. Clients can likewise be routinely educated about the conveyance times of the booked items. Indeed, even the compartments themselves are currently furnished with tables of constrained limit, which open conceivable outcomes for following and sorting out articles in a strategic chain of capacity and conveyance.

Various Data Categories in IoT

In IoT conditions, information originates from various sort of gadgets and speaks to billions of items. IoT information can be grouped into a few classes. A few information is discrete or nonstop, others are created naturally, and a few others presented by clients. Radio Frequency distinguishing proof (RFID) information Radio Frequency Identification alludes to ID and following utilizing radio waves. RFID labels can be embedded into items and used to transmit and get information. The RFID tag is situated in an incorporated circuit that can store information and a receiving wire to get and transmit signals. Labels can be scaled down to scarcely any millimetres long and width, consequently empowering their omnipresent use for regular articles. A tag is enacted by radio waves produced from a RFID peruse. The peruse discusses remotely with the tag. When actuated, the tag sends information put away in its memory identifying with the thing back to the peruse.

RFID labels can be dynamic or inactive. Dynamic RFID labels contain a battery and can work independently. Aloof RFID labels are possibly initiated when they get a radio wave sent by a RFID peruse. The innovation is presently utilized in numerous territories, for example, visas, animals following, street tolling, store network the board, coordination, stock control, and medicinal services. Expressive information about Objects, Processes, and frameworks Much of the intensity of IoT will originate from information or metadata that will be recorded on the taking part articles, procedures, and frameworks. Metadata is information about information and is fundamental to empower clients to discover and get to the proper information. There are look into inquiries on how the information will be put away, spoke to, and approved, to guarantee most extreme productivity and nonrepudiation in its recovery and update. Items should act naturally depicting and can provide details regarding dynamic qualities to augment sharing. Data about essential items, however information about procedures and frameworks will likewise should be put away. Frameworks and procedures can be viewed as extraordinary sorts of items, in spite of the fact that objects of a more mind boggling nature than fundamental articles. It is critical to store information about items, procedures, and frameworks, with the goal that clients realize how to exploit the administrations and offices offered by IoT. IoT administrations will permit clients to find in which procedures and frameworks an article partake. Metadata about procedures and self-depicting information, together with great ordering frameworks, will be useful. An intriguing examination territory will be the improvement of reasonable portrayal plans to catch various kinds of items and their metadata to augment use and ease of use.

IoT data Requirements for Processing and Storage

Today, with the quickened development of IoT hardware, a lot of data are created (Big Data idea). The advancement of these sorts of gear and various information sources has brought an incredible assorted variety of kinds of information that are in various arrangements (organized, unstructured, semi-organized and blended information). When IoT gadgets interface, the measure of information produced turns out to be so huge. The speed of age of IoT information contrasted with conventional exchange handling is very surprising in light of the fact that the gadgets catch information persistently. This speed of creation of IoT information increments exponentially. These high information volumes, joined with speeding up, just as an expanded assortment of information, produce an enormous measure of crude information that requires a truly great explanatory treatment to make included worth. This likewise forces prerequisites for information stockpiling and preparing for dynamic adjustment to the information position. In spite of the fact that, the need to rapidly process these undeniably assorted, mind boggling and less organized information and to store them productively turns into an extremely solid prerequisite for existing IoT information the executives arrangements, it would be in a general sense important to redesign or propose dispersed structures with greatly equal preparing that will meet these necessities. Right now, sorts of costs must be considered, the expense of correspondence and the expense of treatment. Since the previous is regularly a lot higher than the last mentioned, these propositions should limit correspondence costs while fulfilling the capacity and application information prerequisites. They will likewise need to consider transmission capacity and inactivity which are two significant system highlights that may influence the expense of correspondence. An overview has been done in these perspectives so as to have a comprehension of the commitments of the current writing. This intensive examination has given an inside and out understanding of the current advancements of IoT information the board methods, which further assists with separating the open holes and constraints in these current literary works to advance a few open arrangements investigate zones. Some exploration has depended on the combination of IoT and Cloud Computing to give asset the board and substantial figuring potential for applications. Nonetheless, the significant imperative noted is that IoT's presentation will rely only upon the limit of server farms in the cloud to fulfil the necessities of associated gadgets and their applications continuously. A few applications, for example, medicinal services checking frameworks, shrewd urban areas, savvy lattices, specially appointed vehicle systems (VANETs), and so forth., require ongoing processing and insignificant reaction time. Right now, utilization of mist processing will take care of the issue of nature of administration (QoS) the executives and dynamic flexibility. Moreover, Table 3 outlines a few necessities for IoT information. Arrangements utilizing future innovations are proposed to manage the identified issues.

Data Indexing Solutions

To perform effective and quick research and revelation of information and administrations in an IoT organize, ceaseless examining of all the associated gadgets seems, by all accounts, to be wasteful and computationally escalated. Truth be told, productive, adaptable, and successful circulated ordering arrangements are required to help the disclosure and access of information in huge scale IoT systems. Numerous accessible systems and IoT ordering arrangements depend on the utilization of predefined asset connects or brought together information areas. Be that as it may, having various lists utilized for various extraction gadgets is basic for dynamic IoT applications. Hence, to accomplish this dynamic and conveyed ordering, the models or systems incorporate sliding window ordering, multi-granule ordering, wave records, and worldly list model. Dynamic ordering is proposed for as often as possible surveyed information. Astute maturing systems are utilized to control the constrained extra room on sensors, putting access on the least helpful or least got to information. Also, total and outlines of information can be utilized to additionally upgrade stockpiling limit. Passages that perform wise space-time storing and ordering result outlines are utilized to legitimately bind together question sees from heterogeneous sensor stages. Appropriated ordering methods of IoT assets can likewise be received. To accomplish this objective the Geographic Hash Table (GHT) is utilized. The center advance in GHT is the hashing of a key k into geographic directions where k is an occasion type name (e.g., high temperature). In GHT a key-esteem pair (esteem is the information area) is put away at a hub in the region of the area to which its key hashes. This permits GHT to assemble hubs with a similar sort of data together, despite the fact that these hubs might be removed. To guarantee both steadiness and consistency when hubs fizzle or move, GHT utilizes a novel border invigorate convention. This convention recreates put away information for key k at hubs around the area to which k hashes, and guarantees that one hub is picked reliably as the home hub for that k, with the goal that all stockpiling solicitations and inquiries for k can be steered to that hub. Greenstein et al. Proposes an answer that expands GHT by presenting a Distributed Index for Features in Sensor Networks (DIFS) so as to help interim solicitations. In their methodologies, files are developed as a tree in which every hub stores data on various qualities in a geographic territory. Therefore, non-root hubs in the structure can have different guardians. Be that as it may, the record (DIFS) is probably going to have a separation affectability issue if a portion of the parent hubs of a kid hub in the tree are situated far away in various geological zones. Accordingly, a Distributed Index for Multidimensional Data is portrayed. The work depends on isolating the whole sensor field into parcels (i.e., territories) and safeguarding the territory of the information by hashing the multi-trait occasions into geographic zones. This permits the development of a multidimensional pursuit tree in which each geographic territory is spoken to by multi-ascribe occasions to help the directing of multidimensional questions. Another disseminated ordering arrangement is proposed. The ordering component expect that there is a balanced connection between hubs (assets and administrations) and their lists. IoT additionally needs components for finding and questioning assets and their information. Subsequently, extraordinary IoT revelation administrations have been recorded. The vast majority of these disclosure administration arrangements are brought together and others offer constrained usefulness.

CONCLUSION

The information the board frameworks utilized in conventional data sets are not commonly appropriate for IoT information given their specificities. In this chapter, information is diverse in their information structures, volume, getting to strategies, and some others angles. At that point, the examination network has given new IoT information the board strategies and ordering techniques for organized and unstructured information, just as supports for NoSQL database. The cycle of urbanization is joined by the advancement of human progress is another highlighted work which is added in background of study. And also, Data frameworks that go about an urban community must have amazing registering, detecting, and information application capacities also mentioned elaborately.

REFERENCES

Data Flair Training. (n.d.). https://data-flair.training/blogs/applications-of-iot-in-transportation

Educba. (n.d.). https://www.educba.com/benefits-of-iot/

Embitel. (n.d.). https://www.embitel.com/blog/ecommerce-blog/how-modern-retailers-can-leverage-the-iot-benefits-in-their-supply-chain-management

Liu, L., Larsson, E., Yu, W., Popovski, P., Stefanović, Č., & de Carvalho, E. (2018). Sparse Signal Processing for Grant-Free Massive Connectivity: A Future Paradigm for Random Access Protocols in the Internet of Things. *IEEE Signal Processing Magazine, 35*(5), 88–99. Advance online publication. doi:10.1109/MSP.2018.2844952

Medium. (n.d.). https://medium.com/tech-lounge/the-concept-of-iot-enabled-smart-city-fe1e104e3ab

Motlagh, H. (2020). Internet of Things (IoT) and the Energy Sector. *Energies, 13*(2), 494. doi:10.3390/en13020494

SDGlobalTech. (n.d.). https://www.sdglobaltech.com/blog/a-guide-to-iot-based-healthcare-apps

Suresh & Kashyap. (2020). Effectively Mining on Utility Itemset by Using Conventional Method. *Test Engineering and Management, 82*, 13062 - 13068.

Suresh & Mohan. (2020). Development of High Utility Itemsets In Streaming Database. *Test Engineering and Management, 82*, 13052 - 13056.

Suresh & Pattabiraman. (2015). An improved utility itemsets mining with respect to positive and negative values using mathematical model. *International Journal of Pure and Applied Mathematics, 101*(5).

Suresh & Pattabiraman. (2016). Reduction of large database and identifying frequent patterns using enhanced high utility mining. *International Journal of Pure and Applied Mathematics, 109*(5), 161-169.

Suresh & Pattabiraman. (2019). Developing a customer model for targeted marketing using association graph mining. *International Journal of Recent Technology and Engineering, 8*(2), 292-296.

Suresh, K., & Praveen, O. (2020). Extracting of Patterns Using Mining Methods Over Damped Window. *2020 Second International Conference on Inventive Research in Computing Applications (ICIRCA)*, 235-241. 10.1109/ICIRCA48905.2020.9182893

Chapter 6
Deep Learning With Analytics on Edge

Kavita Srivastava
Institute of Information Technology and Management, GGSIP University, India

EXECUTIVE SUMMARY

The steep rise in autonomous systems and the internet of things in recent years has influenced the way in which computation has performed. With built-in AI (artificial intelligence) in IoT and cyber-physical systems, the need for high-performance computing has emerged. Cloud computing is no longer sufficient for the sensor-driven systems which continuously keep on collecting data from the environment. The sensor-based systems such as autonomous vehicles require analysis of data and predictions in real-time which is not possible only with the centralized cloud. This scenario has given rise to a new computing paradigm called edge computing. Edge computing requires the storage of data, analysis, and prediction performed on the network edge as opposed to a cloud server thereby enabling quick response and less storage overhead. The intelligence at the edge can be obtained through deep learning. This chapter contains information about various deep learning frameworks, hardware, and systems for edge computing and examples of deep neural network training using the Caffe 2 framework.

INTRODUCTION

Deep Learning is a subset of Machine Learning which is being used widely in many applications related to Computer Vision (CV) and Speech Processing. There are several techniques that belong to Deep Learning. These techniques include Deep

DOI: 10.4018/978-1-7998-4873-8.ch006

Neural Network (DNN), Convolution Neural Network (CNN), Recurrent Neural Networks (RNN), Long Short Term Memory (LSTM) and Transfer Learning.

All of the deep learning methods have similar characteristics. That is, these methods are data hungry. They perform better with more data. These methods require high computation power and need longer time for training and inferences.

Since deep learning methods are resource intensive in terms of both computing power and storage requirement they often need high performance of cloud server. However, the enabling applications of deep learning such as autonomous vehicles and self-driving cars, home automation and security systems, face detection applications and speech recognition systems require quick response which is not possible when the analysis is done on the cloud server because of latency inherent with cloud processing. Another problem associated with the analysis done on cloud server is that network connectivity is not available all the time.

Addressing of all these issues require the analysis and computation part to be done locally at the network edge. With data analysis and predictions done near the location of data collection, the response time can be reduced substantially. This scenario leads to the emergence of a new computing paradigm called Edge Computing.

Edge computing is distributed in nature as opposed to the Cloud Computing which makes use of a centralized cloud server. Edge computing is mostly applicable to Autonomous Systems (AS), Cyber-Physical Systems and Internet of Things (IoT) applications.

IoT applications comprise of an embedded system, communication system and several sensors. Sensor nodes don't either need extensive computing power offered by the cloud server or the storage space offered by cloud. The concept of Edge Computing refers that the computation is performed in close proximity to the end user. It means the computation is either performed locally on the sensor nodes or on a server near to these nodes, that is, at the network edge.

Edge computing offers a number of benefits to the end user. Edge computing preserves the privacy of personal data of users. The user data need not be sent to the cloud server for training of model. Only the model information is transferred to the cloud server. Since bulk data is not transferred, less number of network resources are required. The edge computing provides scalability as more edge devices can be added easily. As shown in Figure intelligent IoT and other applications can utilize Edge Intelligence. The pre-trained Neural Network Model is deployed at the network edge whereas the model training is performed the backend cloud server.

In the rest of this chapter, state-of-the-art literature survey is provided in section 2. Section 3 describes several application use cases which require the usage of deep learning along with computation on an edge device. Section 4 describes hardware systems and platforms that run deep learning applications. Section 5 provides a comprehensive discussion on various Deep Learning Frameworks both for training and deployment of Deep Neural Network Model. Section 6 presents the strategies for making inferences on edge device with pre-trained model. Section 7 describes how the training of a Deep Neural Network (DNN) takes place using a well-known framework. Section 8 provides some optimization techniques for edge computing. Section 9 provides the real-life examples of using Deep Learning techniques with Edge Computing. Section 10 presents several issues and challenges where further research is required. Finally, the chapter is concluded in section 11.

Figure 1. Intelligent Applications with Edge-Cloud Computing

Literature Survey

When the computing task has to be done at cloud server, it the only decision need to be taken. But in case of fog computing, there are several choices for offloading. Josilo et al. (2018) proposed an offloading approach that works on minimizing the computation time. This technique is decentralized in nature and is based on a game theoretical model.

Li et al. (2018) presented a survey on design and management of Edge Computing Architecture. Their survey highlighted the key differences between existing Fog architectures and presented the detailed architecture for fog-edge computing paradigm. This survey also discussed the various resource management methods and provided various optimization solutions.

Merlino et al. (2019) proposed an OpenStack based middleware for enabling the edge computing. This paper highlighted that the raw data is first pre-processed at the edge server before being offloaded to Fog or Cloud server. Here the horizontal offloading is described for clustering of nearby devices and how the horizontal and vertical offloading can be combined. The architecture of a middleware platform is also presented.

Peng et al. (2018) presented a survey on Mobile Edge Computing (MEC). The survey highlighted the research on service adoption and service provisioning. Mobile Edge Computing (MEC) not only addresses the latency issues but also provides scalability in architecture of IoT applications.

Sodhro et al. (2019) proposed an approach for Industrial IoT (IIoT) platforms for edge computing which are AI enabled. The proposed approach promises to enhance the battery life of the sensor nodes. The Forward Central Dynamic and Available Approach (FCDAA) focuses on controlling the processing time of data sensing and data transmission functions. This approach is applied on AI based IIoT applications. In this paper a system level battery life model is also proposed for edge computing based AI systems. A data reliability model is also provided. The theoretical analysis and MATLAB simulation of these models is provided in this paper.

Sonmez et al. (2019) proposed a workload orchestration approach for edge infrastructure. In this approach the execution location for incoming tasks has been determined with a fuzzy logic based technique. The computation and network resources are taken into consideration and the off loaded tasks are examined by their properties. Edge computing provides the computational offloading service. The dynamic execution of tasks are handled such that user expectations are fulfilled. The significance of edge orchestration and various schemes of edge orchestration are provided. The workload orchestration involves considerable uncertainty in allocating network resources. The number of users and bandwidth utilization may fluctuate. Moreover, CPU utilization is dependent on the specific application. A fuzzy logic based workload orchestration scheme (Sonmez et al., 2019) may be appropriate for handling uncertainty and imprecision.

Wu et al. (2019) proposed hybrid edge-cloud IoT Base Station System. The edge nodes are implemented as embedded programmable logic controllers. The integration between edge nodes and cloud servers is established with dynamic programming method. It has been emphasized that if the cloud service is used, it is not practically possible to respond every alarm or even the most critical alarms. Therefore urgent and time-critical tasks should be delegated to edge servers. An architecture of base station management is proposed that combines the edge and cloud computing with the aim of minimizing false arms thereby increasing the system reliability, scalability, and empowering the edge nodes with increased capability. The choice of ePLC as edge nodes increases the system reliability. Use of Extensible Markup Language (XML) increases the scalability. The response time by employing edge nodes is reduced to 0.1s and number of alarms generated is reduced to 60%.

Yousefpour et al. (2019) presented a thorough discussion on fog computing and other computing paradigms. The similarities and differences among fog computing, edge computing, cloud computing, mobile computing, mist computing and other hybrid configuration is provided in this paper. This paper also presents the fog computing taxonomy through a detailed survey. The survey highlighted the research work under several aspects of fog computing. The survey on foundation of fog computing along with its definition and standardization is provided. The survey on existing surveys pertaining to edge computing applications, research areas, industrial efforts, application use-case, challenges, architecture and design goals, fog computing models and key technologies is provided. The survey on fog computing architecture includes general architecture, resource model, ICN (Information Centric Networking) based architecture and resource allocation framework is provided. The programming models surveyed include vehicular fog computing, fog for transport computing, volunteer edge computing, path computing, fog software stack for android, service modelling, PaaS and so on. Survey on infrastructure design comprised of virtualization-based infrastructure, capacity planning etc. The survey on resource planning involves resource pricing, energy and resource estimation and load and resource time estimation. The survey on resource management and provisioning involves service provisioning, placement and control and monitoring. In this context the studies on service provisioning and migration, orchestration frameworks, virtualization technologies, IoT devices provisioning, handover, service placement, virual machine placement, caching and other related work are described in detail. The survey on operations include scheduling, offloading, load balancing, and applications is provided. The survey on software and tools involve simulation and emulation tools, edge computing middleware, data analytics tools and so on. The survey on test-beds and experiments is also provided. The survey on security and privacy involves location and data privacy, intrusion detection and so on. This paper also highlighted various challenges and research directions on fog computing including the fog design schemes, monitoring, and green fog computing, offloading, security, trust and authentication, standardization and hardware technologies.

Han et al. (2019) proposed an Industrial IoT (IIoT) based architecture. This architecture is based on big data analytics. The architecture is applied on a smart factory which is 5G enabled. The requirement and design aspects of the proposed architecture are described. The requirements suggested the use of fog nodes that reduces the delay for real time analysis. The use of tools for handling high volume of data is also indicated. Integration involves for handling data obtained from different devices. The requirement of application specific visualization is also highlighted.

Crăciunescu et al. (2019) proposed a gateway for IIoT applications. This gateway is based on edge computing. A model for Mist Edge Gateway (MEC) is proposed which makes use of Access Edge and Aggregation Edge. The three case studies on the MEC architecture namely Hydroponic Greenhouse, Power Microgrid and Multi- Camera Surveillance System are provided.

Stojanovic (2019) proposed the intelligence at edge level processing for self-healing manufacturing. It helps in early prediction of equipment conditions. This system also provides recommendations for maintenance. This paper also highlighted the use of semantic technologies for handling unstructured, semi-structured and structured data so that integration of data from many sources can be achieved. The proposed scheme makes use of four layers. The Plug-In/Out Management layer allows enabling and disabling of sensor nodes easily. The knowledge extraction layer employs a number of data extraction methods to retrieve the desired data from sensor nodes. The data obtained from sensors is usually structured data since it is retrieved in predefined format except the videos obtained from camera sensors which is a form of unstructured data. Whereas the data coming from logs and error reports is unstructured data. The Smart Integration Layer provides the data fusion capability. This layer is responsible for integrating data from diverse sources and computing the unique result. The Intelligent Service Layer allows for applying predictive models on data and works on improving edge analytics. Several industrial strength smart applications are described which make use of the proposed model.

With this background on edge computing, the next section presents several application use cases which requires the computation to be done on the network edge rather than on a cloud server. The applications presented here also makes use of Deep Learning techniques in order to incorporate intelligence.

Deep Learning Applications on Edge Computing (DL on Edge)

The applications which are most appropriate to utilize the deep learning technique are computer vision and natural language processing. examples of computer vision applications are given below.

Edge Computing in Computer Vision

Edge computing can offer solutions when there is limited or no connectivity to the Internet so that communication with cloud servers becomes impossible. Apart from this edge computing is also useful when data becomes too large to be financially viable to transfer on the cloud.

Edge Camera Processing

CCTV Camera is used to capture video clips in a surveillance system. An Edge computing based solution can perform video analysis and sends only analytics results and the alerts on a cloud server. This approach can substantially reduce the volume of data transferred and saved on the cloud server.

Local Processing

In a manufacturing production line the processing can be done locally so that any fault can be detected early. It can improve Quality Assurance (QA) process.

Video Analysis

Video Analysis has a number of applications ranging from surveillance systems, attendance system using face recognition and road safety. Edge computing solutions to these applications makes them fast, more efficient and cosy effective.

Smart Living Room and Smart Devices

Smart living room has many smart devices that monitors the environment continuously. The processing required to control these devices can be performed at network edge for immediate response and action. Also the unnecessary data transfer to the cloud server can be avoided. Machine learning techniques can be applied on the network edge. This forms the Smart Edge AI.

Voice Identification

Smart speakers and other smart home devices use voice assistants which can be integrated on the edge computing servers. Smart TV can recognize the voice of a person and can present the smart content. All this can be done in the privacy of the home with all learning and computation done on the edge device. This enables the protection of privacy for a person and quick response therefore achieving the improved user experience.

Face Identification

Camera and Computer vision Intelligence can be used in face recognition which has a number of applications. Above mentioned smart TV application can also utilize face recognition technique so that as soon as a person comes in front of the TV, the personalized content is presented to him or her. All th computation and machine learning tasks can be done on the edge.

Logo Detection

The Smart Edge AI technology can be used to detect what is playing on the smart TV. Based on the user's preference the appropriate advertisements can be delivered.

Event Detection

User's preference for watching specific event can be recognized and learned by Smart Edge AI. The next time user watches his favourite sports, the specific event can be identified and the user can be alerted.

Automated Packaging

The camera can be used as a sensor. It has several use cases. The packaging person will hold the packaging box in front of the camera. Using the Smart Edge AI technique automated bin packaging can be done. It also helps in creating smart conveyer belt and used to identify the missing inventory.

Event Management

The distributed AI vision can be leveraged in event management. We must do as much as possible computing on the edge. It will reduce the cost greatly and increase the speed. Most important use case of edge computing is the computer vision. We can get instant results. If we need to do real time video stream analysis, it should be done on edge only. In this scenario the cloud computing will not work due to latency.

Neural Compute Stick 2 (NCS 2) is a device manufactured by Intel that helps in creating AI algorithms at the network edge. We can also build computer vision algorithms. This device also enables deep neural network testing.

With the potential deep learning applications identified, the next section provides a detailed description of hardware systems which are specifically designed for implementing deep learning on the network edge.

Deep Learning with Edge Computing

Ubiquitous computing and smart factories are on the rise day by day. The sensors collect massive data every moment. This data need to be analysed for smart operation. This gives rise the need of computing at the network edge. In recent years Edge intelligence has emerged that facilitates machine learning and deep learning services at the network edge thereby enabling the distributed computing. There four significant enablers for adaptation of edge computing nearly in every smart and intelligent applications. These enablers are cost, latency, reliability and privacy.

Deep learning at the edge makes it intelligent edge. However, it demands significant change in hardware resources in order to execute deep learning algorithms. In recent years there have been significant development in edge computing hardware and systems. Several AI chips for edge devices have been manufactured. There are GPU based chips such as NVIDIA, Customized chips based on FPGA and ASIC based chips such as Google's TPU (Tensor Processing Unit).

The edge nodes are required to have both computing capabilities as well as the caching capabilities. For instance in case of Smart Transportation System, safety in the current state of the vehicle also depends on its past state such as driver's behaviour and road condition. Therefore, the caching capability must be there in order to store data of the recent past.

There are several Deep Learning (DL) Frameworks that support edge computing. These frameworks include TensorFlow from Google, MxNet from Apache Incubator, PyTorch from Facebook, CoreML from Apple, SNPE from Qualcomm, NCNN from Tencent, MNN from Alibaba and so on. Figure 2 gives the layered architecture for software stack that enables intelligence on the edge. The topmost layer of the architecture represents deep learning applications in several domains. The next layer describes the Deep Learning Frameworks which contain libraries for various deep neural network architectures. Since the training of deep neural network takes place on a cloud server, a software container runtime is required. Whenever the model training takes place a new instance of cloud service is created. Each new instance requires all the framework libraries to be installed from scratch. The Docker Software Container provides an instance of containerized application with no need of installing the libraries again. The bottom-most layer consists of hardware systems such as CPU and GPU available at the cloud server.

Figure 2. Software Stack for Intelligent Edge Computing

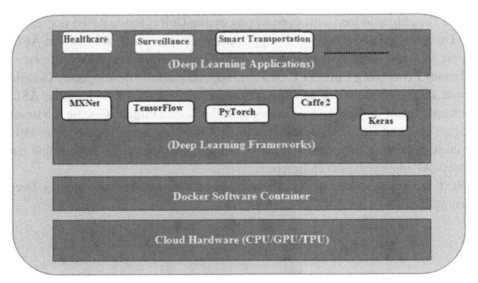

The application specific hardware systems which can be used to train the network model at cloud server and to deploy the trained model at mobile edge device are described in the next section.

Hardware Specific to Deep Learning at Network Edge

This section describes few hardware chips and systems specific to support Deep Learning (DL) on Edge devices.

Huawei Atlas AI Computing Platform is built on Huawei Ascend Series processors and other components. It provides a complete AI-Infrastructure solutions for computation on device-edge-cloud and enables edge computing for smart city, safe transportation, smart-healthcare. The in-built processors speed up AI inference and real-time video analytics. The chip supports 16 TeraOPS (TOPS) on INT8 with very low power consumption.

Kirin 990 5G is world's first flagship 5G System on Chip (SoC) for mobile edge devices that supports 5G connectivity and AI processing. the chip is desined for ultra-low power consumption. Kirin 810 has system level AI capabilities built on it. Kirin 980 had improved performance and energy efficiency. This chip makes use of GPU powered with dual NPU and i8 sensor coprocessor. It is the fastest and most intelligent chipset in the market with very high performance, energy efficiency and low-power consumption. The kirin series chips enable the AI powered scene recognition for photography.

MediaTek Helio P60 makes use of MediaTek NeuroPilot AI technology to enable smart imaging, video analytics and face recognition on the smart phone. The chip has Edge AI processing capability that enables machine learning on the device. The chip also has multi-core AI processing Unit (Mobile APU) that allows for AI and Augmented Reality (AR) application enhancements. The built-in APUs support common AI platforms such ad TensorFlow, TensorFlow Lite, Caffe etc.

Tensor Processing Unit (TPU) is a hardware AI platform developed by Google. Google TPU is cloud based platform implemented with machine learning ASIC which are custom-designed. Google products like Search Engine, Google Assistant, Google Drive and Gmail, Google Assistant and Translate are powered by the TPU. The chip supports common AI and Deep Learning platforms like TensorFlow and supports AI application development.

Next section describes in detail the common software frameworks for Deep Learning (DL).

Deep Learning Frameworks

This section describes various Deep Learning Frameworks that enable AI and deep learning on edge devices.

CNTK or The Microsoft Cognitive Toolkit allows the users to easily realize complex neural networks such as feed-forward Deep Neural Network (DNN), Convolution Neural Networks (CNN), Recurrent Neural Network (RNN), Long-Short Term Memory (LSTM). CNTK implements SGD (Stochastic Gradient Descent) learning. The parallelization is automatically performed by multiple GPUs. SNTK is available as python, C# and C++ libraries. CNTK also supports ONNX (Open Neural Network Exchange) format for interoperability and optimization.

Chainer is a python based framework for neural networks. This framework also makes use of multiple GPUs for parallelization and fast processing. This framework also supports different neural network architectures such as DNN, CNN and RNN. It has functions defined for both forward propagation and back propagation. In Chainer framework the neural network is dynamically defined.

TensorFlow is the Google's framework for machine learning. It is implemented in all products of Google to provide AI experience to users. TensorFlow can run on multiple CPUs and GPUs. It is available as a library in python, C++ and Java. TensorFlow performs preprocessing of the data, builds the model, train and evaluates the model. The input data is accepted as multidimensional arrays called tensors. Then, a number of operations are performed on the tensors. Training of model can be done on desktop or laptop whereas the run can be performed on cloud or mobile devices or on a PC. TensorBoard is another component that allows us to visualize what the TensorFlow is doing. TensorFlow has APIs available for common deep learning architectures such as DNN, CNN or RNN. The TensorFlow libraries can be deployed easily at scale.

DL4J or Deep Learning for Java is a deep learning framework which is based on vectors and tensor. The library used by DL4J framework is ND4J. Loading data is separate process from training data in DL4J framework. Deep Neural Network model is built in DL4J using layers. DL4J also has separate process for optimization and updating of neural network.

TensorFlow Lite

Machine learned models can be run on mobile devices with low latency using TensorFlow Lite framework. It is supported as API for both Android and iOS devices. The runtime is available which allows pre-trained models to run on mobile devices. However training of model is not supported. This framework is still evolving.

MXNet is a deep learning neural network framework that allows users to define the model, train it and deploy the trained model. MXNet has several features that makes it a better framework compared to other frameworks. These features are programmability, portability and scalability. MXNet is available in several languages such as Python, R, Julia, C++ etc. the model can be trained on a cloud platform with multiple GPUs and can be deployed on a smartphone or any other connected device.

PyTorch

PyTorch is a simple and flexible deep learning library. It allows building the neural network from scratch. It is a python based library. The paradigm followed by PyTorch is imperative/eager. Each line of code for building the graph defines a part of the graph. PyTorch framework also works with tensors. The main elements in PyTorch framework are tensors for input data, mathematical operations, Autograd module for computing differentiation automatically for computing gradients, an optimization module and nn module for implementing neural network layers. PyTorch libraries outperform several other deep learning librraies. However, PyTorch should not be used to deploy a model. In order to deploy the trained model, it should be converted to some other model such as Caffe 2.

SNPE or Snapdragon Neural Processing Engine is a deep learning framework for executing an arbitrary deep neural network on Snapdragon CPU, Ardeno GPU or the Hexagon DSP. The models from other frameworks like Caffe 2, TensorFlow or ONNX can be converted to SNPE Deep Learning Container (DLC) file. SNPE runtime is used to execute models trained on other frameworks like TensorFlow.

NCNN is a neural network computing framework optimized for mobile platforms. NCNN gives high performance all nearly all mobile phone CPUs. Deep learning models can be easily deployed on NCNN and developers can build intelligent mobile apps.

MNN or Mobile Neural Networks is another framework developed for deploying neural network models on a mobile device. MNN has also been used on devices other than mobile phones such as IoT devices. MNN is lightweight and can easily deploy a trained model. MNN supports trained models from common frameworks such as Caffe, Caffe 2 and TensorFlow. MNN allows common neural networks such as CNN, RNN and GAN to be deployed on mobile device. It is applicable for both Android and iOS.

Paddle Lite is a deep learning framework for performing inference on mobile devices, embedded systems and IoT devices. It is a lightweight.

The trained Deep Neural Network can be deployed on an edge device for performing the inferences. However, it is a time consuming task which can effect the application response time. This issue need to be addressed. The next section provides few strategies to speed-up the inference process.

Deep Learning Inference in Edge (DL in Edge)

As already mentioned deep learning model can be trained by a framework like TensorFlow before going into the production environment where the trained model; can be used to perform inferences. In the production environment there are a number of issues that need to be addressed so that the application can perform efficiently. The latency is the most significant factor that effects the performance of an application. The deep learning framework which is used to train a model gives the trained model in the form of a collection of weights. These weights are often real numbers such as double or float. Since the computation has shifted to network edge rather than being performed on cloud serve, there are few constraints in terms of speed, memory and computing power. The trained model must be fast enough to produce the prediction results in reasonable time to enhance the user experience. There are several strategies that can contribute in speeding up the computation that need to be performed for providing the prediction. These strategies are discussed below

(1)   Cropping /Pruning Insignificant Neurons

This strategy identifies which neurons have little or no impact on the final output. Once those neurons are identified, their weight can be made zero so that these neurons don't contribute the computation which leads to final output. By making the weights of insignificant neurons to zero, the weight matrix may have substantial number of zeros. Therefore the weight matrix becomes sparse and it can be easily compressed. This process speeds up the computation with slight reduction in performance. However, the latency can be reduced as the number of effective neurons are reduced to several times.

(2)   Quantization

The trained model can be optimized for the available hardware on which it is going to run. For a CPU, 8-bit integer representation is required and for a GPU, 16-bit floating point representation is required. If the trained models consists of weights in terms of 32-bit floating point values, they can be converted in appropriate format according to the available hardware. It would speed up the multiplication and activation operations since the hardware latency is reduced. The model size will decrease with slight reduction in accuracy. The quantization technique also results in low power consumption thus making the application energy-efficient.

(3)   Weight Clustering

The interconnections in a neural network that connect its different layers have weights which can be shared. The weights can be clustered together with the help of any clustering technique such as K-Means clustering. This strategy creates the clusters of neuron weights by determining the cluster centroid. The cluster centroid is that weight tht can be shared by all members of the cluster. This technique also results in substantial reduction in the size of neural network model. Therefor it will lead to fast execution of the application.

Once the trained model is optimized, inference can be made with Google Accelerator. The trained model can be compiled in a format appropriate for target environment. The converted model can be loaded to the edge device such as Raspberri Pi where it can execute. Figure 3 shows the complete process of execution of a deep learning application on the edge device. The training dataset is loaded on a cloud server for building the initial model of deep neural network. After the initial model is trained, cross-validation and testing of the model takes place by using the test dataset. These steps are performed on a cloud server. The output of this process is a model file containing the static weight matrix and biases. The weights represent the trained model. This model is now ready for deployment on the edge device. Since for deployment the frameworks being used are different from the frameworks used for training, model conversion is required. This is followed by model optimization, quantization and compression. These steps are required to make the inference and predictions fast. The deployed application now can be used by intelligent applications running on the edge device.

Next section presents the training of neural network model.

Deep Learning Training at Edge (DL at Edge)

In this section training of a deep neural network model has been demonstrated using Caffe 2 Framework.

Caffe 2 (Convolution Architecture for Fast Feature Embedding) can be used for both deep neural network learning or training the model as well as it can be used for performing inferences. Caffe 2 is cross-platform. Caffe 2 supports training Deep Neural Networks (DNN) in a distributed manner. It can utilize several GPUs for training.

The environment setup can be done as follows. First of all, download the Google Cloud SDK and unzip the tar file and then install it. Then install the NVIDIA Graphics Driver and CUDA toolkit. Then install the Caffe 2 dependencies as well as the Caffe 2. Now you can open the Jupyter Notebook and import the library.

Figure 3. Execution of Deep Learning Application.

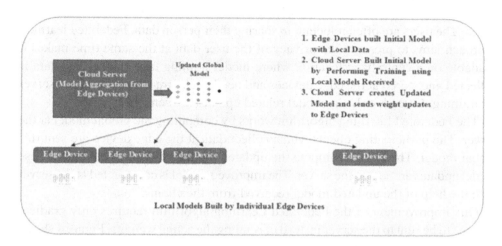

For Example,

```
Import caffe2
Import caffe2.python
```

We don't want to install Caffe 2 and Caffe 2 dependencies each time we install our application in Google Cloud. Hence we need to install Docker container. Whenever we start a new cloud instance to train our model we need Caffe 2 and Caffe 2 dependencies installed on that instance. Since each cloud instance is independent of each other, every time we need to install all libraries. Docker container provides virtualization on operating system level. Docker is basically a virtual environment for running a software.

Next the dataset for training can be read and prepared for processing. The dataset may be converted to an appropriate format. Now define the layers of neural network and start training till the network converges. The trained model can be optimized for the edge.

Deep Learning for Optimizing Edge (DL for Edge)

Deep Learning can also be used to perform optimization on the edge. Federated Learning is one such approach that enables optimization.

Federated Learning is an approach for training deep neural networks specifically on edge devices. This technique was developed by the Google. Training of a neural network model is heavily dependent on the data available. The data is fetched from various devices essentially from the edge devices. Therefore the issue of data privacy arises. The users are often reluctant in sharing their person data. Federated learning approach aims to preserve the privacy of the user data at the same time makes it available on a centralized location where model training takes place. The data is collected and stored at the edge devices and need not be transferred to cloud server for training. Instead, only the model related updates are sent.

The Federated Learning algorithm works by computing the global model at the server. The participating clients which collect data at the edge device are sent this global model. The clients compute the updated model using the local data. These model updates are sent to the server. The improved model is constructed at the server with the help of the updated model received from the clients.

One improvement of the Federated Learning algorithm requires only gradient updates to be sent to the server instead of sending the actual weights. Figure 4 shows the optimization done by Federated Learning. The initial model is constructed at the cloud. The individual edge devices construct the local model with the help of data available locally at that device. These locally build network models are transferred to the cloud server in the form of weights. Therefore, there is no need of sharing the actual data. The cloud server receives the local model from edge devices and creates the updated model which in turn is sent to each edge device which participates in the training process.

Figure 4. Federated Learning for Edge Optimization

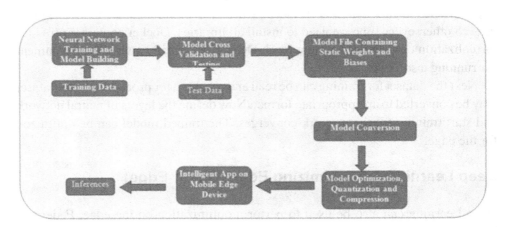

Federated Learning also has several challenges related to the security and privacy. These challenges are discussed below.

(1) Inference Attack

Since training a neural network model require large number of iterations, the continuous sending of model weights my reveal the properties of individual client. The personal information of clients can be obtained from this auxiliary information. A solution of this kind of attack is to use differential privacy where a random noise is mixed with the data. It makes it difficult for adversary to breach the privacy, since whatever the adversary receives appears noisy and imprecise to him.

(2) Model Poisoning

Adversary can mount a Sybil to poison the global model. Therefore additional overhead of overcoming the Sybil attack is also required.

Deep Reinforcement Learning based Online Offloading Framework is proposed in earlier research work. With this approach all computations have been performed either locally or on a MEC (Mobile-Edge-Computing) server.

In recent years the focus of AI research has been shifted to Deep Learning. As a result numerous frameworks and hardware and software platforms have been developed. This also gives rise to the possibility of several new kinds of security breaches and attacks. There several open challenges and issues that require further research. Some of these issues and challenges are discussed in the next section.

Real Life Examples Deep Learning in Edge Computing

This section presents several scenarios of real-life application making use of deep learning techniques and are empowered by the Edge computing Technology. As a matter of fact, the Edge Computing has become essential in implementing the solutions for many smart applications. For instance, it is not possible to realize fully autonomous vehicles without using Edge Computing since relying only on centralized cloud server will make these applications ineffective.

Edge Computing allows users to obtain real-time insights through real-time data availability and applications of AI and deep learning. Hence, Edge Computing is an enabler for IoT based applications which generate huge volume of data largely consisting images. In particular edge computing based solutions for smart homes, home surveillance, autonomous vehicles and smart farming are in demand.

In general, edge computing solutions are provided by the cloud service providers. Also many cloud based solutions are extended to offer the edge computing solutions. As a result, many AI and machine learning application providers have partnered with the Edge Computing Solution Providers. Some use cases of such applications are given below.

Autonomous Vehicle Solution by Renovo and EdgeConnX

Connected Autonomous Vehicles require real-time analytics to operate. The data these vehicles generate is mostly in the form of images. **Renovo** is a platform for commercial deployment of fully autonomous vehicles. A single vehicle could generate up to 50TB of data per day. Most of this data is in the form of image files. Mostly, the data is required only when the vehicle is running. However, some data is also required after that, when the journey is over for further analysis.

As most of this data is generated by car's cameras, if we process this data on vehicle itself it would result in reduction of the cost and delay associated with uploading data on the cloud server. However, it will drain out or deplete the power of vehicle. Therefore, it doesn't make much sense to perform this kind of data analysis on the vehicle itself. **EdgeConnX** is a Data Centre Solution Provider company that brings together Deep Learning with Edge Computing. It provides Edge Computing solutions for the Service Provider customers. EdgeConnX deploys its computing nodes where the cars are parked at charging points. It gives enough time to transfer the data and it is done far faster than it could be uploaded on a cloud server.

AI-Powered Smart Home Camera - SimCam

The AI-powered home security cameras can also make effective use of Edge Computing. For instance, **SimShine** has developed an AI-powered smart home camera system called **SimCam**. The SimCam is featured by its ability of running AI on the local device using edge Computing. The SimCam provides double benefits to the customers by reducing the latency in uploading the data on the cloud server as well as protecting their privacy by retaining the data on local devices. Also, the Simcam makes use of latest deep learning algorithms. SimCam can recognize the faces of family members and trusted ones. The SimCam can also track other objects that are selected in the camera view. It makes SimCam a god real-life example of using Deep Learning with Edge Computing.

Edge Computing Solutions for Smart Farming by AeroFarm

Another real-life example where Edge Computing has been used is the Smart farming. A New Jersey based company, **AeroFarm** has been using edge computing for managing vertical farming and sustainable agriculture. In order to apply edge computing, AeroFarm creates its edge-to-core-to-cloud infrastructure with the help of Dell EMC IoT Technology. One application, in which this technology has been applied is about the improvement in the tracking of seeds to package through each distinct stage of farming – seeding, germination, growing, harvesting and packaging. Another application, in which edge computing has been applied to leverage the deep learning tasks is for improving real-time quality control through multi-spectral imaging of grow trays. In this application, the images are analysed using machine learning techniques.

The other applications of Edge Computing Technology with Deep Learning consists of applications in industrial control, IoT, Drones, Robotics and smart cities. Following is a list of some of the companies which offer edge computing solutions for AI and Deep Learning.

- **Omron** uses edge devices for industrial control, in particular, for controlling of production equipment with a robust, low-latency connectivity.
- **Mutable** is a microservices provider offering Platform as a Service (PaaS) solutions with Edge Technology.
- **SWIM.AI** provides edge-based solutions for the execution of real-time analytics and machine learning for enterprises in the field of equipment manufacturing, Smart Cities and IoT.
- **Affirmed Network** provides a fully virtualized Cloud Edge Solution as well as Mobile Edge Connectivity (MEC) for Content Delivery Networks (CDN), Augmented Reality and Virtual Reality, IoT, drones, autonomous vehicles etc.
- **Hanger** provides Robotics-as-a-Service (RaaS) for enabling drones without human intervention and also provides services for real-time data analysis. The combination of hardware, software and services in a single platform enables delivery of 4D Visual Insights.
- German Edge Cloud has developed an industrial edge cloud appliance called ONCITE. It enables users to find information from their production data using AI, Machine Learning and Deep Learning as the real-time data becomes available.
- AlefEdge is a 5G applications provider through open APIs at the edge for AI, Smart Cities, IoT, AR/VR etc. It provides the services through edge gateways and edge cloud and can be used in Smart Cities, Industry 4.0, IoT etc.

Future Research Directions

- **Innovation in Edge Technology**

The applications running on network edge are leveraged by several enabling technologies such as Cloudlets, Cloud of Things, Fog Computing, Mobile Edge Computing and Edge Specific Hardware. Future research in this direction will lead to faster application deployment and greater user experience.

- **Application-Specific Processing**

Application Specific Mobile Edge Computing architecture has been discussed in several research papers in recent years. There are many more application specific optimization use cases that can be explored in further research.

- **General Purpose Edge Computing Infrastructure**

Currently the development in edge computing is application specific. There is a need to develop an edge computing infrastructure that serves large number of applications.

- **Offloading the Computing Tasks**

Edge computing enables distributed processing. Therefore both horizontal and vertical offloading of tasks is required. In this direction, future research is required to develop more efficient algorithms that perform offloading tasks.

- **Security and Privacy**

There are several security and privacy related concerns related to edge computing. For instance in a healthcare application, data may be required from several unrelated places. The users may show their reluctance in sharing their personal data.

Apart from this there are a number of new kind of security breaches such as model poisoning and inference attack that need to be addressed.

- **Energy Conservation**

Mobile Edge device deploy the trained model for performing inferences and predictions. This process may be time consuming and resource intensive. Therefore future research will involve determining the new techniques for model optimization and therefore reducing the size of model.

CONCLUSION

This chapter gives insight into a very important technique for imparting intelligence at network edge – the Deep Learning technique. Deep Learning (DL) is a subset of a broader component of AI (Artificial Intelligence) call Machine Learning. The chapter describes several aspects of Deep Learning which are applicable for Edge Computing.

The chapter starts with introduction of Edge Computing and Deep Learning. How the Deep Learning can leverage Intelligent Edge Applications is described. It is followed by Literature Review section. Literature Review presents state-of-the-art research work done in recent few years on edge computing.

The next section describes Deep Learning on the Edge where several edge computing applications are highlighted that can be benefitted by using Deep Learning Techniques. This section emphasized that computer vision is the most prominent application area which requires deep learning for inferences and predictions.

The next section describes Deep Learning with Edge Computing. In this section a number of hardware systems and chips are discussed which can make training a Deep Neural Network fast. These hardware systems can be the part of cloud infrastructure where training of neural network model takes place.

Several Deep Learning Frameworks are described next. The frameworks described in this section can be used for either performing training at cloud server or deployment at the edge device or both.

The next section discusses how inferences are obtained by the deployed model at the edge device. This section provides several strategies such as neuron cropping/pruning, quantization and weight clustering so that the deployed model can be executed faster.

How to train a DNN is described in the next section. Here an example of usage of Caffe 2 and PyTorch framework is described.

The next section discusses the optimization techniques for edge computing is described. This section provides an important scheme called Federated Learning that can be used for the optimization of the computation performed on the Edge.

Finally, few real-life applications of the usage of Deep Learning with Edge Computing are presented.

The last section provides future research direction in the field of deep learning with edge computing.

REFERENCES

Crăciunescu, M., Chenaru, O., Dobrescu, R., Florea, G., & Mocanu, Ş. (2020). IIoT Gateway for Edge Computing Applications. In T. Borangiu, D. Trentesaux, P. Leitão, A. Giret Boggino, & V. Botti (Eds.), *Service Oriented, Holonic and Multi-agent Manufacturing Systems for Industry of the Future. SOHOMA 2019. Studies in Computational Intelligence* (Vol. 853). Springer.

Han, Y., Park, B., & Jeong, J. (2019). Fog Based IIoT Architecture Based on Big Data Analytics for 5G-networked Smart Factory. In Lecture Notes in Computer Science: Vol. 11620. *Computational Science and Its Applications – ICCSA 2019. ICCSA 2019*. Springer. doi:10.1007/978-3-030-24296-1_5

Jošilo, S., & Dán, G. (2018). Decentralized algorithm for randomized task allocation in fog computing systems. *IEEE/ACM Transactions on Networking, 27*(1), 85–97. doi:10.1109/TNET.2018.2880874

Li, C., Xue, Y., Wang, J., Zhang, W., & Li, T. (2018). Edge-oriented computing paradigms: A survey on architecture design and system management. *ACM Computing Surveys, 51*(2), 39. doi:10.1145/3154815

Merlino, G., Dautov, R., Distefano, S., & Bruneo, D. (2019). Enabling Workload Engineering in Edge, Fog, and Cloud Computing through OpenStack-based Middleware. *ACM Transactions on Internet Technology, 19*(2), 28. doi:10.1145/3309705

Peng, K., Leung, V., Xu, X., Zheng, L., Wang, J., & Huang, Q. (2018). A Survey on Mobile Edge Computing: Focusing on Service Adoption and Provision. *Wireless Communications and Mobile Computing, 2018*, 2018. doi:10.1155/2018/8267838

Sodhro, A. H., Pirbhulal, S., & de Albuquerque, V. H. C. (2019). Artificial intelligence driven mechanism for edge computing based industrial applications. *IEEE Transactions on Industrial Informatics, 15*(7), 4235–4243. doi:10.1109/TII.2019.2902878

Sonmez, C., Ozgovde, A., & Ersoy, C. (2019). Fuzzy Workload Orchestration for Edge Computing. *IEEE eTransactions on Network and Service Management, 16*(2), 769–782. doi:10.1109/TNSM.2019.2901346

Stojanovic, L. (2020). Intelligent edge processing. In Machine Learning for Cyber Physical Systems. Technologien für die intelligente Automation (Technologies for Intelligent Automation) (vol. 11). Springer Vieweg. doi:10.1007/978-3-662-59084-3_5

Wu, H., Hu, J., Sun, J., & Sun, D. (2019). Edge Computing in an IoT Base Station System: Reprogramming and Real-Time Tasks. *Complexity*, *2019*, 2019. doi:10.1155/2019/4027638

Yousefpour, A., Fung, C., Nguyen, T., Kadiyala, K., Jalali, F., Niakanlahiji, A., Kong, J., & Jue, J. P. (2019). All One Needs to Know about Fog Computing and Related Edge Computing Paradigms. *Journal of Systems Architecture*, *98*, 289–330. doi:10.1016/j.sysarc.2019.02.009

Chapter 7
Innovative Concepts and Techniques of Data Analytics in Edge Computing Paradigms

Soumya K.
Kristu Jayanti College, India

Magaret Mary T.
https://orcid.org/0000-0001-5756-266X
Kristu Jayanti College, India

Clinton G.
Sambhram Institute of Technology, India

EXECUTIVE SUMMARY

Edge analytics is an approach to data collection and analysis in which an automated analytical computation is performed on data at a sensor, network switch, or other device instead of waiting for the data to be sent back to a centralized data store. Cloud computing has revolutionized how people store and use their data; however, there are some areas where cloud is limited; latency, bandwidth, security, and a lack of offline access can be problematic. To solve this problem, users need robust, secure, and intelligent on-premise infrastructure for edge computing. When data is physically located closer to the users who connected to it, information can be shared quickly, securely, and without latency. In financial services, gaming, healthcare, and retail, low levels of latency are vital for a great digital customer experience. To improve reliability and faster response times, combing cloud with edge infrastructure from APC by Schneider electrical is proposed.

DOI: 10.4018/978-1-7998-4873-8.ch007

Edge analytics is a technique of information assortment and analysis during which an automatic analytical computation is performed on the information on a detector, network adapter, or different device instead of looking forward to knowledge/the info/the information to be came back to a central data store(Keithshaw,2019). Cloud computing has revolutionized however individuals store and use their knowledge, however there square measure some areas wherever the cloud is proscribed, bandwidth, security, and latency, and lack of offline access is a haul. to unravel this drawback, the user desires a strong, secure and intelligent high-end computing infrastructure. Once knowledge is physically placed in shut proximity to the users connected to that, the knowledge is shared quickly, firmly and at once in money services, play aid and low-latency retail square measure very important to a good digital client expertise. To boost irresponsibleness and quicker response times, sweep the cloud with advanced infrastructure from APC by Schneider(electrical).Edge analytics is that the assortment, processing, and analysis of information at the sting of a network at or close to a detector, network switch, or different connected device. Edge computing directs computational data, applications, and services away from Cloud servers to the network edge. The substance suppliers and application designers can utilize the Edge figuring frameworks by offering the clients benefits nearer to them. Edge computing is portrayed regarding high data transfer capacity, super low inactivity, and ongoing admittance to the organization data that can be utilized by a few applications (WazirZada Khan et al.,2019). Edge analysis is descriptive or diagnostic or prophetical analytics.

WHY EDGE ANALYTICS?

Is edge analysis another fun term coined to complicate our lives? Not really. Associations are quickly sending a huge amount of sensors or other shrewd gadgets at their organization edge, and the operational information they gather at this scale could be a significant administration issue. Edge Analytics offers several important benefits:

The first is to minimize data analysis latency. In many environments like oil platforms, airplanes, and CCTV cameras. In far off assembling conditions, there may not be adequate opportunity to send information to the focal information investigation climate and trust that the outcomes will impact choices to be made nearby in an ideal way. As mentioned in the drilling rig example, analyzing the data on the defective devices there and closing the valve immediately can be more efficient if needed.

Secondly the scalability of the analysis. As per increasing sensors and network devices, the volume of data they collect increases exponentially, and the burden on central data analytics resources to process this massive amounts of data increases.

Edge computing can satisfy the developing need of applications with privacy, strict latency, and bandwidth requirements (AshkanYousefpour et al.,2019).

Third, edge analytics helps to overcome the problem of low-bandwidth environments. The bandwidth required to send all the information gathered by a great many these fringe gadgets will also increase exponentially as the count of these devices increases. What's more, a significant number of these far off destinations might not have the transmission capacity to push information and examination to and from. Edge Analytics mitigates this issue by providing analytics capabilities in these remote sites.

Recently, edge scanning has the potential to condense overall costs by minimizing bandwidth, scaling operations, and reducing latency for critical decisions. It can also solve the issue of extreme energy utilization in cloud computing, reduce costs, and reduce the pressure of network bandwidth. Edge computing is applied in many fields such as production, energy, smart home, and transportation.(Keyan Cao et al.,2020)

When Should Edge Analytics be Considered?

While edge analytics is an interesting area, it should not be considered as a possible alternative to fundamental data analytics. Both can complement each other to provide data insights, and both models have a place in organizations. One tradeoff foredge analysis is that only a subset of data can be prepared and dissected at theat the edge and results can only be transmitted over the network to HQ. This will output in the "loss" of raw data that may never be stored or processed. Therefore, edge analysis is a good thing if this "data loss" is acceptable.Compared with traditional cloud computing, edge computing has advantages in response speed and real-time. Edge computing is closer to the data source, data storage and computing tasks can be carried out in the edge computing node, which reduces the intermediate data transmission process. (KEYAN CAO et al.,2020)

Who are the Players in Edge Analytics?

Notwithstanding shrewd smart sensors and connected devices to collect data, edge analysis requires hardware and software platforms to data, prepare data, train algorithms, and process algorithms. Most of these features are increasingly being provided on server and client, generic software platforms. Intel, Cisco, IBM, HP and Dell are some of the leading companies in advanced analytics.

Where is Edge Analytics Conveyed the Most?

Since perimeter analysis is beneficial for organizations where data insight is needed, the vertical segments of Retail, Manufacturing, Energy, Smart Cities, Transportation and Logistics are at the forefront of implementing scope analysis. Some use cases are: analysis of retail customer behavior, remote checking and support as well as maintenance of energy operations, fraud detection in financial places (ATMs, etc.) and production monitoring. Web based shopping could profit by edge registering. For instance, a client may make continuous shopping basket changes. Authorities could get help from Edge analytics to find missing kids. Today, cameras conveyed in open territories in urban communities—just as cameras in certain vehicles—could catch a missing youngster's picture (Weisong Shi&Schahram Dustdar,2016).

Delivering Edge Analytics

Reaching edge analysis is not an immediate task. Usually, the analysis model is built, the model is deployed, and the model runs on the edge. In every one of these regions, decisions need to be made about how to collect data, how to prepare data, how to choose algorithms, how to consistently train algorithms, how to publish / republish models, etc. Processing / memory capacity at the edge also plays a major role. Some of the built-in publishing models include decentralized publishing models and peer-to-peer publishing models with pros and cons for each model.

How Edge Analytics Work for all Industries

Edge analytics is beneficial for establishments where data intuitions are mandatory at the edge. The assembling, retail, brilliant urban communities, energy, utilities, transportation and coordinations sections are driving the path in executing edge examination.

Retail: Brick-and-mortar businesses are rich in edge devices like beacons, cameras, sensors, Wi-Fi networks, etc. They are searching for upper hands that can help them defeat online business organizations, and edge analytics in Real-time can give you simply that.Edge Analytics is utilized to make deals information, pictures, coupons utilized, traffic examples and recordings to give remarkable experiences into customer conduct. You have the perfect infrastructure and equipment to explore edge analytics. Additionally, customers' mobile devices and the data produced by store apps add to this number. Real-time insights are paramount as retail stores need to know their customers' needs as soon as they walk in to keep them in business. A recommendation or offer that comes after the customer has left the store cannot be of any use. Identifying customer behavioral data requires high processing power in the cloud. It can be a good idea to take privilegeof some processing features like tracking items viewed, picked, and purchased. Otherwise, metadata can be sent to the Cloud Lake for recommendations, offers, etc. so that the whole process stays near real-time. A distributed edge computing architecture can further improve this. The increasing video data traffic year by year will occupy more Internet bandwidth resources. When a user sends out a video playing request, the video resource can achieve the effect of loading from the local, thus not only saving bandwidth, but also greatly falls down the waiting time of the user. Thus network efficiency is achieved(K. Cao et al.,2020).

2)   Manufacturing:

Manufacturing is associate business that needs analytics and computing at the sting. Take associate example, a median offshore oil rig has nearly thirty,000 sensors. They live gas emission, pressure, temperature, etc., unceasingly. Connecting these to cloud lake and derivation analysis are going to be too expensive and long. A majority of this knowledge is really not needed for analytics; hardly 1-3% of information is employed for analysis once cleansing the information. It will bring tremendous blessings if these edge devices knew what analysis has to be performed and what knowledge has to be sent to the cloud, therefore saving ample information measure. Embedding computing capability within the kind of advanced event process (CPE), edge devices will separate out howling knowledge and collect solely info that's deemed helpful. Within the absence of cloud, the distributed edge computing will method this knowledge for analysis, take essential actions, and may later advise the cloud regarding the updates.

Smart industry has stringent requirements in terms of reliability and real-time accessibility that cannot be fulfilled by cloud computing alone. FOG Computing has been used to meet these necessities in applications, for example, shrewd support the executives, Efficient Manufacture Inspection System and energy-consumption management and scheduling (Anderson Carvalho et al.,2019).Another example is that the good assembly line. We all know that in an exceedingly assembly line, every method is time-bound. Each action should be taken in line with production processes. Hence, it becomes vital to derive analysis at the sting. Remarking producing defects or anomalies, badly written stickers, packaging, etc., in time period will be achieved mistreatment edge analytics.

3)   Healthcare:

Healthcare is another domain wherever we tend to are seeing an enormous surge within the variety of connected devices. Within the close to future, a room on a median can have fifteen to twenty medical devices, a majority of which can be networked. An outsized hospital will have as several as eighty-five, connected medical and IoT devices, swing a colossal strain on the cloud network. Edge computing and analytics will cut back this burden to a good extent. Here again, time period analytics can carry a lot of importance than delayed analytics. For instance, a clinician's mobile device is that the edge between the patient UN agency is that the information supply and therefore the cloud. Arctician treating a patient with a pill are going to be able to enter patient information into the analytics platform at the sting wherever it's processed and displayed in close to time period. Patients not ought to watch for analytics results, which can cut back theirvarietyofvisits.

In addition, edge computing in care offers another thought referred to as cooperative edge. in a very cooperative edge, geographically spread information may be amalgamated by making virtual shared views. This shared information is exposed to the users through some pre-defined interfaces thatedge devices will directly consume.

To add this up, with edge computing practitioners and patients will get the most effective response times from the info that's generated and picked up by care facilities. Because the care sector is exploitation a lot of and a lot of medical devices that are connected to a typical network, edge computing is near to become a customary in health IT infrastructure.A medical application can include a check-up, a specialist examination, bio-signal or genomic measurement. By utilizing Grid computing, all the assessments and estimations can be connected utilizing geologically disseminated using geographically-distributed computing resources, intelligent analysis software and algorithms, and databases via secure and reliable wired or wirelessnetworks. (FlaviaDonno&ElisabettaRonchieri,2009)

What is the Difference Between Edge Analytics and Edge Computing?

Edge analyticsis a way to do contextual data analysis on sensing devices (sensors, actuators, con-trollers, concentrators), network switches or other devices instead of sending the whole data to a centralized computing environment/Cloud(Satyanarayanan M et al.,2015).Edge computing and edge analysis are not mutually exclusive, according to Bernhardy, but are two phases of the same wall. "Edge computing uses devices only to behave like computers, to record events and to track communications between devices and the site. Edge analysis takes the same device or devices and uses them to process the calculated data and turn it into actionable information right on that device, "said Bernhardy. While edge analysis can perform some analysis functions, analysis requires edge analysis on the edge computing next level, as Paul Butterworth, co-founder and CTO of Walnut Creek, CA, Vantiq explains, "Edge analytics takes edge computing to the next level by collecting more data on the edge and applying more complex analytics to it," said Butterworth. He went on to give an example of a machine tension sensor that uses edge analysis. "Edge computing can apply an algorithm that shuts down a machine when a sensor indicates that the power supply is not providing the required voltage based on the last two or three sensor readings. Similarly, edge analysis could do a long-term analysis of the voltages accumulated over the past month trying to predict [possible] voltage anomalies in the near future.

Edge Vs Cloud: Which Is Better for Data Analytics

Edge Computing and Cloud Computing technologies are similar regarding the methods of storing and processing data. However, the differences between these technologies are related to the physical locations of storing and processing, the amount of analysed data, processing speed and so on(BojanaBajic et al.,2019).When the premise of stories for fiction films, computerized reasoning (AI) presently has valuable applications that are changing the manner in which organizations are run. Designers are looking at approaches to combine AI with regular gadgets to help organizations maintain their organizations. In this scenario, cloud computing plays an important role in making the best possible decisions.

A cloud-based platform enables developers to quickly create, deploy, and manage their applications, such as serving as a data platform for applications, building an application to scale and support millions of users and interactions, and more. You can analyze bulk amounts of data and perform analysis, create powerful visualizations, and more. Then there's state-of-the- computing, which meansservices, applications and analytical data processing are done outside of a centralized data center and closer to end clients.

Edge computing closely aligns the IoT. It's a level back from the modern cloud computing model, where all the cool bits happen in data centers. Rather than using local resources to collect data and send it to the cloud, some of the processing is done on the local resources themselves.

Latency Problems in Cloud vs Edge

We all know the value of data analytics cloud computing, and how widely it is used across businesses. On the other hand, companies may sometimes encounter the problem of having to collect transportation and analyze all that data.

Despite the fact that the computing has the incredible potential torelieve the pressure on core networks, its fundamental bottle neck is the restricted calculation and communications limits as compared with the cloud computing. Therefore, in the cloudand edge coexistence system, hierarchical computing can berealized in which tasks can be opportunistically processedby both the edge node and the cloud server(JinkeRen et al.,2019)

Suppose you have some internet-connected sensors in your repository, and they send a lot of data back to some servers. When data is transferred to a remote cloud server, you can implement complex machine learning algorithms to try to predict the maintenance needs of the warehouse. All of these helpful analyzes are then sent to a dashboard on your personal computer where you can decide what actions to take next, all from the comfort of your office or home.

This is the intensity of distributed computing; notwithstanding, as you scale up activities at the stockroom, you may begin to run into actual impediments in your organization transfer speed, and idleness issues.

Figure 1. Cloud Latency(Mitch,2019)

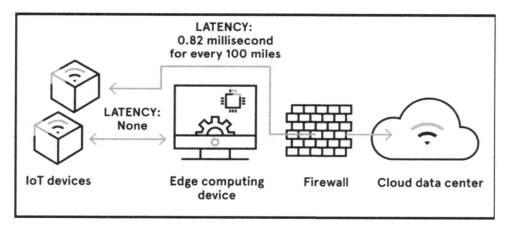

Rather than communicating your information the nation over when you transfer to the cloud, you can likewise do information handling at the edge, similar to a brilliant camera with facial acknowledgment where sending huge loads of information to an Amazon server farm probably won't be so helpful.

Edge computing attempts to bridge the gap by having that server more local, sometimes even on the device itself (Zai,2020). This takes care of the issue of inactivity to the detriment of the sheer preparing power you get by means of the cloud. Additionally, with the data collection and processing capacity now available at the edge, companies can significantly reduce the amount of data that must be uploaded and stored in the cloud, saving time and money in the process.

While edge applications don't need correspondence with the cloud, they can at present speak with online applications and workers. Huge numbers of the average edge gadgets have actual sensors, for example, temperature, lights, speakers, and information handling abilities running nearer to these sensors in the actual climate. It is this edge computing capability that is transformative and used to run intelligent artificial intelligence algorithms and real-time data processing on autonomous driving, drones and smart devices.

Edge computing may not be as strongest as remote servers,be that as it may, it can help mitigate a portion of the transmission capacity prerequisites. These edge servers can collect, organize and perform some basic analysis of the data before sending it to the remote server.

The Cloud Trend for Data Processing Will Continue Except In Special Edge Cases

It will be more interesting when we run machine learning algorithms on the edge devices, as long as the processing power allows us to do some core data analysis and retention before sending it to our servers. If you're looking for a more familiar Edge example, you can take a look at the nearest smart speaker that has a preprogrammed pattern waiting for a wake-up word or phrase. Once that word is heard, your voice is broadcast over the internet to a server where the entire request is handled remotely.

On cloud platforms like Amazon Web Services (AWS), Microsoft Azure, Google Cloud Platform, and other cloud service providers, most of the data from connected devices in the IoT network is collected and sent to the cloud for processing and analysis(Von et al.,2020). In the processing and storage capacity of the cloud data center, data is aggregated and AI-compatible models are created to make valuable decisions.

Whereas this approach is still sturdy, the time it takes for data to move in and out of the cloud generates potential issues that can impact the real-time decision-making processes required by many autonomous systems. The further geologically from a cloud data center, the more latency is added. For every 100 miles of data transfer, the speed will lose about 0.82 milliseconds. Cloud computing is agile, but it cannot meet the increasing demands of large workloads that IoT applications require for industries such as healthcare, manufacturing and transportation.

As the amount and practicality of AI-enabledIoT solutions keeps on developing, distributed computing will be a fundamental piece of the IoT biological system for intricate and recorded processing. In order to be able to make decisions in real time, edge computing is a good and more agile way of providing end devices with computer and analysis functions for many applications.Empowered by the emerging technologies such as NFV and SDN, edge cloud and edge computing technologies are privileged to address different challenges with the current cloud computing model facing with the future IoTworld(Jianli Pan& James McElhannon,2017).

IoT Edge Analytics

Edge Computing / Edge Analytics is a relatively new approach for many businesses. Most architecture is used to send all data to the Cloud / Lake. But in high-tech computing, that doesn't happen. That is to say. The data can be processed close to the source and not all the data is sent back to the cloud. For large-scale IoT deployments, this functionality is critical due to the volumes of data generated.

Figure 2. Iot Edge Analytics Factors

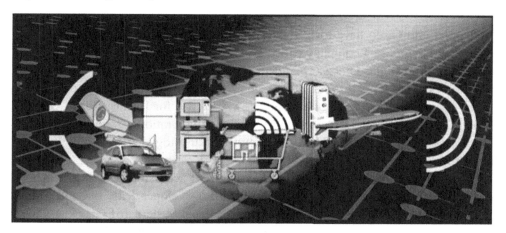

The importance and evolution of IoT edge analytics is that hardware capabilities will converge with major vendors (Cisco, Dell, HPE, Intel, IBM, etc.). Hence, IoT analytics will be the main distinguishing factor, as companies like Cisco, Intel, and other early computing backers have positioned their portals as Edge devices**(Aji,2016).**

Historically, gates served the function of aggregating and directing traffic. In the advanced computing paradigm, the basic gateway functions have evolved. Portals not only route data but also store data and perform mathematical operations on the data as well. Edge Analytics allows us to do some preprocessing or filter data near where the data is created(Newman,2020). Thus, data that falls within normal parameters can be discarded or stored in low-cost storage and abnormal readings can be sent to Lake or the in-memory database. Now, a new segment of the market is being developed that is led by resellers like Dell, HPE and others. These vendors position their servers as Edge devices by adding additional storage, computing, and analytics capabilities. This has implications for Edge Analytics for IoT.

Edge Analytics typically applies to oil platforms, mines, and plants operating in low-bandwidth and low-latency environments. Edge Analytics can be applied not only to sensor data but also to richer forms of data such as video analytics. IoT datasets are huge. The Formula One concept car has 150-300 sensors.

An airline, for example, the current Airbus A350 model contains nearly 6,000 sensors and generates 2.5 terabytes of data per day. The smart cities have a network of more than 25,000 sensors. To avoid the situation of constantly testing your cloud connection, it is necessary to do interim processing. Hence, need to address the edge in IoT analytics. We can consider Edge devices from two perspectives: the evolution of traditional portal vendors and the evolution of traditional server vendors.

Evolution of the Gateway

Both Intel and Cisco have long collaborated with IoT Edge analytics and Cisco incubated / acquired a company called Parstream(Agb et al,2020). ParStream has created a lightweight database platform (less than 50MB) mainly for use in IoT platforms such as wind turbines etc. Cisco also includes IoT analytics products for specific verticals such as: Cisco Connected Analytics for Events, Retail, Service Providers, IT, Network Deployment, Mobility, Collaboration, Contact Center, etc. More recently, Cisco and IBM have begun working together to bring Watson's capabilities to the Edge.

The Intel product suite is based on a number of acquisitions such as mashery (API), MacAfee (security) etc. through the IoT Developer Kits, the end to end platform includes: The Wind River Edge Management System, IoT Gateway, Cloud Analytics, McAfee Security for IoT Gateways, Privacy Identity (EPID) modules, API and Traffic Management (based on Mashery) and possibly with synergies with Cloudera, where Intel is an investor. Of course, there are other players on the Edge who can incorporate Edge analysis as well. For example: The Access netfrontbrowser, widely used in set top boxes and automotive applications, could also perform edge analysis functions.

This offers the ability to implement IoT analytics using web technology, such as node.js or PhantomJS based JavaScript engines. Similarly, SAP has implemented functionality in HANA (in-memory database), which enables data synchronization between the company and remote locations at the edge of the network.

Evolution of the Server

More recently, we've been seeing traditional server providers deploy their servers as edge devices. On the hardware side, devices such as the Dell Edge Gateway 5000 series are specially developed for building and industrial automation. The HPE Edgeline series is also in the same room. The analysis strategy is much more interesting - for example, the use of Statistica by Dell. Dell uses Dell Statistica. As a middleware solution to provide peripheral analyzes. In this way, Dell can use a hardware / software solution for analysis (particularly relevant for IoT analysis). In particular, this enables an analysis model to be created at one location (e.g. in the cloud) and provisioned in other parts of the ecosystem (e.g. on the edge device or at the actual sensor location itself - e.g. a windmill) using technologies such as PMML (e.g. in a windmill). More on this below). Impact on IoT Analysis

So, the real question is: What does it mean for IoT Analytics?

An adaptable and proficient arrangement, both at the organization and cloud level, is to convey the IoT examination between the center cloud and the edge of the organization . For an efficient distribution of IoT analytics and use of network resources, it requires to integrate the control of the transport networks with the distributed edge and cloud resources in order to deploy dynamic and efficient IoT services(Raül Muñoz et al.,2018).

- First, we must distinguish between two stages: creating the analysis model and running the analysis model. Building the analytical model involves: collecting data, storing data, preparing the data for analysis (some ETL functions), choosing the analytical algorithm, training the algorithms, validating the analytical goodness of fit, etc. The result of this trained model will be rules, recommendations, scores, etc. Only then can we implement this model. So when we say that we are implementing analytics at the "edge", what exactly are we doing? If you follow the examples above, for example from Dell, the most general case is: build the model at one location and potentially deploy the model at multiple points (e.g. cloud to gateway, server, factory, etc.)

- PMML becomes important for the ability to distribute models in multiple locations: PMML (Predictive Model Markup Language) PMML is an XML-based predictive model interchange format. PMML permits scientific applications to depict and trade prescient models created by information mining and AI calculations. It supports ordinary models such as logistic regression and feedforward neural networks.

- Reorganizeddispensation is inherently intricate: when you decentralize processing, some innately complex situations arise - e.g. For example, master data regulation and replication, security, storage, and so on. You must also create the analysis model on a computer and deploy it on a computer another machine is new.

- Peer-to-peer node communication can be a real leeway over time: Today, IoT is implemented in silos. Edge networks offer the ability for peer-to-peer communication using edge devices if they have enough processing power.

Figure 3. Iot Analytics Server(Aji,2016)

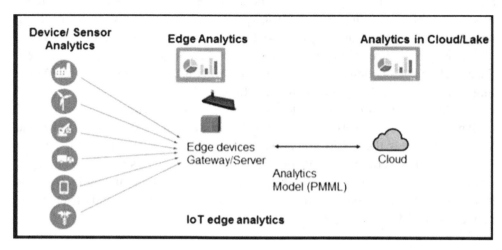

4 Emerging Use Cases for IoT Data Analytics

Use Case #1: Consumer Product Usage Analysis for Marketing

IoT solutions have the probable to entirely rewrite the way industries think about their consumers.

This is already trendy by analyzing information about how consumers use a company's internet-connected products. As an example, take the following dashboard from Birst, a developer of self-service and guided analytics solutions:

Figure 4. Marketing Analysis

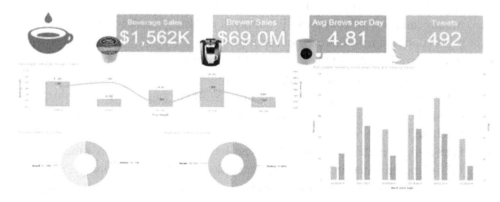

FarnazIrfan, Birst's Senior Product Strategy Manager, explains how IoT-related espresso makers transmit records to the producer approximately what number of espresso pots a purchaser brews in step with day, and that records can then be related to social media records to decide if customers are Brew greater espresso than probable to actively speak the emblem on social media. In addition, the vendor can see if the variations in the quantity of espresso brewed through the customers in shape the quantity of espresso pills that the vendor additionally sells(**Man,2020**).

Use Case #2: Serving Consumers and Business Users with the Same Analytics

One of the great aspects of Irfan'sIoT data analytics is that the analyzes can be both business and consumer oriented, for example, Irfan mentions a Birst distribution to an accompanying customer selling smart energy meters that don't require a meter. Readers: "They sell to state and county governments as well as private energy suppliers, so organizations can conduct fraud detection on meter data and revenue projections(Ana,2020)." "However, the other channel is consumer oriented," he says, "where the analyzes allow consumers to manage their energy consumption, see what's up and down other households in the neighborhood, turn appliances on and off to determine how they affect energy consumption, etc."

"In this case, the company generates value from the same analysis in two ways:

1. Traditional data mining to identifydeceit
2. Permitting a new amenity for its customers, which appeals both prudent patrons than natural ones?

Use Case #3: Sensors and Cameras Enable Connected Events

One of the most interesting domains of IoT analysis is the emerging field of social analysis. Social data analytics uses sensor data, video data, social media data, etc. To provide useful information's on the personalities, behaviors of individuals and of other groups. Facial recognition and motion detection are crucial areas for enabling social analytics through video. In the case of fashion shows, we can use motion detection to determine where the audience is actually trying to detect events that grab the group's attention. We measure this by looking at their faces and using the position of their eyes and mouth to understand the person's focus and level of interest. Today, social analytics is creating business value by supporting video capture of important moments during events. By analyzing a crowd's emotions, behaviors, and focal points to identify event highlights, you can create video clips that naturally relate to the interests of the crowd (and, by extension, online viewers too).

Use Case #4: Video Analytics for Surveillance and Safety

Video analytics is the use of software algorithms to identify, classify, and track objects or people. The scrutiny is carried out in the form of software or hardware. It is either integrated into the camera (on the edge - which provides entry points into central corporate or service provider networks) or centrally in video processing systems such as DVRs and NVRs or the servers, video security systems smarter and more efficient than ever. From telling individuals to checking and overseeing traffic, to investigating movement by season of day and different factors, video examination has carried business security to a more significant level of sagacity. Advantages of Edge Analytics

In edge analytics, however, the devices or the gateways can handle the analysis. Advantages in doing so include:

- **Reducing network bottlenecks:** Low latency examination on geologically conveyed datasets (across datacenters, edge bunches) is a forthcoming and progressively significant test.The dominant approach of aggregating all the data to a single datacenter significantly inflates the timeliness of analytics(QifanPu et al.,2015).Some data, for example video used in smart city submissions like traffic running, is so large that it can devastate the network. A network with a 100 Gbps bandwidth, for example, can support 1080p upload from 12,000 users with a YouTube recommended upload speed of 8.5 Mbps, bestowing to a recent article in Mainstream Computing. 1 million simultaneous downloads will require 8.5 terabytes per second.

Rapid Response Times: Tenders such as spawning power from wind or solar power plants and watching sick patients require response times of one minute or less. When this data is sent to a central location for analysis, it loses its value.

Data Filter: Consents studies to be performed on actionable data; only the necessary data is analyzed or sent for further analysis. "What happens is that the [analytical] model may be produced in the cloud and then instantiated in an edge or gateway device. However, where the analysis is to be performed depends on the working condition and the effectiveness of the terminal device or gate. Certain types of edge gravity analyzes cannot be performed. Sometimes an edge device, such as a smart meter, is not sufficiently capable of running analyzes. For example, in the case of power consumption, John Thompson, General Manager of Advanced Analytics at Dell, said: "Usually smart meters in homes are not capable enough to run analytical models." Smart meter data can be sent to a gateway that filters the data, and then it is sent Data to a server running at the city or district level. "We don't really need 10 million data points to say the smart bulb is on.

The Pros—

- Too much "connection" has created, for many organizations, a clogged data transmission pipeline that can be not only cumbersome but also expensive to manage. By running data through an analytics algorithm as it is created, at the edge of a corporate network, companies can set parameters on what information is worth sending to a local cloud or data warehouse for later use, and which is not.
- Better and more Effective decision making is a direct result of edge analytics. Reducing latency due to the ability to interpret data at the edge of the network is key to making smarter and more productive decisions than ever before. taken with all subsequent analysis in a central location.
- Edge analysis diminishes the expense of information stockpiling and the executives. It likewise decreases working expenses, limits fundamental transfer speed, and lessens assets spent on information examination. All of these factors combine to provide significant financial savings. "

The Cons –

- Executing a well-thought-out edge computing policy is complex and can be expensive given the additional scheduling, resources, and apparatus required to deploy analytics at the edge. The result, of course, is to improve proficiency and hopefully lower costs. But be aware that a significant initial investment will often be necessary.
- "Not all edge analysis is good; the efficiency they bring at a cost. Only a subset of the data will be processed and analyzed, the results being sent over the network," explains Zhang. "In effect, this means that the raw data is deleted, which inevitably results in the loss of some information it might have provided. Device type and data usage must be considered - data loss is it a critical issue or a necessary aspect to increase efficiency?"
- "There is a borderline skills gap. Quite simply, many organizations are still learning to make full use of the data from which they acquire or distribute edge locations. And there is a dearth of developers who can write new applications for emerging use cases, including the "killer" applications that many companies hope to develop for true business transformation.

What Are The Limitations of Edge Analytics?

Edge analysis is a relatively new technology. Bernhardy stated that currently not all hardware "is able to your data or perform complex processing and analysis". However, we can assume that hardware manufacturers will change this fact in the months and years to come. Califano also says that while the architecture of edge computing is not "inherently bad", there are two questions to consider before investing in edge analytics(Blesson Varghese et al,2016). "The first question to be checked is whether it makes sense to invest in edge analysis for a particular application. In general, it's best for scenarios that need to be optimized for a combination of speed, efficiency, and security," Califano said. "The second question is how an IoT application can be built that includes an element of edge intelligence. Since we are relatively early in the lifecycle of adopting edge computing architectures, there are many practical hurdles that engineers (of all kinds) must overcome in this way to successfully implement an IoT application of this kind.

CONCLUSION

edge analysis is an exciting area, with organizations in the Industrial Internet of Things (IIOT) field increasing their investments year on year. Major vendors are investing broadly in this rapidly developing area in specific segments such as manufacturing, energy and logistics, retail, edge analytics delivers quantifiable business benefits by reducing decision latency, increasing scan resources, solving bandwidth issues and potentially reducing expenses.

REFERENCES

Agbehadji, I. E., Frimpong, S. O., Millham, R. C., Fong, S. J., & Jung, J. J. (2020). Intelligent energy optimization for advanced IoT analytics edge computing on wireless sensor networks. *International Journal of Distributed Sensor Networks*, *16*(7), 1550147720908772.

Amos, B. (2015). Edge analytics in the internet of things. *IEEE Pervasive Computing*, *14*(2), 24–31.

Anagnostopoulos, C. (2020). Edge-centric inferential modeling & analytics. *Journal of Network and Computer Applications*.

Carvalho, & O' Mahony, Krpalkova, Campbell, Walsh, & Doody (2019). Edge Computing Applied to Industrial Machines. *Procedia Manufacturing, 38*, 178–185.

Donno & Ronchieri. (2009). *The Impact of Grid on Health Care Digital Repositories*. Doi:10.1109/HICSS.2009.435

Gracie, M. (2019). *The Case for Computing at the Edge*. Retrieved, 2 Nov 2020 https://www.kdnuggets.com/2016/09/evolution-iot-edge-analytics.html

Khan. (2019). Edge computing. *Survey*.

Manish. (2020). *IoT Analytics – 3 Major Uses Cases of Internet of Things Analytics*. Retrieved, 2 Nov 2020 from https://data-flair.training/blogs/iot-analytics

Muñoz, Vilalta, Yoshikane, Casellas, Martínez, Tsuritani, & Morita. (2018). *Integration of IoT, Transport SDN, and Edge/Cloud Computing for Dynamic Distribution of IoT Analytics and Efficient Use of Network Resources*. Academic Press.

Newman, D. M. (2020). *Bayesian edge analytics of machine process and health status in an IoT framework* (Doctoral dissertation). Georgia Institute of Technology.

Pan & McElhannon. (n.d.). *Future Edge Cloud and Edge Computing for Internet of Things Applications*. doi:10.1109/JIOT.2017.2767608

Pu. (n.d.). *Low Latency Geo-distributed Data Analytics*. doi:10.1145/2829988.2787505

Ren. (2019). *Collaborative Cloud and Edge Computing for Latency Minimization*. doi:10.1109/TVT.2019.2904244

Ren, Bajic, Cosic, Katalinic, Moraca, Lazarevic, & Rikalovic. (n.d.). *Edge computing vs. cloud computing: Challenges and opportunities in Industry 4.0*. Doi:10.2507/30th. daaam.proceedings.120

Shaw, K. (2019). *What is edge computing and why it matters*. Retrieved, 14 Nov 2020 from https://www.networkworld.com/article/3224893/what-is-edge-computing-and-how-it-s-changing-the-network.html

Shi & Dustdar. (2016). The Promise of Edge Computing. *Computer, 49*(5), 78–81. doi:10.1109/MC.2016.145

Varghese, B. (2016). Challenges and Opportunities in Edge Computing. Academic Press.

vonStietencron, M., Lewandowski, M., Lepenioti, K., Bousdekis, A., Hribernik, K., Apostolou, D., & Mentzas, G. (2020, August). Streaming Analytics in Edge-Cloud Environment for Logistics Processes.In *IFIP International Conference on Advances in Production Management Systems* (pp. 245-253).Springer.

Yousefpour, Fung, Nguyen, Kadiyala, Jalali, Niakanlahiji, … Jue. (2019). *All one needs to know about fog computing and related edge computing paradigms: A complete survey*. Academic Press.

ZAID, M. A., Faizal, M., Maheswar, R., & Abdullaziz, O. I. (2020). Toward Smart Urban Development Through Intelligent Edge Analytics. In *Integration of WSN and IoT for Smart Cities* (pp. 129–150). Springer. doi:10.1007/978-3-030-38516-3_8

Chapter 8
Generic Issue in Edge Computing and Use Cases

Sunita Panda
GITAM University (Deemed), India

Padma Charan Sahu
Godavari Institute of Engineering and Technology, India

Kamalanathan Chandran
GITAM University (Deemed), India

EXECUTIVE SUMMARY

Edge computing (EC) is a rising innovation that has made it conceivable to deal with the huge volume of information generated by terminal devices connected with the internet. Here the authors represent the issues of EC. The reconciliation of EC in those settings would suggest an improvement of the cycles that are ordinarily executed in a distributed computing condition, bringing impressive favorable circumstances. Before they are sent to the cloud or central server, the primary commitment of EC is a superior preprocessing of the information gathered through gadgets.

INTRODUCTION:

With the advancement of intelligent society and the constant improvement of individuals' needs, insight has included different businesses and individuals' day by day lives in the public eye. Edge devices have spread to all parts of society, for example, keen homes and self-ruling vehicles in the field of transportation, camera, shrewd creation robot in wise assembling, and so on. Thus, the quantity of gadgets associated with the Internet has expanded significantly. Cisco brought up

DOI: 10.4018/978-1-7998-4873-8.ch008

in the Global Cloud Index (K. Ashton, 2009, pp. 97–114,) that in 2016, there were 17.1 billion gadgets associated with the Internet,by 2019, the complete number of information traffic in worldwide server farms will arrive at 10.4 Zettabyte (ZB), 45% of the information will be put away, handled and broke down on the edge of the system, and by 2020, the quantity of remote gadgets associated with the system will surpass 50 billion. The measure of information created by gadgets worldwide has additionally expanded from 218ZB in 2016 to 847 ZB in 2021. Universal information organization Internet Data Center measurements show that by 2020, the quantity of terminals and gadgets associated with the system will surpass 50 billion, and the complete worldwide information in 2020 will likewise surpass 40 ZB (H. Sundmaeker et al, 2010.). In light of the nonstop and massive growth of data volume and various data processing requirements, cloud-based large information handling has demonstrated numerous weaknesses, for example,

Real-Time

For processing of data, a large number of terminal devices transmitted the data if the number of devises is increased. Hence the transmission performance is reduced which ultimately effect to bandwidth that used for transmission, resulting some delay. Some criteria that cloud computing does not meet real-time requirements such as Security and privacy: such as, By using number applications in smart phones, Both user data and privacy data of user is required. There is a high danger of security spillage or assault on this information when transferred to the cloud community. The quantity of keen gadgets keeps on expanding, and the force utilization of server farms in China has expanded significantly. Improving the utilization efficiency of distributed computing vitality utilization (J. Gubbi et al, 2013) can't satisfy the expanding need for information vitality utilization. The quickly creating keen society will have higher prerequisites for the vitality utilization of distributed computing.

Literature Review on Edge Computing

The idea of MEC was firstly proposed by the European Telecommunications Standard Institute (ETSI) in 2014, and was defined as another stage that "gives IT and distributed computing capacities inside the Radio Access Network (RAN) in nearness to portable endorsers". The first definition of MEC alludes to the utilization of BSs for off stacking calculation undertakings from cell phones. As of late, the idea of Fog Computing has been proposed by Cisco as a summed up type of MEC where the definition of edge gadgets gets more extensive, extending from PDAs to set-top boxes . This prompted the rise of another examination zone called Fog Computing and Networking. Nonetheless, the territories of Fog Computing and MEC are covering and the phrasings are much of the time utilized reciprocally. In this paper, we center around MEC yet numerous innovations examined are additionally material to Fog Computing. MEC is executed dependent on a virtualized stage that use ongoing headways in network capacities virtualization (NFV), data driven organizations (ICN) and programming defined networks (SDN). Specifically, NFV empowers a solitary edge gadget to give processing administrations to numerous cell phones by making various virtual machines (VMs)1 for at the same time performing various assignments or working diverse organization capacities . Then again, ICN gives an elective start to finish administration acknowledgment worldview for MEC, moving from a host-driven to a data driven one for executing setting mindful figuring. Last, SDN permits MEC network directors to oversee administrations by means of capacity reflection, accomplishing versatile and dynamic processing. A fundamental focal point of MEC research is to build up these overall organization advancements so they can be actualized at the organization edges.

Concept on Edge Computing

Edge Computing is changing the utilization and estimation of information inside the venture and, simultaneously, featuring the two chances and worries that operational, data, and business chiefs need to consider pushing ahead. Edge processing is not quite the same as conventional distributed computing. It is another processing worldview that performs figuring at the edge of the system. Its center thought is to cause figuring nearer to the wellspring of the information (D. Evans et al, 2014). Researchers to have various dentitions of edge processing. (Shi et al. 2017) presented the rise of the idea of edge figuring

Edge Computing is transforming the use and value of data within the enterprise and, in the process, highlighting both opportunities and concerns that operational, information, and business executives need to consider moving forward. Edge computing is different from traditional cloud computing. It is a new computing paradigm that performs computing at the edge of the network. Its core idea is to make computing closer to the source of the data (D. Evans et al, 2014).Researchers have different dentitions of edge computing. (Shi et al, 2017) the emergence of the concept of edge computing 'Edge figuring is another processing method of system edge execution. The downlink information of edge registering speaks to cloud administration, the uplink information speaks to the Internet of Everything, and the edge of edge figuring alludes to the discretionary processing and system assets between the information source and the way of distributed computing place.'' Satyanarayanan, a teacher at Carnegie Mellon college in the United States, depicts edge registering as: ''Edge processing is another figuring model that conveys processing and capacity assets, (for example, cloudlets, miniaturized scale server farms, or haze hubs, and so on.)

at the edge of the system closer to cell phones or sensors''(D. Evans et al, 2014). Zha et al. (D. Evans et al, 2016) proposed based on the over two definitions: ''Edge registering is another figuring model that unifies asset that are near the client in topographical separation or system separation to give processing, stockpiling, and system for applications administration.'' China's edge figuring industry collusion defines edge registering as: ''close to the edge of the net work or the wellspring of the information,an open plat structure that coordinates center capacities, for example, organizing, registering, capacity, applications, and gives edge wise administrations close by to meet the business dexterity key necessities in association, continuous business, information enhancement, application insight, security and protection'' (V. Turner,2018). As such, edge registering is to offer types of assistance and perform computations at the edge of the system and information age. Edge figuring is to relocate the cloud's system, registering, capacity abilities and assets to the edge of the system, and offer wise types of assistance at the edge to meet the critical need so the IT industry in age linking, real- time business, data optimization, application intelligence, security and protection, and meets the necessities of low dormancy and high transfer speed on the system. Edge processing has become an exploration hotspot these days.

Scope of Edge Computing

MEC has risen as a key empowering innovation for understanding the IoT and 5G dreams . MEC research lies at the convergence of versatile processing and remote correspondences, where the presence of many exploration openings has brought about an exceptionally dynamic zone. As of late, scientists from both scholarly community and industry have examined a widerange of issues identified with MEC, including framework and organization demonstrating, ideal control, multiuser asset assignment, execution and normalization.review articles have been distributed to furnish outlines of the MEC zone with various centers, including framework models, structures, empowering methods, applications, edge storing, edge calculation offloading, and associations with IoT and 5G . Their subjects are summed up as follows. A review of MEC stages is introduced where diverse existing MEC structures, models, and their application situations, including FemtoClouds, REPLISM, and ME-VOLTE, are examined. The study centers around the empowering procedures in MEC, for example, distributed computing, VM, NFV, SDN that permit the flexible control and multi-tenure help. Liu et al.categorize assorted MEC applications, administration organization situations, just as organization structures. The overview shows presents a scientific classification for MEC applications and identifies likely bearings for innovative work, for example, content scaling, neighborhood network, enlargement, and information conglomeration and examination. The rising strategies of edge registering, storing, and interchanges (3C) in MEC are reviewed, demonstrating the union of 3C. Furthermore, key empowering agents of MEC, for example, cloud innovation, SDN/NFV, and shrewd gadgets are likewise examined. The overview centers around three basic plan issues in calculation off stacked for MEC, specifically, the off stacked choice, computational asset distribution, and portability the board. What's more, the function of MEC in IoT, i.e., making new IoT administrations, is featured through MEC sending models regarding IoT use cases. A few alluring use situations of MEC in 5G networks are additionally presented in going from versatile edge coordination, collective reserving and handling, and multi-layer obstruction scratch-off. Moreover, potential business openings identified with MEC are talked about from the viewpoints of utilization designers, specialist organizations, and organization gear merchants. Considering earlier work, there still does not have a deliberate review article giving complete and solid conversations on specific MEC research results with a profound reconciliation of portable processing and remote correspondences, which propels the ebb and flow work. This paper contrasts from existing reviews on MEC in the accompanying perspectives. To begin with, the momentum overview sums up existing models of processing and interchanges in MEC to encourage hypothetical examination and give a speedy reference to the two scientists and experts. Next, we present an extensive writing survey on joint radio-and-computational asset portion for MEC, which is the focal topic of the current paper. The writing audit in our paper will be an important expansion to the current overview writing on MEC, which can benefit perusers from the exploration network in working up a deliberate comprehension of the cutting edge asset the board strategies for MEC frameworks. Besides, we distinguish and examine a few exploration difficulties and openings in MEC from the correspondence point of view, for which potential arrangements are expounded. Also, to overcome any barrier between hypothetical examination and genuine execution of MEC, ongoing normalization endeavors and use situations of MEC will at that point be presented.

Edge Computing Architecture

The architecture of Edge computing is a combined system structure that stretches out cloud administrations to the edge of the system by presenting edge gadgets between terminal gadgets and distributed computing. The structure of cloud-edge joint effort is commonly separated into terminal layer, edge layer and distributed computing layer. Coming up next is a concise prologue to the structure and elements of each layer in the edge architecture.

- **Terminal layer** This layer contains many devices to connect the corresponding network. In this layer the particular device act like as both data consumer as well as provider in order to reduce the delay. Here the basic concept of different terminal devices are considered, which results many terminal devices are collected the actually data and uploaded in the upper layer for the purpose of calculation.

- **Boundary layer:** This layer plays an important role among the total architecture of edge computing. This layer consist the edge node which are distributed among various terminal devices as well as cloud. It consists of gateways, routers, access points and base stations, etc. This layer supports the access of terminal for downward transmission, and also support to in the terminal devices. It also helps to both connection (A. S. Gomes et al, 2017) and uploading the data in the cloud. As this layer is very close to the terminals, for real time application the data transmission is easy and also more helpful for processing the data.

- **Cloud layer:** Comparing to many services in the present era, cloud computing is most powerful for processing of data as a center . The cloud computing layer consists of a number of high-performance servers and storage devices, with powerful computing and storage capabilities, and can play a good role in areas requiring large amounts of data analysis such as regular maintenance and business decision support. The cloud computing center can permanently store the reported data of the edge computing layer, and it can also complete the analysis tasks that the edge computing layer cannot handle and the processing tasks that integrate the global information. In addition, the cloud module can also dynamically adjust the deployment strategy and algorithm of the edge computing layer according to the control policy.

Edge computing refers to the enabling technologies allowing computation to be performed at the edge of the network, on downstream data on behalf of cloud services and upstream data on behalf of IoT services. Here we define "edge" as any computing and network resources along the path between data sources and cloud data centers. For example, a smart phone is the edge between body things and cloud, a gateway in a smart home is the edge between home things and cloud, a micro data center and a cloudlet is the edge between a mobile device and cloud. The rationale of edge computing is that computing should happen at the proximity of data sources. From our point of view, edge computing is interchangeable with fog computing (W. Shi et al,2017), but edge computing focus more toward the things side, while fog computing focus more on the infrastructure side. We envision that edge computing could have as big an impact on our society as has the cloud computing. Fig. 1 illustrates the two-way computing streams in edge computing. In the edge computing paradigm, the things not only are data consumers, but also play as data producers. At the edge, the things can not only request service and content from the cloud but also perform the computing tasks from the cloud. Edge can perform computing offloading, data storage, caching and processing, as well as distribute request and delivery service from cloud to user. With those jobs in the network, the edge itself needs to be well designed to meet the requirement efficiently in service such as reliability, security, and privacy protection.

Figure 1.

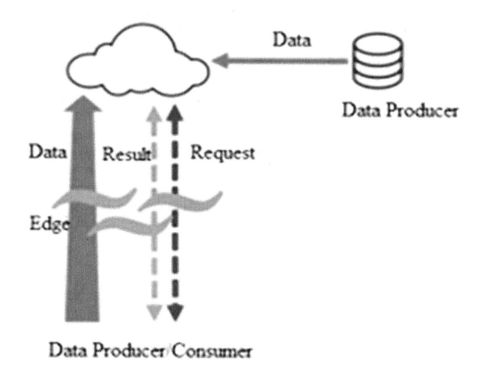

Generic Issues on Edge Computing and Use Cases

Generic Issues:

The basic generic issue of EDGE technology belongs to

❖ **Edge computing as an enabler**

Edge Computing is more than change itself, it is enabling change – including the value – of other systems.

159

The value of Edge Computing is not in the technology itself but on where it is delivered, and what it enables. Edge Computing is going where the data is created, transforming it, and giving it new value. And it's doing it in stages.

❖ The operations challenge

IT may not be driving the adoption of Edge Computing but ends up owning it.

Edge Computing frequently enters the enterprise through an individual Business Unit or to address a specific operational requirement. But even if IT doesn't initiate the process, it often responsible for the ongoing management.

❖ Barriers and drivers

Edge Computing is believed to offer increased Security, Reliability, and Performance to existing IoT and sensor-collected data.

The key drivers of Edge Computing are similar to what we've seen in previous research for other emerging technologies—securing data, improving operational reliability and efficiency, and driving application performance are all important factors. But while security is a top driver, it is also considered a top barrier, and this is a cause which is to be informed sooner rather than later.

❖ Adoption and budgets

Edge computing deployment is projected to increase considerably and budgets appear to match. Close alignment of overall budgets and Edge Computing budgets indicates a proactive approach to funding, particularly as Edge Computing is expected to continue to increase over the coming years. But an overall due to increase of data, and a pattern of relying on IT for management expertise, indicates there may be a surprise funding issue down the road.

❖ Embarking on the edge computing journey

Edge Computing is being driven by operations, driven not by IT, but by the business.

While many technology implementations today are driven by broad-based performance improvement requirements (faster, more reliable, more secure, etc.), Edge Computing is being driven by operational needs that can best or only be met through the processing of data where it originates, at the edge.

Apart from these issues some additional issues are mentioned below.

- **Deployment of MEC Systems**

The essential inspiration of MEC is to move the Cloud Computing ability to the organization edges so as to lessen the inactivity brought about by blockage and proliferation delays in the center organization. Nonetheless, there is no proper definition of what a MEC worker ought to be, and the worker areas in the framework are not specified. These conjure the site choice issues for MEC workers, which are significantly unique in relation to the traditional BS site determination issues, as the ideal arrangement of edge workers is combined with the computational asset provisioning, and them two are obliged by the sending spending plan. The efficiency of a MEC framework depends vigorously on its engineering, which should represent different viewpoints, for example, remaining task at hand force and correspondence rate measurements. What's more, it is basic for MEC merchants to decide the necessary worker thickness for providing food the administration request, which is firmly identified with the foundation sending expenses and promoting methodologies. (X. Sun et al, 2017) In any case, the huge scope nature of MEC frameworks makes customary reenactment based strategies irrelevant, and along these lines arrangements dependent on network-scale examination are liked. In this subsection, we will examine three exploration issues identified with MEC arrangement, including the site choice for MEC workers, the MEC network design, and worker thickness arranging.

- **Cache-Enabled MEC**

It has been anticipated by Cisco that portable video web based will involve up to 72% of the whole versatile information traffic by 2019. One interesting property of such administrations is that the substance demands are profoundly thought and some well known substance will be nonconcurrently and consistently mentioned. Inspired by this reality, remote substance storing or FemtoCaching was proposed to maintain a strategic distance from continuous replication for similar substance by reserving them at BSs. This innovation has pulled in broad consideration from both scholarly world and industry because of its striking focal points on decreasing substance procurement idleness, just as assuaging weighty overhead weight of the organization backhaul. While reserving is to move well known substance near end clients, (Z. Han et al, 2016) MEC is to convey edge workers to deal with calculation escalated assignments for edge clients to upgrade client experience. Note that these two procedures appear to focus for differing research headings, i.e., one for mainstream content conveyance and the other for singular calculation off stacked. Nonetheless, they will be coordinated consistently in this subsection and imagined to make another exploration region, in particular, the store empowered MEC.

- **Mobility Management**

For MEC Mobility is a characteristic attribute of numerous MEC applications, for example, AR helped gallery visit to improve insight of guests. In these applications, the development and direction of clients give area and individual inclination data for the edge workers to improve the efficiency of dealing with clients' calculation demands. Then again, versatility additionally presents significant challenges for acknowledging universal and dependable registering (i.e., without interferences and blunders) because of the accompanying reasons. To begin with, MEC will be commonly executed in the HetNet design involving different full scale, little cell BSs and WiFi APs(J. Xu et al, 2016) Subsequently, clients' development will call for successive handovers among the little inclusion edge workers, which is profoundly confounded because of the assorted framework configurations and client worker affiliation arrangements. Next, clients moving among various cells will acquire serious impedance and pilot tainting, which will incredibly debase the correspondence execution. Last, incessant handovers will build the calculation dormancy and subsequently break down clients.

- **Green MEC**

MEC workers are little scope server farms, every one of which devours generously less vitality than the ordinary cloud server farm. Be that as it may, their thick organization design raises a major worry on the framework wide vitality utilization. Subsequently, it is irrefutably critical to create imaginative methods for accomplishing green MEC . Shockingly, planning green MEC is significantly more testing contrasted with green correspondence frameworks or green DCNs. Contrasted with green correspondence frameworks, the computational asset should be figured out how to ensure good calculation execution, making the customary green radio procedures not promptly appropriate. Then again, the past exploration endeavors on green DCNs have not thought about the radio asset the executives, which makes them not reasonable for green MEC. Additionally, the profoundly unusual calculation remaining task at hand design in MEC workers represents another huge test for asset the board in MEC frameworks, calling for cutting edge assessment and streamlining procedures. In this subsection, we will present various methodologies on planning green MEC frameworks, including dynamic right-measuring for vitality corresponding MEC, geological burden adjusting (GLB) for MEC, and MEC frameworks fueled by sustainable power source

- **Security and Privacy Issues**

MEC There are expanding requests for secure and privacy preserving portable administrations. While MEC empowers new sorts of administrations, its special highlights additionally bring new security and protection issues. Above all else, the natural heterogeneity of MEC frameworks makes the ordinary trust and validation systems irrelevant. Second, the decent variety of correspondence advancements that help MEC and the product idea of the systems administration the executives instruments bring new security dangers. Also, secure and private calculation instruments become exceptionally attractive as the edge workers might be a snoop or an assailant (S.-W. Ko, K. Huang et al, 2017). These rouse us to create viable instruments as depicted in the accompanying.

- ❖ **Trust and Authentication Mechanisms**: Trust is a significant security component in pretty much every versatile framework, behind which, the essential thought is to know the personality of the element that the framework is cooperating with. Validation the executives gives a potential answer for guarantee "trust"
- ❖ Networking Security:

The correspondence advances to help MEC frameworks, e.g., WiFi, LTE and 5G, have their own security conventions to shield the framework from assaults and interruptions. Notwithstanding, these conventions unavoidably make distinctive trust areas. The first challenge of systems administration security in MEC frameworks originates from the difficulties in the dissemination of qualifications, which can be utilized to arrange meeting keys among various trust areas . In existing arrangements, the certification authority can just convey the qualifications to all the components situated inside its own trust area, making it difficult to ensure the security and information trustworthiness for correspondences among various trust areas. To address this issue, we can utilize the cryptographic credits as accreditations so as to trade meeting keys. Likewise, the idea of unified substance organizations, which defines how various trust areas can arrange and keep up between space certifications can be used.

- ❖ **Secure and Private Compensation**

Relocating calculation escalated applications to the edge workers is the most significant capacity and inspiration of building MEC frameworks. By and by, the undertaking input information generally contains touchy and private data, for example, individual clinical information and business financial records. Subsequently, such information ought to be appropriately pre-handled before being off stacked to edge workers, particularly the untrusted ones, so as to keep away from data spillage.

Serious Over Emphasis and Under Emphasis of any Issue

In the writing of MCC, correspondence channels between the cell phones and cloud workers are commonly preoccupied as touch pipes with either consistent rates or arbitrary rates with given dispersions. Such coarse models are received for manageability and might be sensible for the plan of MCC frameworks where the centers are to handle the inertness in the center organizations and the executives of huge scope cloud yet not the remote correspondence inactivity. The situation is distinctive for MEC frameworks. Given little scope edge mists and focusing on inertness basic applications, decreasing correspondence dormancy by planning an exceptionally efficient air interface is the principle configuration center (]. R. Wang et al, 2016). Therefore, the referenced piece pipe models are insufficient as they disregard some essential properties of remote proliferation and are too simplified to permit the usage of cutting edge correspondence procedures. To be specific, remote channels contrast from the wired partners in the accompanying key viewpoints: Due to climatic ducting, reflection and refraction from dispersing objects in nature (e.g., structures, dividers and trees), there exists the notable multipath blurring in remote channels, making the channels profoundly time-changing and can cause extreme between image impedance (ISI). Hence, successful ISI concealment methods, for example, balance and spread range, are required for dependable transmissions. The transmission idea of remote transmissions brings about a sign being meddled by different signs involving a similar range, which lessens their separate get signal-to-obstruction in addition to commotion proportions (SINRs) and in this manner brings about the probabilities of blunder in discovery. To adapt to the presentation corruption, impedance the executives gets one of the most significant plan issues for remote correspondence frameworks and has pulled in broad examination endeavors. Spectrum lack has been the principle adversary for exceptionally high-rate radio access, propelling broad exploration on misusing new range assets, planning novel handset structures and organization standards to improve the range efficiency, just as creating range sharing and total procedures to encourage efficient utilization of divided and underutilized range assets . The irregular varieties of remote diverts in time, recurrence and space make it significant for planning efficient MEC frameworks to consistently coordinate control of calculation off stacked and radio asset the executives. For example, when the remote direct is in profound blur, the decrease on execution inertness by distant execution may not be sufficient to make up for the expansion of transmission idleness because of the lofty drop in transmission-information rates (Z. Chang et al, 2016). For such cases, it is attractive to concede off stacked till the channel gain is good or change to an elective recurrence/spatial channel with a superior quality for off stacked. Besides, expanding transmission force can build the information rate, yet additionally lead to a bigger transmission vitality utilization. The above contemplations require the joint plan of off stacked and remote transmissions, which ought to be versatile to the time-changing channels dependent on the precise channel-state data (CSI). In (]. R. Wang et al, 2016) MEC frameworks, interchanges are commonly among APs and cell phones with the chance of direct D2D correspondences. The MEC workers are little scope server farms conveyed by the Cloud Computing/telecom administrators, which can be co-situated with the remote APs, e.g., the public WiFi switches and BSs, as so to diminish the capital use (CAPEX) (e.g., site rental). The remote APs not just give the remote interface to the MEC workers, yet additionally empower the admittance to the far off server farm through backhaul joins, which could help the MEC worker to additionally off stacked some calculation errands to other MEC workers or to enormous scope cloud server farms. For the cell phones that can't speak with MEC workers straightforwardly because of insufficient remote interfaces, D2D correspondences with neighboring gadgets give the chance to advance the calculation assignments to MEC workers. Besides, D2D interchanges likewise empower the distributed participation on asset sharing and calculation load adjusting inside a bunch of cell phones.

Use Cases

There are presumably many approaches to portray use cases and this paper is too short to even consider providing a thorough rundown. Yet, here are a few guides to help explain thinking and feature open doors for cooperation

Data Collection and Analytics

IoT, where information is frequently gathered from a huge system of microsites, is a case of an application that profits by the edge figuring model. Sending masses of information over frequently restricted system associations with an examination motor situated in a brought together server farm is counterproductive; it may not be responsive enough, could add to unreasonable dormancy, and squanders valuable transfer speed. Since edge gadgets can likewise deliver terabytes of information, taking the examination closer to the wellspring of the information on the edge can be more financially savy by breaking down information close to the source and just sending little clumps of consolidated data back to the concentrated frameworks. There is a tradeoff here—adjusting the expense of moving information to the center against losing some information

Security:

As edge gadgets multiply – including versatile handsets and IoT sensors– – new assault vectors are rising that exploit the expansion of endpoints. Edge figuring offers the capacity to draw security components nearer to the starting wellspring of assault, empowers better security applications, and builds the quantity of layers that help guard the center against penetrates and hazard

Compliance requirements:

Consistence covers an expansive scope of prerequisites, extending from geofencing, information power, and copyright requirement. Confining admittance to information dependent on geology and political limits, restricting information streams relying upon copyright constraints, and putting away information in places with explicit guidelines are generally feasible and enforceable with edge processing framework.

Network function virtualization:

This is at its heart the quintessential edge registering application since it gives foundation usefulness. Telecom administrators are hoping to change their administration conveyance models by running virtual system capacities as a component of, or layered on head of, an edge registering foundation. To augment productivity and limit cost/multifaceted nature, running NFV tense processing framework bodes well.

Real-time:

Constant applications, for example, AR/VR, associated vehicles, telemedicine, material web Industry 4.0 and shrewd urban communities, can't endure in excess of a couple of milliseconds of inertness and can be amazingly delicate to jitter, or dormancy variety. For instance, associated vehicles will require low inactivity and high transfer speed, and rely upon calculation and substance reserving close to the client, making edge limit a need. In numerous situations, especially where shut circle robotization is utilized to keep up high accessibility, reaction times in many milliseconds are required, and can't be met without edge processing framework.

Immersive:

Edge computing grows data transfer capacity abilities, opening the capability of new vivid applications. A portion of these incorporate AR/VR, 4K video, and 360° imaging for verticals like human services. Reserving and advancing substance at the edge is now turning into a need since conventions like TCP don't react well to abrupt changes in radio system traffic. Edge processing foundation, integrated with ongoing admittance to radio/organize data can lessen slows down and delays in video by up to 20% during top review hours, and can likewise differ the video feed bit rate dependent on radio conditions.

Network efficiency:

Numerous applications are not touchy to inactivity and don't need a lot of close by figure or capacity limit, so they could hypothetically run in a concentrated cloud, however the data transmission prerequisites as well as register necessities may even now make edge processing a more effective methodology. A portion of these remaining burdens are normal today, including video reconnaissance and IoT doors, while others, including facial acknowledgment and vehicle number plate acknowledgment, are developing abilities. With huge numbers of these, the edge processing framework .decreases data transmission prerequisites, yet can likewise give a stage to capacities that empower the estimation of the application—for instance, video reconnaissance movement location and danger acknowledgment. In a considerable lot of these applications, 90% of the information is standard and insignificant, so sending it to an incorporated cloud is restrictively costly and inefficient of frequently scant system data transmission.

Self-contained and autonomous site operations:

Numerous conditions, even today, have restricted, temperamental or unusual network. These could incorporate transportation (planes, transports, ships), mining tasks (oil rigs, pipelines, mines), power framework (wind ranches, sunlight based force plants), and even situations that ought to commonly have great availability, similar to stores. Edge figuring flawlessly supports such situations by permitting locales to remain semi-independent and practical when required or when the system availability isn't accessible. The best case of this methodology is the requirement for retail stores to keep up their place of deals (POS) frameworks, in any event, when there is incidentally no system availability.

Privacy:

organisation may have requirements for edge computing limit contingent upon remaining tasks at hand, availability cutoff points and security. For instance, clinical applications that need to anonymize individual wellbeing data before sending it to the cloud could do this using edge registering foundation. Another approach to take a gander at prerequisites that would profit by cloud edge figuring is by the sort of organization that would send them. Administrator applications are outstanding burdens set off registering framework that is constructed and overseen by administrators—media communications organizations, for instance. Outsider applications are worked by associations to run on existing edge foundation, so as to use others' edge registering framework. It is important that any applications could use any or the entirety of the capacities gave by a cloud—figure, square stockpiling, object stockpiling, virtual systems administration, uncovered metal, or holders.

CONCLUSION

As technology advances and the ability to monitor, measure, and analyze becomes increasingly embedded into business and consumer behavior, real-time insights will become part of all business processes. And as intelligent and autonomous systems become more commonplace, the need for computing resources at the point of data generation will become critical. While the cloud has many benefits, and is often favored as the centralized single source of record, we believe Edge Computing offers a complimentary type of value that extends and augments the cloud, or hybrid cloud, value proposition.

REFERENCES

Ashton, K. (2009). That Internet of Things thing. *RFiD J.*, *22*(7), 97–114.

Chang, Z., Gong, J., Li, Y., Zhou, Z., Ristaniemi, T., Shi, G., Han, Z., & Niu, Z. (2016, December). Energy efficient resource allocation for wireless power transfer enabled collaborative mobile clouds. *IEEE Journal on Selected Areas in Communications*, *34*(12), 3438–3450. doi:10.1109/JSAC.2016.2611843

Evans, D. (2014). Cisco global cloud index: Forecast and methodology, 2014–2019 white paper. In *The Internet of Things: How the next evolution of the Internet is changing everything*. CISCO White Paper.

Evans, D. (n.d.). *The Internet of Things How The Next Evolution of the Internet is Changing Everything*. Available: https://www.researchgate.net/publication/30612290

Gao, Y. Q., Bguan, H., & Qi, Z. W. (2014). Service level agreement based energy-Effificient resource man agreement in cloud data centers. Comput. Elect. Eng., 40(5), 1621–1633. doi: .compeleceng.2013.11.001 doi:10.1016/j

Gomes, A. S., Sousa, B., Palma, D., Fonseca, V., Zhao, Z., Monteiro, E., Braun, T., Simoes, P., & Cordeiro, L. (2017, May). Edge caching with mobility prediction in virtualized LTE mobile networks. *Future Generation Computer Systems*, *70*, 148–162. doi:10.1016/j.future.2016.06.022

Greenberg, A., Hamilton, J., Maltz, D. A., & Patel, P. (2008). The cost of a cloud: Research problems in data center networks. *SIGCOMM Comput. Commun. Rev., 39*(1), 68–73. Available: https://doi.acm.org/10.1145/1496091.1496103

Gubbi, J., Buyya, R., Marusic, S., & Palaniswami, M. (2013). Internet of Things (IoT): A vision, architectural elements, and future directions. *Future Generation Computer Systems, 29*(7), 1645–1660. doi:10.1016/j.future.2013.01.010

Han, Z. (2016). Dynamic virtual machine management via approximate Markov decision process. *Proc. IEEE Int. Conf. Comput. Commun. (INFOCOM),* 1–9. 10.1109/INFOCOM.2016.7524384

Ko, S.-W., Huang, K., Kim, S.-L., & Chae, H. (2017, May). Live prefetching for mobile computation offloading. *IEEE Transactions on Wireless Communications, 16*(5), 3057–3071. doi:10.1109/TWC.2017.2674665

Li, A., Yang, X., Kandula, S., & Zhang, M. (2010). *CloudCmp: Comparing public cloud providers. In Proc. 10th ACM SIGCOMM Conf. Internet Meas.* doi:10.1145/1879141.1879143

Satyanarayanan, M. (2019). The emergence of edge computing. *Computer, 50*(1), 30–39.

Satyanarayanan, M. (2011). Mobile computing: The next decade. *SIGMOBILE Mobile Comput. Commun. Rev., 15*(2), 2–10. Available: http://doi.acm.org/10.1145/2016598.2016600

Shi, W., Sun, H., Cao, J., Zhang, Q., & Liu, W. (2016, October). Edge computing-an emergingcomputingmodelfortheInternetofeverythingera. *J. Comput. Res. Develop., 54*(5), 907–924.

Shi, Zhang, & Wang. (n.d.). Edgecomputing:State-of-the-art and future directions. J. Comput. Res. Develop., 56(1), 1–21.

Shi, Cao, Zhang, Li, & Xu. (n.d.). Edge computing: Vision and challenges. IEEE Internet of Things Journal, 3(5), 637–646. doi:10.1109/JIOT.2016.2579198

Sun, X., & Ansari, N. (2017, January/February). Green cloudlet network: A distributed green mobile cloud network. *IEEE Network, 31*(1), 64–70. doi:10.1109/MNET.2017.1500293NM

Sundmaeker, H., Guillemin, P., Friess, P., & Woelfflé, S. (2010). Vision and challenges for realising the Internet of things. Academic Press.

Turner, V., Gantz, J. F., & Reinsel, D. (2018). *The digital universe of opportunities: Rich Data and the Increasing Value of the Internet of Things*. Available: https://www.emc.com/leadership/ digitaluniverse/2014iview/index.htm

Wang, R., Peng, X., Zhang, J., & Letaief, K. B. (2016, August). Mobilityaware caching for content-centric wireless networks: Modeling and methodology. *IEEE Communications Magazine*, *54*(8), 77–83. doi:10.1109/MCOM.2016.7537180

Xu, J., & Ren, S. (2016). Online learning for offloading and autoscaling in renewable-powered mobile edge computing. *Proc. IEEE Glob. Commun. Conf. (GLOBECOM)*, 1–6. 10.1109/GLOCOM.2016.7842069

Zha, Z. M., & Liu, F. (2018). Edgecomputing:Platforms;Applications and challenges. *J. Comput. Res. Develop.*, *55*(2), 327–337.

Chapter 9

Data Security and Privacy Requirements in Edge Computing:
A Systemic Review

Chinnasamy Ponnusamy
iD https://orcid.org/0000-0002-3202-4299
Sri Shakthi Institute of Engineering and Technology, India

Rojaramani D.
Sethu Institute of Technology, India

Praveena V.
Dr. N. G. P. Institute of Technology, India

Annlin Jeba S. V.
Sree Buddha College of Engineering, India

Bensujin B.
University of Technology and Applied Sciences, Nizwa, Oman

EXECUTIVE SUMMARY

Several researchers analyzed the information security problems in edge computing, though not all studied the criteria for security and confidentiality in detail. This chapter intends to extensively evaluate the edge computing protection and confidentiality standards and the different technical approaches utilized by the technologies often used mitigate the risks. This study describes the latest research and emphasizes the following: (1) the definition of edge computing protection and confidentiality criteria, (2) state-of-the-art strategies used to mitigate protection and privacy risks, (3)

DOI: 10.4018/978-1-7998-4873-8.ch009

developments in technical approaches, (4) measures used to measure the efficiency of interventions, (5) the categorization of threats on the edge device and the related technical pattern used to mitigate the attackers, and (6) research directions for potential professionals in the field of edge devices privacy and security.

INTRODUCTION

Edge computing approach is introduced with the aim of resolving the cloud technology based disadvantages. The edge network in distributed computing falls between all the cloud and end-users, putting end-users with cloud services much closed (Sayad, 2018). Hence this offers enormous real-time data collection, reduces latency, low operating costs, high interoperability and increases consumer satisfaction. The most difficult issue impacting edge technology's performance is a violation of the security and confidentiality of almost all the devices which are connected with it. This research looks at eight protection and security criteria of a traditional edge computing network. Privacy and security considerations may be called the measurement of the functionality and operations a program could perform to remove loopholes in protection and privacy (Zhang, 2018). The program effectively cooperates only with requisite secret and stable goals along with legislative requirements and guidance (Roman, 2018), when the criteria are met. The specifications entail confidentiality, and credibility, identification of attacks, honesty, efficiency, message integrity, and performance. In sections III the specifics within each condition would be addressed.

Several research studies addressed the security and privacy challenges in edge computing; furthermore, almost all of these previous researches significantly ignored the investigations into the edge computing program's compliance and security criteria. Moreover, in survey reports, work on the state-of-the-art regulating approaches with the associated tools and methods was really insufficient. In (Zhang, 2018), addressed a research on privacy concerns in edge devices, even cryptography-based approaches remained emphasized were identified the criteria for confidentiality. In (Guan, 2019), his squad studied and discussed the vulnerabilities involved in different methodologies relevant to edge computing, like fog and mobile computing. Nevertheless, the research study perceived authenticity-related techniques, so although little attention is being paid to all other prerequisites. In (Guan, 2019) addressed key data owed in the energy industry, but everyone's fieldwork primarily focused on security and privacy concerns focuses on the application of cutting edge computer technology in the energy market. In (Rapuzzi, 2018) also analyzed the technological constraints with the emerging fog / edge strategies of existing cyber-security methodologies. The survey research was focused on providing a framework for developing novel cyber-security approaches, but a comprehensive analysis of the criteria regarding

172

protection was lacking. In this other study, In (Xiao, 2019) discussed a need to build and examine important security aimed at reducing techniques in the evolving field of edge / fog technology in various modern computing frameworks. The different survey researchers have reported a concrete foundation for identifying concerns about privacy in edge devices. Some of these reports, though, presented minimal details about the edge computing program's security and privacy requirements. Moreover, much of the research was very partly addressed or checked at a preliminary phase whenever the issue emerged. This analytical work would encapsulate the present condition-of-the-art privacy and security guidelines, but also the pattern of the technical strategies adopted by the approaches to mitigate the related threats to future investigations in edge computing to explore. A systematic analysis framework that defines all appropriate processes required to achieve the survey's objectives and targets would be established and recognized again from the initiation phase before another data preparation phase begins. This method would facilitate accurate analysis and retention of the data. Responding to the research objectives and questions should meet the involvement of this research study:

1. What are protection and privacy parameters of edge computing network architecture design?
2. Which approaches are presented to safeguard the specified standards?
3. Which pattern of various techniques is used with the techniques identified?
4. What are the correct measurement criteria used for the success appraisal of the technologies?
5. What are the types of attacks that impact edge computing systems, along with the correct preventive advanced technology?
6. What are the promising future prospects for efforts in the field of edge computing safety and confidentiality?

The rest of this article is summarized as follows: an explanation of edge computing concepts will really be presented in section II, and an analysis of edge computing privacy and security considerations will be provided in Section III. Section IV should demonstrate the procedures for conducting the review of relevant literature, statistical analysis will also be presented in Section V, interpretation of the evaluated outcome would be presented in Section VI, and Section VII may highlight the open research objectives, and summary would be presented finally in Section VIII.

2. RELATED WORKS ON EDGE COMPUTING

This section introduces specific methodologies in edge devices which are recognized as post-cloud computing methodologies. With the rapid growth and comprehensive deployment of the IoT, data analytics and 5 G wireless architectures, the vast data gathered by the networks required to complete and the real-time system constraints are beyond the capabilities of the conventional cloud computing technology. Existing study, including micro server farm mobile computing (Zhou, 2019), fog computing (Ghobaei, 2020), cloudlet, and web-sea computing was implemented to minimize cloud services storage and computational charges. Edge computing (Zhou, 2019) has newly emerged introduced as a new framework to enable the concept of data dumping that stretches cloud computing technology to the edge of networks. We address momentarily an analysis of the edge computing throughout this article. First of all, by describing the developing processes we clarify why we need edge technology so urgently. Then we'll give edge technology a description and a four-layer architectures. We also implement certain modules that have gained tremendous interest from academia and the industry, like cloud hauling, video monitoring, electricity cities, intelligent vehicle and many more.

Elements of Edge Computing

1. Cloud Computing

The conventional cloud computing framework for data processing at the datacenter is an excellent technique. This would pose several disadvantages given the prevalence of IoT and the vast information collected by the large sensor nodes. Initially, IoT 's auditory layer infrastructure is at a significant scale and there is constant disagreement and collaboration among data (Chinnasamy, 2018), indicating that computing capacities of centralized cloud services growth retardation cannot fulfil the multi - sensor data acquisition demand of large edge processing. Furthermore, due to the extreme mass scale of access privileges and the long-distance data transfer among consumer and cloud services centre, communication bandwidth and connectivity speeds have come to a standstill, this phenomenon would contribute to higher processing time and a misuse of processing power. Third, many other end-users with in network edge are typically resource-constrained connected phones with low memory and computational capabilities and short battery life, but that some computing responsibilities need to be offloaded to the edge without long-distance transmission to the cloud database server. Finally, data protection and confidentiality are significant challenges in cloud services despite the long-distance transmission and procurement functionality, thus the chance of security breaches in the edges.

2.   **The Era of Internet**

As per Cisco Global Cloud Index (GCI) and Network Technology Services Community estimates, data collected from IoT devices will surpass 500 Zettabytes (ZB) while IP Addresses data center congestion would only hit 15,3 ZB by 2020, there will be over 50 billion Network linked devices (Roman, 2018). Moreover, the principle of "victimization" has begun to slowly expand to the IoT ecosystem that would accelerate the arrival of the Internet of Everything era.

3.   **Change Between Customer To Business**

Typically the cloud provider plays an important role as the service provider in the conventional cloud computing technology, including searching photos in an internet browser, streaming YouTube videos or reading documents in a file system. Nevertheless, the function of the cloud services shifts from the service provider to the internet and digital data, which assumes that customers often generate data on its sensor nodes at the edge of networks.

EDGE COMPUTING

The Pacific Northwest National Laboratory (PNNL) is developing edge computing as a strategy to moving the limits of smart devices, data and resources away from the conventional networks to the absurd conclusions of a network operation, allowing analysis and information creation to take place at the data provider. The Edge Computing Convergence (ECC) describes edge computing as just an interactive network distributed at the edge of networks adjacent to the data provider and offers sophisticated solutions to fulfill real-time processing, data storage, protection and security demands across edge cloud's modernization framework. In overview, we could conclude that edge computing is a revolutionary, disruptive technology that needs to be stored and processed at the edge devices, and therefore by integrating with cloud technology to provide smart services beyond the data provider.

Fig. 2 demonstrates the important edge computing layout, that consisting of a scalable four-layer structural system: core system, edge processors, edge node and fog nodes. Second, the core platforms offer central data transmission and integrated cloud - based solutions and edge cloud system information management. Second, edge servers built and run by the application owner and fitted with cloud computing for multitenant users are responsible for securing Virtual Machines (VMs) and various technology solutions. The edge can also install several edge cloud services that collaborate with one another won't detach from its conventional cloud. Moreover, edge com-positioning system links access to modern, edge centers and core networks with wireless network, data virtual routers and the Cloud. Lastly, fog nodes involve all kinds of systems attached to the edges network (e.g. mobile terminals, IoT devices) that it not only play an important role as user data, but rather as end - users for all 4 levels to interact in the virtualized environment.

Figure 1. Edge Computing Architecture

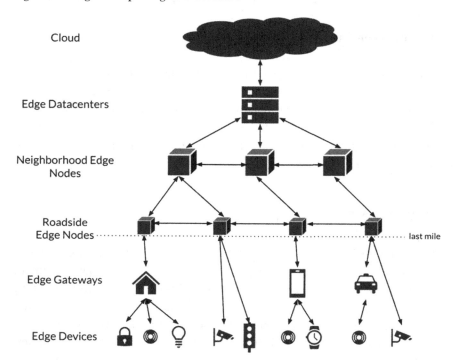

APPLICATIONS OF EDGE COMPUTING

Researchers discovered edge computing has lots of wonderful applications in various fields compared to existing decentralized cloud services architecture. After that, we'll explain some case studies of new technology circumstances.

a.   Cloud Offloading

With the exponential rise of peripheral devices many low-latency applications need real-time processing for these systems to make the right choices. Typically, the data and inquiries generated by end customers are managed in the cloud in the conventional cloud service provider, which ensures longer latency will occur in a quite clustered computing infrastructure due to long vast benefits. In edge devices, the edge organizations typically have other processing tools that will provide an ability to offload most or all of the workflows by storing data and activities at the edges of a cloud. This offloading concept is very similar to a conventional content delivery network (CDN) (Yu, 2020), but the discrepancy would be that the information and its subsequent storage are all required to be preserved in cloud computing since only the information are compressed in CDN. The consistency of the computational performance and the customer engagement for time-sensitive applications might be dramatically enhanced by exploiting edge computing.

b.   Video Analytics

As an innovative technology, video analytics could be broadly described as an intelligent recollection of events arising within a sequence tracked by several surveillance cameras. Video monitoring system (Ashkan, 2019) is one possible application of computer vision that Cloud benefits through edge computing. Realistic monitoring systems introduced nowadays are still not responsible for proper understanding of the various activities in large cameras due to the exponential escalation in IoT nodes. Conventional cloud computing seems to have a significant shortcoming that video updates from billions of security cameras can't be processed in real time and increase data transfer rate and legal issues. With edge computing integration, video analytics reports could be created from the clouds and dispersed over a given locality to the specific data centers. Any consumer can run on these local edge devices with the requirements and could only transmit the operating performance to the clouds.

c.   Smart Grid

Smart grid, as first-generation solution to producing power to millions of people worldwide around the country, is a mix of electricity supply and resource networks, complemented by ICT. Each smart grid network is composed of many processing elements, like specific operating centers, transmission nodes, and end consumers, who are tributary cloud services connections. Here all confidential data obtained by the smart grids, along with details on electricity costs, could be used for demonstrative evidence or for marketing. With edge computing environments, the power efficiency details on the edge devices can be stored and processed (Yang, 2019).

d.   Intelligent Vehicle

Due to the rapid growth of the Internet of Vehicles (IoV) (Liu, 2020), increasingly small devices are both on the roads and all of these vehicles is fitted with such a computing device to recognize the traffic management services. In this model, the vehicle system could achieve excellent two-way communication by installing edge servers on the RSUs and, whereas, by combining networking and computing processes, drive the cloud storage service to the edge of a RSUs. Additionally, the advanced Internet of vehicle technologies, like automated cars, data processing in real time, and transport-aware computing, might be getting best by exploiting edge computing.

Several other smart technologies, including such smart healthcare, home automation, smart city (Liu, 2020), and blockchain (Chinnasamy, 2016) would need a connection among cloud centers and sensor to enable cloud technology for effective services.

SECURITY AND PRIVACY ISSUES ON EDGE COMPUTING

Edge computing will migrate certain storage and computational activities through cloud servers to the edge devices, and that could pose several security and privacy associated responsibilities. Security and privacy issues in general seem to be the most relevant services (Donald, 2016) in terms of edge computing, which would be our major consideration throughout this study. This paper highlights the edge computing information security criteria, as well as threats. We have also developed a data protection development system in edge computing, covering confidentiality, integrity, authorization, preventing from unauthorized user access and encryption techniques.

REQUIREMENTS OF SECURITY AND PRIVACY

If either cloud storage or edge computing, the information of the authorized body must be explicitly or implicitly outsourced to private entities, and their ownership of property is divided, which could also ultimately lead to loss of data, security breaches, unauthorized data activities and other information privacy problems, data integrity and anonymity could not be assured. Consequently, distributing data protection still is a central question of information security in edges computing (Caprolu, 2019). The following parameters should consider to enhance the security of edge computing.

1) **Confidentiality:** It is a basic necessity which really guarantees that certain data owners and operators can obtain personal data just at edges of computing. It prohibits unwanted users from gaining access content whenever sensitive information is exchanged and retrieved by clients mostly in edge or central data centers and retained or discontinued also at the edges or cloud service.

2) **Integrity:** consistency is required to ensure that data is transmitted properly and reliably to the authors even without unrecognized data alteration. The lack of traditional authentication procedures may harm the privacy of personal information.

3) **Availability:** The mobility for edge computing means that almost all approved users can access the edge and storage resources anywhere at location as required by a clients. Then it ensures, in general, that user information that has been maintained in edge or cloud storage provider of encrypted structure could be analyzed within various performance standards.

4) **Authentication:** Authorization guarantees that a customer's identity is allowed that suggests that it must be a mechanism of proving the identity of the user.

5) **Access Control:** In addition, access management serves as a strengthening mechanism for both protection and privacy considerations through the control laws, it defines who might access the information and also what types of skills including reading and writing may undertake.

6) **Privacy Requirement:** The security protocols can be used to ensuring that almost all customer distribution data, including data, personal identity, and location, is kept confidential against truthful though suspicious opponents. Additionally, data security solutions including certain encoding, reliability internal audit, authorization, and unauthorized access may explicitly or implicitly protect consumer privacy through edge computing.

CHALLENGES IN DATA SECURITY AND ISSUES

Edge computing uses some of the new technology, like data transfer, cloud computing, and privatization, to bring computation close to datasets. In this case, the basic criteria for protecting consumers in the sector, economy, and real activities have been data protection and privacy preservation. In addition, in developing edge computing systems, we have to accept that protection and security will be mentioned in each and every level. In this section we illustrate the possible security and privacy concerns centered on the architecture of edge computing as shown in Figure 1. A description of the identification of data protection and privacy issues is shown in Table 1.

Table 1. Classification of edge computing challenges

Core Infrastructure	Edge Servers	Edge Network	Edge Devices
Privacy Leakage Data Tampering Denial of Service	Privacy leakage Denial of Service Access Control Authorization	Denial of Service Man-in-the-Middle attack	Injection in information Service manipulation

Security of Core Infrastructure

It is important to remember that multiple core services and infrastructure, including decentralized cloud service delivery systems, can endorse all edge methodologies, similar core systems can be operated by same third-party providers, like telecommunications operators. This will pose major challenges, including certain data breaches, data theft, denial of service attacks, and database exploitation, since these core networks could be semi-confident or totally mistrusted. Second, sensitive and confidential details of the consumer may be manipulated by illegal users or trustworthy yet suspicious opponents, or confiscated. That will lead to information leakage and data manipulation vulnerabilities. In addition, edge computing permits for mutual information sharing among edge nodes and edge storage systems that can circumvent the centralized networks. Core networks could provide and share erroneous data if the systems are hacked and blocked, which might lead to denial of attacks on a systems. Furthermore, the data flow could be abused via an inner attacker with ample privileged access that provide many organizations with erroneous information and fake resources. This form of security breach may not have been able to effect the entire system due to its distributed and scalable aspects of edge computing, however this is a potential threat that couldn't be neglected.

Security of Edge Servers

Edge servers are responsible for virtual server networks and multiple monitoring systems by installing edge storage systems in same geographical region as cloud - based scenarios. For this scenario, all internally and externally opponents will control the edge servers and snatch or interfere with the sensitive material. Unless the opponents has acquired adequate edge data center access rights now they can either misuse their rights as a genuine controller or exploit the resources. As a result, the opponents will perform many forms of assaults, like man-in-the-middle attacks, denial of services and so forth. In addition, there will be an absurd example where an opponent can access the whole edge server or create an artificial network, as well as the intruder could fully monitor all of the resources and guide the flow of data to a malicious cloud server. Other protection problem is indeed a remote data centre's physical violence. It is important to realize that such a physical threat is restricted to a narrow local area but that according to the dispersed distribution of edge devices, just the networks in a specific geographical location would be crippled.

Security of Edge Networks

As described above, edge computing recognizes the interconnectedness of IoT sensors and devices through the integration of various communication networks (e.g. Wired, Wireless), that creates several network security problems for all these communications technologies. The conventional network threats, including DOS and DDOS attacks, could be effectively restricted by using the servers at the edge of network. Such activities could only disturb the proximity of an edge devices and have little impact on the data center, therefore the DOS or DDOS attackers in network topology may not seriously interfere with edge data center protection. In addition, intrusive attackers may initiate operations to manipulate the communications infrastructure, like eavesdroppers or traffic amplification threats.

Security of Edge Devices

In edge computing, the fog nodes acted as contributing members at multiple levels as in mobile edge world, since even smaller amounts of breached edge nodes may manifest in deleterious consequences for entire edge system. For instance, any systems infiltrated via an opponent could attempt to interfere with resources by injecting misleading information or encroach the framework with certain maliciousness operations. In general, destructive systems can exploit networks in certain unique situations where each of those systems has been granted the privilege of access by the malicious opponents. An edge node connects to one trusted domain, for example, can serve as an edge cloud server for all other systems.

MECHANISMS FOR DATA SECURITY AND PRIVACY

To build a secure edge model network with protection and convenient access, introducing multiple types of privacy and security technologies and preventing attention from malicious adversaries is essential. This section discusses the current frameworks of security and privacy which could be used in edge computing paradigms. In addition, we have developed an edge computing information security analysis framework, as seen in Fig. 2.

Figure 2. The Architecture of Data Security in Edge Computing

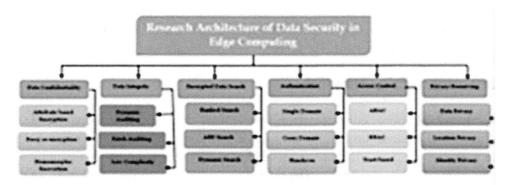

A.   Confidentiality of Data

Customer sensitive information is exported to an edge node in edge computing, as well as its government ownership is divided, allowing customers to sacrifice the direct possession over outsourced data. In addition, confidential data in the export computing state eventually led to significant security breaches, data theft, and unauthorized data processes (e.g. copying, deleting, and sharing of information). To counter those risks, an effective data protection mechanism must be introduced in the sense of edge computing to secure confidential data, which means that client-sensitive data across edge devices must be protected until being exported to edge server. The conventional encryption method incorporates the secret key algorithms and the asymmetric techniques, but typically the functionality of the encrypted data collected by the conventional cryptographic algorithms is limited, creating serious challenges to an eventual data processing. In recent days, several innovative cryptographic algorithms have been incorporated to establish multiple data encryption technology for safe storing data and encourage users to manage their personal information as encrypted data on unreliable server.

B.   Integrity of Data

Data integrity is an essential problem of edge computing reliability as customer data is exported to an edge devices, although the integrity of the participants may be breached throughout this operation. It refers to the processes by which data providers verify the quality and efficiency of outsourced information to determine that either unauthorized people or devices have unrecognized configuration changes. In edge computing, data integrity analysis must concentrate on 4 main factors: batch auditing, dynamic auditing, privacy-conserving and minimal complexity (Wazir, 2019).

C. **Secure Retrieval of Data**

Another key problem that needs to be resolved in edge computing is stable data storage. End-user sensitive data are typically exported to edge encryption-form computation systems. For this situation, secured retrieval is the primary hindrance, meaning the consumer will have to overcome the keyword based problems over the protected file system. With authors' contributions, numerous searchable encryption algorithms were introduced to help secure search of encrypted files via queries before decryption like rank based, wild keyword (Caprolu, 2019), dynamic search etc.,

D. Authentication

Cloud computing is an emerging collaborative technology system of numerous confidence environments whereby various processing participants, programs, and communications infrastructure exist peacefully (Donald, 2016). Without even any user authentication, exterior competitors are very able to view the essential resources of the network service, and inner competitors may remove the indications of unauthorized behavior because of their authorized access. In this case, solutions for implementation of authorization in edge computing need to be explored to protect the consumer across emerging privacy and security problems and reduce threats and vulnerabilities.

E. Access Control

Because of the procurement function of edge computing, some unauthorized attacker via an approved identification may misuse the resources and services in edge or providing grants if there are too many secure authorization procedures at a certain location. This poses a major security vulnerability for the protected authorized user, such as the edge node network virtual machines service being manipulated, misconstrued, and updated through edge nodes unless they have some rights. Fortunately, most of conventional access controls are typically handled in one step in risk, but are not appropriate for edge computation multiple security environments. Some of the access control models are discussed in (Chinnasamy, 2018).

F. Privacy-Preserving

Privacy is among the biggest problems in many other computer methodologies, as confidential information is moved from edge computers to multiple computers by the users and private information. In edge devices, the privacy issue is much more critical since there are a range of reasonable but interesting opponents, like edge nodes, network operators, network operators as well as some clients. Typically these perpetrators are approved organizations which second objective is to obtain additional personal information which could be used in different selfish behavior. For this case, this is not difficult to confirm if a network operator in an open environment with various confidence ecosystems is reputable (Wasir, 2019).

FUTURE RESEARCH DIRECTIONS

Depending on a basic factors overviews, the conservative establishment and the major challenges of preserving edge computing systems, it can be concluded that analysis on edge computing integrity and confidentiality seems far from satisfactory and the future avenues of investigation reside on addressing the significant obstacles and the current deficiencies and limitations. Mostly on other side, stronger protection strategies, particularly defensive techniques, are certainly required to minimize physical attacks; but in the other hand, new frameworks are interesting to explore which can implement security measures to safeguard the existing network in a more consistent fashion. Most notably, the protection-by-design principle must be widely embraced and often retrospective. We highlight a fundamental principle that ensures effective edge computer programs with a coherent model and to propose research trends across that research study. The system comprises three layers: an external, fine-grained access control layer, a functionality layer with mid-security, and an internal device-isolated OS layer.

The exterior layer emphasizes on fine-grained access control that acts as a "door" to impede the external attackers' penetrations. We recognize a template to execute a framework per mission which can integrate at least the details from the five essential inputs: who, where, what, when, and how. If properly constructed and successfully controlled, a really fine-grained access control system might have the ability to alleviate strikes caused by configuration-level design issues, development-level faults, and poor user access, leading to flood-based DDoS, activities that manipulate maneuverable malicious attacks, intrusion detection, and threats on identification and authorization. The inner layer aims to incorporate robust full-bodied security frameworks. We consider adopting SDN and Networking Function Virtualization (NFV) just at edge server side, whereby SDN is embraced to manage anomalous attacks per-packet basis, whereas the NFV embraces quite advanced technologies like deep learning to autonomously and self-revoltingly recognize suspicious behaviors. The edge devices facilitated by SDN and NFV could have the ability to inhibit the growth packet-based threats like DDoS, synchronized defraud and poor access controls.

The innermost layer addresses the bugs that are inevitable on the compiled code. We comprehend that a feasible solution will be to build a firmware-isolation, enabled Application at the edge device level. Even an operating system segregates the OS kernel and all critical device-level information in separate protected environments employing hardware insulation to prevent software problems. This architecture may be able to minimize security concerns exacerbated by deficiencies at the assembly level, like zero-day cyberattacks and zero-day malicious insider attacks.

The main aim of introducing the above discussed three-layer security architecture is to "throw stones and get sylvan." Research and development on edge computing vulnerability still in its embryonic stages. Also in near future would succeed powered by new technologies and also developments in cryptographic algorithms, groundbreaking prototypes and deployment to secure edge computing.

CONCLUSION

In this report, from a comprehensive viewpoint, we examine and describe the data protection and privacy-conserving threats and defensive measures in edge computing system. Initially, defining edge computing definitions are presented along with the limitations of cloud technology, the approaching era of IoE, as well as the shift towards user to consumer, therefore we introduce the concept, architectures and a few critical edge computing applications. Next, we are evaluating the security threats to data protection and privacy, and the practicable security protocols are being provided. In addition, cryptographic-based solutions are outlined to address data protection and privacy problems, and a comprehensive analysis on the legislature-of-the-art security requirements is thoroughly researched and categorized.

REFERENCES

Caprolu, D. P., Lombardi, & Raponi. (2019). Edge Computing Perspectives: Architectures, Technologies, and Open Security Issues. *2019 IEEE International Conference on Edge Computing (EDGE)*, 116-123. doi: 10.1109/EDGE.2019.00035

Chinnasamy, Deepalakshmi, & Praveena, Rajakumari, & Hamsagayathri. (2019). Blockchain Technology: A Step Towards Sustainable Development. *International Journal of Innovative Technology and Exploring Engineering*, 9(S2).

Chinnasamy, P., & Deepalakshmi, P. (2018a). A scalable multilabel-based access control as a service for the cloud (SMBACaaS). *Transactions on Emerging Telecommunications Technologies*, *29*(8), e3458. doi:10.1002/ett.3458

Chinnasamy & Deepalakshmi. (2018b). A Survey on Enhancing Cloud Security through Access Control Models and Technologies. *International Journal on Computer Science and Engineering*, *9*(5), 326–331.

Donald, A. C., & Arockiam, L. (2016). Key Based Mutual Authentication (KBMA) Mechanism for Secured Access in MobiCloud Environment. In *MATEC Web of Conferences* (Vol. 40, p. 09002). EDP Sciences.

El-Sayed, Sankar, Prasad, Puthal, Gupta, Mohanty, & Lin. (2018). Edge of things: The big picture on the integration of edge, IoT and the cloud in a distributed computing environment. *IEEE Access, 6*, 1706-1717.

Ghobaei-Arani, M., Souri, A., & Rahmanian, A. A. (2020). Resource Management Approaches in Fog Computing: A Comprehensive Review. *Journal of Grid Computing*, *18*(1), 1–42. doi:10.100710723-019-09491-1

Guan, Zhang, Si, Zhou, Wu, Mumtaz, & Rodriguez. (2019). ECOSECURITY: Tackling challenges related to data exchange and security: An edge-computing-enabled secure and efficient data exchange architecture for the energy Internet. *IEEE Consum. Electron. Mag., 8*(2), 61-65.

Khan, Ahmed, & Hakak, Yaqoob, & Ahmed. (2019). Edge computing: A survey. *Future Generation Computer Systems*, *97*, 219–235.

Liu, L., Chen, C., & Pei, Q. (2020). Vehicular Edge Computing and Networking: A Survey. *Mobile Netw Appl.* doi:10.100711036-020-01624-1

Rapuzzi & Repetto. (2018). Building situational awareness for network threats in fog/edge computing: Emerging paradigms beyond the security perimeter model. *Future Gener. Comput. Syst., 85*, 235-249.

Roman, Lopez, & Mambo. (2018). Mobile edge computing, fog et al.: A survey and analysis of security threats and challenges. *Future Gener. Comput. Syst., 78*, 680-698.

Xiao, Y., Jia, Y., Liu, C., Cheng, X., Yu, J., & Lv, W. (2019). Edge Computing Security: State of the Art and Challenges. *Proceedings of the IEEE*, *107*(8), 1608-1631. 10.1109/JPROC.2019.2918437

Yang, Yu, Si, Yang, & Zhang. (2019). Integrated Blockchain and Edge Computing Systems: A Survey, Some Research Issues and Challenges. *IEEE Communications Surveys and Tutorials*, *21*(2), 1508–1532. doi:10.1109/COMST.2019.2894727

Yousefpour, Fung, Nguyen, Kadiyala, & Jalali, Niakanlahiji, Kong, & Jue. (2019). All one needs to know about fog computing and related edge computing paradigms: A complete survey. *Journal of Systems Architecture, 98,* 289–330.

Yu, T., & Zha, Z., Song, & Han. (2020). An EPEC Analysis among Mobile Edge Caching, Content Delivery Network and Data Center. 2020 IEEE Wireless Communications and Networking Conference (WCNC), 1-6. doi: 10.1109/WCNC45663.2020.9120613

Zhang, Chen, Zhao, Cheng, & Hu. (2018). Data security and privacy-preserving in edge computing paradigm: Survey and open issues. *IEEE Access, 6,* 18209-18237.

Zhou, Y., Tian, L., Liu, L., & Qi, Y. (2019). Fog Computing Enabled Future Mobile Communication Networks: A Convergence of Communication and Computing. IEEE Communications Magazine, 57(5), 20-27. doi:10.1109/MCOM.2019.1800235

Chapter 10
Data Security and Privacy–
Preserving in Edge Computing:
Cryptography and Trust
Management Systems

Manoranjini J.
Swami Vivekananda Institute of Technology, India

Anbuchelian S.
Anna University, India

EXECUTIVE SUMMARY

The rapid massive growth of IoT and the explosive increase in the data used and created in the edge networks led to several complications in the cloud technology. Edge computing is an emerging technology which is ensuring itself as a promising technology. The authors mainly focus on the security and privacy issues and their solutions. There are a lot of important features which make edge computing the most promising technology. In this chapter, they emphasize the security and privacy issues. They also discuss various architectures that enable us to ensure safe technologies and also provide an analysis on various designs that enable strong security models. Next, they make a detailed study on different cryptographic techniques and trust management systems. This study helps us to identify the pros and cons that led us to promising implementations of edge computing in the current scenario. At the end of the chapter, the authors discuss on various open research areas which could be the thrust areas for the next era.

DOI: 10.4018/978-1-7998-4873-8.ch010

INTRODUCTION

Edge computing is the new era of computing. Over the period cloud computing has become the massive storage and the data warehousing was another notable factor of research with the cloud. However, the cloud has its disadvantages like effective bandwidth utilization, limited usage of resources. IoT has been a new working methodology that can perform massive growth in technical systems. However, there are several limitations in IoT as these devices incorporate only the cloud and the security issue in the cloud has always been the major limitation. To address these complexities edge computing came as a boon to the technical world.

The basic working of edge computing defines a device to process its data within itself or to the closest point near the device. This working principle has brought the data warehousing also to grow in a new way. So the data is processed somewhere between the device and the cloud repository. Generally, edge computing uses devices that act as an intermediate level for processing data. The cloud computing provisionally pictured few problems like the bandwidth maintenance and also not able to meet the data processing requirements. The problems faced while processing the data was mainly because of the size of data which was huge in size. Moreover this data processing consumed large amount of utilization capacity. So the cloud faced more challenges.

In edge computing the devices (Al-Fuqaha et al., 2015) are placed such that the data is either processed within the devices or at its close proximity. Sometimes we call it as data being processed at the corner or edge of the network. The edge computing network refers to the devices which are in close association with the devices. The devices which belong to the edge computing form a network with few ideal factors like the storage capacity speed or we can call it as computational speed which is required for fast data processing.

Edge computing architecture helps to reduce the computational processing in a large manner. Effective communication is also trusted as the network has its devices in close proximity. These flexibilities in the network contribute to the massive growth of this edge technology. In cloud technology the preserving of data was a challenge and secures data storage was always under a scrutiny. In particular the edge networks reduced these challenges in the cloud by offering efficient data storage .The cloud also had issues in access control which was another important privacy factor. However the upcoming edge computing offers stringent access control which maintain the privacy in a structured manner.

However, the edge computing had its own challenges. Since the data is processed in close proximities, every device has to be communicating and coordinating among them to ensure the flow of data processing without any security challenges. So the devices had to authenticate themselves. The authentication should be flexible so that there are no constraints with regard to specific domains. These contribute to the new challenges of maintaining an ideal security and privacy preservation. This chapter enables to understand mainly the five critical privacy factors which are authentication, access control, integrity, availability and confidentiality.

The need for edge computing mainly developed due to the change in the use of data by the end user. Social media and YouTube and several platforms use huge amount of data which requires effective processing in less time. The Edge Computing Consortium (ECC) defines edge computing as the source of data at a very close network which is very close to the source device of the data and process it to meet the end requirements of the user. We can also define edge computing as intelligent devices collaborating for effective computational processing. The edge network collaborates with the cloud. So all the devices in the edge network are also a part of the cloud.

Figure 1. Architecture diagram for edge computing

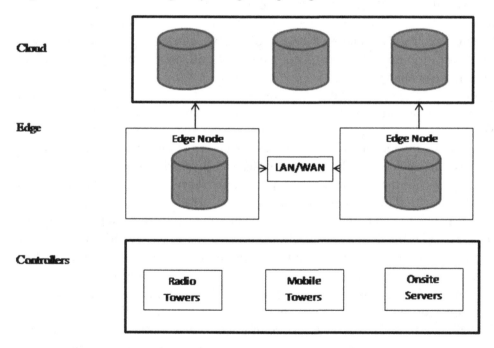

The architecture diagram of the edge network is depicted above. The figure mentions the base has the different controllers or sensors. They are connected to the edge networks as and when required and do not stay connected always. Now the Edge networks forms several nodes which are connected by means of LAN or

WAN or SAN or PAN. LAN is Local area networks which connects the systems in same area. WAN is wide area network which connects between two metropolitan cities. SAN is small area network and PAN is personal area network like Bluetooth. The edge nodes are all connected to the cloud.

Data Security and Privacy issues

1.   Edge Security and Privacy

Data security is defined as the art of protecting the data in fact the digital data in a structured security process like encryption or hashing techniques or several other cryptographic and trust management systems or using the network firewalls. Firewalls literally stop the network from accessing the other networks and are more effective in their performances over the decade. However the current technology has vast growth from securing data. We have the cloud infrastructure, edge computing and fog computing which are several new technical growths in the computer world. Most of the working computer world is greatly using the IoT where they connect their laptops and computers and mobiles and data is shared among them. There is an average increase in the number of devices which are interconnected in 2020. This led to the edge computing which makes use of all these potentials.

Edge computing is extended to its security which is Edge security which identifies the computers or computer nodes which are at the edge network. The security in edge follows all the security practices used in the computer network world like firewalls and other network monitoring tools. The edge computing also maintains a browser. Hence there should be assurance of a secure edge browser. Thus to ensure edge security and edge browser security the edge computing maintained an edge firewall which is similar to the firewalls used in computer networks which acts as a bridge connecting the networks be it internal or external. To ensure a better and efficient security of data we should be able to develop a trusted network. To do this, the monitoring of network should maintained and the network should be labelled as malicious free and the allowed to participate in the edge computing. The several internet protocols are implemented to maintain the security at every network. Further in this chapter we would be going through the maintenance of edge data security and the methodologies which could be adopted to enhance the security of edge computing.

2.   Requirements to maintain privacy

Data is always sent to various other networks for its various usages. So there is definitely a large loss of data and serious data misuse happening in large in the digital world. So the basic essential security factors in any network are the following:

1.   Availability

Availability ensures the edge computing networks to be available at all times as and when needed. This should be ideal in all networks. As the data transmission in any type of network is the main concern, if the network is not available for a short period then the data transmission would affect the total performance of the network. So availability of the network should be the primary security concern.

2.   Access control

Edge computing should have structured access controls defined for their networks. Access control defines the permission given by the network on who can actually access the data and who have the authority to modify or only to send or read the data. This is actually a key factor in edge network which helps in ideal data transmission without the intervention of malicious users.

3.   Confidentiality

Edge computing has several interconnected devices and confidentiality should be ensured such that the communicating devices should have all the information sharing in a right way. The sharing of information should only be between the communicating devices. Confidentiality is very important to be maintained such that communicating devices transfer the confidential data only between themselves.

4.   Authentication

This security factor is mainly about authorizing the identity of the network. Only when the computers in the networks are able to identify the other computers in another network then there will efficient data transmission. Usually this communication fails if they are not able to prove their identity. Therefore authentication between edge networks is highly an important security concern.

5. Integrity

Integrity is very important to be maintained in edge computing as the data should not be altered while it is being transmitted between the edge networks. The networks are often affected by data inconsistency. This inconsistency in data led to ineffective communication.

Security Challenges

The most important challenge is having a full view of the network, enhanced operating systems, encryption and decryption techniques, and the trust management mechanisms. As edge networks are being used now a day the main focus is on data security. The security of data builds the trust of the network. It is more important to maintain same security scheme throughout the network. As many devices are connected to form the edge network there is more security issues. Generally the IoT devices are the ones which can form edge networks. IoT devices do not have consistent connections which leds to security breaches.

Every network (Evans, D., 2011) should be transparent for working. The administrator should be able to understand all the operations in the network for which there should be transparency. The cloud receives the data from various edge devices and they should be operated efficiently in the network to ensure data security.The operating system is the heart of any network operation. Ensuring an encrypted OS will enhance the effective transfer of data from sender to receiver. The system can include encrypted nodes and form an encrypted network.

Encryption of data is the main security challenge to be addressed. Data misuse, data leakage, data tampering is some of the possible security challenges in an edge network. The integrity ensures secure transfer of data without any modification. The encrypted data offers secure transmission of data using intergrity audit trials method or some encryption techniques or authentication methods.

Table 1. Edge Network Challenges

Edge Network Challenges				
Cloud Infrastructure Challenges	Data Misuse	Inappropriate identity	Viruses and other malware attacks	Distrusted or mistrusted device
Client Security Challenges	Viruses	Data Leakage	SQL Injection	Data manipulation
Server Security Challenges	DOS	Physical Damage	Meet in middle attack	Manipulation of Server identity

Edge Network: Cloud Infrastructure Challenges

Any device in the edge network has its infrastructure based on the cloud. The cloud is the technology used for massive data storage in almost most of the devices. Generally the technical world has moved their massive data into the cloud. The data security inabilities in cloud are,

1. Data misuse

Data misuse happens in almost any network. The data are collected and they are tampered or altered. This kind of data misuse is highly critical challenge to any network. With regard to the edge network, since these computing devices are near the other devices and also since they form an edge network where scalability is often ensured in the network more possibility of data misuse takes place.

2. Inappropriate identity

The edge computing devices are scalable so reliability is also a great challenge. This uncertainty is due to the loss of identity of a device which could be the source or destination device. Loss of the identity by a device is possible when the device is being infected by any intervention of technical hackers.

3. Viruses and other malware attacks

The main challenge faced by the edge network which is globally aligned to the cloud is the attack of viruses and other different kinds of malware attacks. There are several viruses which attack the core device participating in the network and making them either unable to perform the data transmission or enable them for a wrong transfer of data or send tampered data. Several malware attacks affect the data such that the data transmission is affected and can bring down the whole performance of the network which leads to degrading of the network performance.

4. Distrusted or mistrusted device

The device can be a trusted or a mistrusted device. Maintaining the trust of a device is the most difficult challenge faced by any edge network. The behaviour of a device in the data transmission directly affects the network efficiency. The devices can be attacked by an intruder and the device can be made inactive.

Edge Network: Client Security Challenges

In the edge network (M. Peng et al., 2016), the devices are our serious concerns with regard to data transmissions. These devices all also in the edge of the network interacting with other edge devices. So the vulnerability of the systems is more prone to attacks. The devices are easily manipulated by intruders as they are available in the edge of the networks. The viruses can also bypass the network easily and enter the most flexible device in the edge network. When the other devices in the network communicate with the infected device then the infected device easily transmits to the other devices in the network and slowly over a period of time they affect and degrade the overall network performance.

Edge Network: Server Security Challenges

The edge servers can also be called as the edge data centres. All the data are being sent and received through the server. Maintaining the security of server is a serious concern. In many cases the edge network mostly tends to attach the server and the cloud in one place. This is a valid reason for data being easily misused. Any intruder can gain access and can start accessing all the important data's that are transferred between the server and client in the edge computing. The popular man in middle attack can be a known attack that can affect the edge servers. This attack generally appears between the communicating devices and the malware device makes itself to appear to the source as the original destination device. So now all the data is sent to the malware device instead of the edge device inside the edge network. Another most difficult challenge is the damage made on the servers physically. Sometimes due to natural calamities or accidents the servers could be damaged manually. So maintaining a second server as a backup is generally done for edge computing networks.

Security Technologies

Edge networking (Chiang, M. et al., 2016) gives more importance to the edge systems in the networks. Several security technologies are given importance to secure the networking however we focus on encryption and trust systems. The main focus is on the cryptographic methods and trusted systems which are the basis for any secure data transmission. Several cryptographic methods are available. We concentrate on reusable encryption method which can reuse successfully transmitted encrypted data. We then include homomorphic encryption which is based on strong calculations using prime orders like in elgamal and RSA algorithms to encrypt data. Next we introduce the trust systems which establish a trust model either by direct, indirect or mutual trust among nodes.

1. Cryptographic methods
    A. Reusable Encryption

We can implement reusable words for encryption process. The data stored in the network is analysed over a period of time and the strong words can be reused. Identifying the strong reusable words is done by using some machine learning concepts in the training phase and enabling the network to learn the frequently used words. These training sets are given into the network so that they learn from the previous datasets and predict the future reusable words also. Searching of encrypted data can also be a part of this reusable encryption. The ciphertext data can be searched and then added to the reusable dictionary.

Reusable Encryption (RE) technology ensures availability and reliability of data on ciphertext. The process is as follows,

1. Encryption technique: The primary technique of encryption is to encrypt the plaintext. In RE, we can convert the plaintext into encrypted format using message digest and assign a structured secret key. These encrypted ciphertext are then stored in the edge computing data centres.
2. Filter mechanism: This is used to capture all the necessary words or contents in the encrypted data and maintain filter storage in the data center. Filter acts like a strong encryption mechanism.
3. Reuse mechanism: The edge server gathers the encrypted filtered data and performs the necessary decryption models and ensures that the data communication takes place effectively with availability and reliability.

Reusable mechanism can be classified based on the cryptographic basic models namely, symmetric and asymmetric. Symmetric method is defined as the same key being used for encryption and decryption process. Asymmetric method uses pair of keys to be used for encryption and decryption process one is private key known only to the owner and the other is public key which is known by everyone who are in the network.

i. **Reusable Symmetric Encryption:**

Reusable Symmetric Encryption works using the same key shared between the sender and the receiver. The same shared key is used by the filter mechanism to filter the ideal ciphertexts only. The working of this mechanism uses the permutation

Figure 2. Reusable Encryption

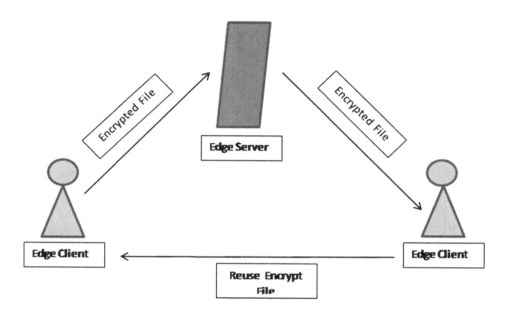

functions and every data is passed to the encryption model to generate the ciphertext and the filter, additionally enables to classify the ciphertext into the essential and non-essential datas. The passing of data into the encryption model should be done based on time fragmentation. So in any communication, the datas are fragmented based on their time frame and length of the data. After fragmentation, the fragments enter the encryption model and the ciphertexts are released into the filter. Now the filter maintains the ciphertexts and sends to the appropriate receiver after refragmenting the ciphertexts. This method stores and maintains the list of datas which are frequently used for that particular communication. So when there is continuous communication in the edge network over a period of time then the filter storage is reused sending the encrypted fragments.

ii.   Reusable Asymmetric Encryption:

Reusable Asymmetric encryption works using a pair of keys, which is a public, private key pair. The asymmetric keys can be generated using different asymmetric encryption algorithms. The public key is generally a known key in the network whereas the private key is known only by the owner of the communication. The reusable mechanism uses this concept as it ensures more security. The public key in the asymmetric encryption is used for generating the ciphertext. These ciphertext

Figure 3. Homomorphic Encryption

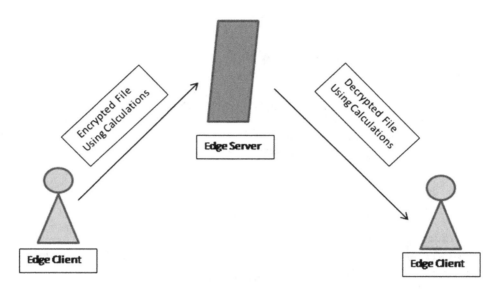

generated are the sent into the filter to be captured for reusing. The filtered required ciphertext are transferred to the storage center in the edge server.

B.   Homomorphic Encryption

This is a technique used by performing calculations on both the encryption and decryption sides. The calculations are matched to identify the ideal data transfer. Generally this kind of encryption methodology allows the edge data transfer in a secure manner. This kind of encryption ensures safe and secure transmission and addresses problems like data leakage and data misuse or data mishandling. But there are limitations when the data gets tampered. We can show the working of the encryption.

We can classify them as fully homomorphic encryption and partially homomorphic. There are several other encryption types also but these are the currently working encryption models. The number of calculation takes place in circuits keeps changing and so the encryption takes place. Partially homomorphic also helps in the calculations and they consist of many types of logic evaluations like logic gates or flip flops.

The following calculations are used in this method. Let us see them one by one.

1. Discrete Logarithm: In this method, consider a set of prime numbers a, and let X*a be a finite field and generate n from X*a, now let us pick an integer which can belong to this calculated X*a set.

2. Integer Factorization: Consider a set of unique prime numbers. Using this method we calculate factor expressions like, $m=(a(e^1)\ 1, a(e^2)\ 2, \ldots\ldots, a(e^n)\ n)$.

3. Decisional Composite Residuosity: Consider A=mn where m and n are two prime numbers chosen. Consider a number b which belongs to $X*A^2$ and this gives us if b is A times the residual value.

2. Trust management models for security

The presence of malicious nodes in the edge network can lead to the cause of data drop or data loss during transmission. There are various methodologies to identify the malicious nodes in an edge network. One such methodology is to establish a strong trust model. Developing a trust relationship between the nodes in a network can impact on the performance of the network and also avoid the network to degrade in its performance. The malicious nodes sometimes act as the replica of the node inside the edge network and capture all the data and degrade the performance of the network.

To ensure efficient data transfer and also to improve the performance of the edge network (Ganz, F et al., 2015), we can build a trust relationship among all nodes in the edge network. Generally there can three types of trust that can be established, they are direct, indirect and mutual trust between the nodes in the edge network and it's supporting neighbour networks. Let us consider each case one by one.

Model Assumption

Edge computing trust model can be implemented based on certain metrics like magnitude trust, potential trust, protection trust, reliability trust, incident trust and rejection trust. Let us understand each trust metric one by one.

i. Magnitude trust is defined as the trust between the source (a) and destination (b) in any edge network when there is achievement of maximum efficiency. Magnitude can also be said to be achieved when there is maximum traffic handled in the edge networks.

ii. Potential trust is defined as the maximum magnitude of data transmission and the exact order of the nodes in the communication path between the the source (a) and destination (b) in any edge network.

iii. Protection trust is defined as the trust between the source (a) and destination (b) in any edge network that ensures the attitude of the nodes in the data transmission.

iv. Reliability trust is defined as the trust established between the source node a and destination node b such that there is always a possibility of one trusted device in any edge network.

v. Incident trust is defined as the trust recorded for every node or device that belongs to the edge network and these recordings of the past incidents helps the network to understand the behaviour of the future behaviour of the devices.

vi. Rejection trust of any device in an edge computing determines the model of behaviour the device exhibits over a period of time.

Based on these assumptions we can classify the trust model into direct, indirect and mutual trust.

Direct Trust:

The direct trust can be established as the communication and cooperation among the nodes which are adjacent to each other in the edge network. Direct trust can also be defined as the direct communication between two neighbouring nodes in the edge network. The total number of nodes which are adjacent to each other is first calculated. This is called as the possibility index. When the possibility index is above a threshold th then the current node in the edge network assumes that there is a high range of adjacent nodes and so the data is not transmitted. When th is low or 1 it is assumed that there is one adjacent node and the data can be transmitted to the neighbouring node.

Indirect Trust:

The edge network has several interconnected networks. Therefore the transmission of data may be through several intermediate nodes. These nodes between the source and destination networks are the reason for indirect trust to be built while data transfer. We need to first identify the path of data transfer. When there is multi path during transfer then we establish the indirect trust to be built. The indirect trust between the nodes in the edge computing always ensures the loss of data integrity. Thus the data transmitted is lost between the middle nodes in the edge network.

Mutual Trust:

The trust between two nodes should agree on mutual basis. Therefore we assign a trusted node pair which agrees on common goals. This is called as mutual trust. To establish the mutual trust between nodes we need to find all the nodes adjacent to the source and destination nodes in the edge network. The indirect trust calculates the nodes in the single and multi-paths based on these we can identify the adjacent nodes and their close proximity towards the source and destinations. The indirect trust model can provide necessary updates to the mutual trust model.

Figure 4. Implementation of Trust Model

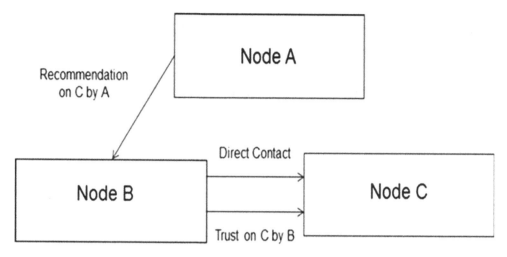

Hence from these models we can get the inferences such as,

i.   When two nodes a and b in any edge computing are in direct communication then the direct trust model can be used.

ii.   When two nodes a and b in any edge computing are in non-directional communication and non-adjacent to each other then we implement the indirect trust model.

iii.   When two nodes a and b in any edge computing don't have the same trust then the mutual trust model can be implemented.

REFERENCES

Al-Fuqaha, A., Guizani, M., Mohammadi, M., Aledhari, M., & Ayyash, M. (2015). Internet of things: A survey on enabling technologies, protocols, and applications. *IEEE Communications Surveys and Tutorials, 17*(4), 2347–2376. doi:10.1109/COMST.2015.2444095

Chiang, M., & Zhang, T. (2016). Fog and IoT: An overview of research opportunities. *IEEE Internet of Things Journal, 3*(6), 854–864. doi:10.1109/JIOT.2016.2584538

Evans, D. (2011). The internet of things: How the next evolution of the internet is changing everything. *CISCO White Paper, 1*(2011), 1-11.

Ganz, F., Puschmann, D., Barnaghi, P., & Carrez, F. (2015). A practical evaluation of information processing and abstraction techniques for the internet of things. *IEEE Internet of Things Journal, 2*(4), 340–354. doi:10.1109/JIOT.2015.2411227

Peng, M., & Zhang, K. (2016). Recent advances in fog radio access networks: Performance analysis and radio resource allocation. *IEEE Access: Practical Innovations, Open Solutions, 4*, 5003–5009. doi:10.1109/ACCESS.2016.2603996

Chapter 11
IoE–Enabled Healthcare 4.0 Systems

Kamatchi Periyasamy
PSG College of Technology, India

Anitha Kumari K.
PSG College of Technology, India

Sebastin Arockia Akash
CRED Club, India

EXECUTIVE SUMMARY

The whole world is changing quickly into a mechanical world. One of the most encouraging innovations is the smart sensor innovation which is presently accessible all over the place. Nowadays the utilization of internet is exaggerated in our lives everywhere so that most of the things we use in our day-to-day lives are dependent on internet, which leads to a new era of internet of everything (IoE). The internet of everything (IoE) has different applications in medication, from far off seeing to smart sensors and clinical appliances. It can ensure and screen patients and improve the degree of care. This technology shows improvements in different sectors, specifically in critical sectors which lead everything in the world to be very smart.

INTRODUCTION

The on-going improvements in biomedical sensors, remote correspondence frameworks, and data systems are changing the customary human services frameworks. The changed social insurance frameworks are empowering circulated human services administrations to patients who may not be co-situated with the

DOI: 10.4018/978-1-7998-4873-8.ch011

medicinal services suppliers, giving early judgments, and lessening the expense in the health awareness segment. The principle objective of the IoE innovation is to change over gathered data into activities, encourage information based dynamic and give new capacities and more extravagant encounters. The Internet of Everything is the associations between people, things, data and processes joined into a typical interrelated framework, the point of which is to improve encounters and settle on more brilliant choices. The IoE reasoning delineates the world where billions of sensors are embedded into billions of gadgets, machines and conventional articles, giving them extended systems administration openings, subsequently making them more intelligent. The advancements in clinical web of things (medical-IoT) would empower a scope of utilizations, including far off wellbeing observing through clinical evaluation wearables to give homecare to elderlies; virtual specialist understanding cooperation to have whenever and place access to clinical experts; remote endoscopic assessment; and distantly worked mechanical medical procedure to stretch out the entrance to profoundly talented specialists. Wireless Body Area Network (WBAN) are key empowering influences of these changes. These systems associate sensors and actuators to outer preparing units, which could be put on the outside of the patient's body or embedded inside the body to interface explicit sensors or potentially actuators inside, on, and around the body to the information assortment focuses. The accomplishment of these systems profoundly depends on the coming of low-power, low-delay, solid, and minimal effort remote availability arrangements. This book covers late advancements in remote human services frameworks to give a knowledge to the mechanical arrangements (for example for body zone channel spread models, correspondence methods, and vitality gathering/move) for remote body region arranges, and rising utilizations of clinical web of things and remote human services frameworks (Masoud et al., 2019).

DEFINITION OF IOE

The Internet of Everything (IoE) is an idea that expands the Internet of Things (IoT) prominence on machine-to-machine (M2M) correspondences to depict a progressively convoluted framework that likewise includes people and procedures.

IoE vs. IoT

To keep away from the misperception between the terms, IoT versus IoE, here is how about that make sense of and in what ways they vary (Chauhan & Jain, 2019).

The major distinction between the Internet of Things and the Internet of Everything is the measure of pillars for these ideas:

- IoT mainly around physical items as it whereas,IoE incorporates four segments (things, procedures, data and people)
- The IoT, fundamentally, is the interconnectivity of physical items that send and get information, while the IoE is a more extensive term that incorporates, aside from IoT, various innovations and individuals as the end-hubs.

In spite of the fact that IoT and IoE are various terms, there are additionally a few resemblances between them:

1. **Decentralization:**The two frameworks are disseminated and don't have a solitary place; every hub fills in as a little administration community and can play out specific tasks autonomously.
2. **Security issues**: Conveyed frameworks are still exceptionally defenceless against entrance and cyber-attacks; the more gadgets are associated with the system, the higher the defencelessness to breaks.

From one perspective, decentralization is one of the IoE and IoT favourable circumstances, since the entire framework doesn't flop regardless of whether there are issues in a few hubs. Then again, such a dissemination causes impediments as dangers for information security and individual protection.

IoE further advances the intensity of the Internet to improve business and industry results, and at last improve individuals' lives by adding to the advancement of IoT.

Background

The advancement of the worldwide web has brought about virtual associations pervasively entering genuine items and exercises. Today, everything can be associated with all the fixings, making another dispersed ecosystem that goes past the recognizable IoT (Internet of Things) idea. Cisco has instituted a unique term — the Internet of Everything (IoE) — to portray this powerfully evolving marvel.

The Internet of Everything (IoE) is an idea that means to take a gander at the master plan in which the Internet of Things fits. However, when it comes to further at IoE, it is noticeable that it truly is likewise about the vision of an appropriated coordinate with a developing spotlight on the edge in the midst of progressing decentralization, some advanced change empowering influences and an attention on IoT business results.

The Internet of Everything (IoE) unites people, process, data, and things to make organized associations more significant and important.While the Internet of Things today mostly is drawn nearer from the viewpoint of associated gadgets, their detecting capacities, correspondence prospects and, at long last, the gadget produced information which are investigated and utilized to control cycles and force various potential IoT use cases, the Internet of Everything idea needs to offer a more extensive view.

The Internet of Everything is instituted by Cisco yet in addition utilized by some different firms once in a while, regardless of whether accepted in the impression of individuals it is fundamentally observed as related with Cisco and most assets originate from Cisco.

Realizing that Cisco isn't only a major part in the Internet of Things scene yet additionally, among others plays a main function in systems, security, advances for human communication (in business) and the improvement of business and modern cycles, there is likewise a marking angle to the Internet of Everything.

Literature Survey

The Author S. Aruna, et.al in the paper **"Academic Workbench for Streetlight Powered by Solar PV System Using Internet of Everything (IoE),"** stated that Sustainable power source is one of the developing pattern in creating nations. Fast improvement of sustainable power source prompts the monetary advantages and decrease ecological contamination. As indicated by current situation 20 to 40 percent of the force produced is devoured by streetlights. The issues looked by the current road lighting frameworks are when there is accessibility of light there is no legitimate usage. Sun force move isn't steady constantly, it differs as the atmosphere changes. Continuous checking and control utilizing astute calculation dodges vitality wastage during day time. ZigBee as a correspondence convention current and voltage esteems are sent and gotten. Base Controller (Single Board Computer) goes about as an interphase between the correspondence convention and the cloud account. Far off customer application is created to control and screen streetlight (Aruna & Venkataswamy, 2018).

The Author A. K. Demir, et.al in the paper **"Fine Tuning Distributed Divergecast Scheduling Algorithms in IEEE 802.1S.4e TSCH for Internet of Everything,"** stated that the idea of the Internet of Everything (IoE) is a zone of extraordinary enthusiasm, with a ton of consideration. The way that it is utilized in practically all territories gains this idea ground a lot quicker. The gadgets utilized in the conditions of this idea are needed to be insignificant as far as equipment just as their vitality utilization. In spite of the fact that there are various methods of limiting vitality utilization in these gadgets, one of the most encouraging conventions that give referenced requests is the IEEE 802.15.4e Time Slotted Channel Hopping (TSCH) Medium Access Control (MAC) convention. This convention runs on 802.15.4 radio and requires a correspondence plan for MAC. How and when these timetables, updates and support will happen are not secured by this convention. A few arrangements are accessible in the writing to tackle these issues. Dispersed divergecast Aloha based planning and DIVA booking calculations are two of these arrangements. The two calculations make their planning as indicated by certain likelihood counts (Demir & Bilgili, 2019). Changing the estimations of these likelihood computations is a novel examination with assessment brings about this paper. The point of this investigation is to inspect the impact of the adjustment in the related likelihood factors on the presentation and attempt to locate the most ideal qualities. It has been seen that the adjustments in these computation esteems affect arrange unite time.

The Author H. Lu, et.al in the paper **"A novel search engine for Internet of Everything based on dynamic prediction,"** stated that As of late, with the fast advancement of detecting innovation and arrangement of different Internet of Everything gadgets, it turns into a urgent and viable test to empower constant quest inquiries for articles, information, and administrations in the Internet of Everything. In addition, such effective question handling methods can give solid encourage the exploration on Internet of Everything security issues (Lu et al., 2019). By investigating the interesting qualities in the IoE application condition, for example, high heterogeneity, high elements, and disseminated, they build up a novel web crawler model, and construct a unique expectation model of the IoE sensor time arrangement to meet the continuous prerequisites for the Internet of Everything search condition. They approved the exactness and adequacy of the dynamic expectation model utilizing an open sensor dataset from Intel Lab.

The Author C. Dai, et.al **"Heuristic computing methods for contact plan design in the spatial-node-based Internet of Everything,"** stated that To fulfill the expanding requests of rapid transmission, high-productivity processing, and constant interchanges in the high-dynamic and heterogeneous systems, the Contact Plan Design (CPD) has pulled in nonstop consideration as of late, particularly for the spatial-hub based Internet of Everything (IoE). In this paper, the authors study the NP-hardness of contact booking and the constriction of environmental precipitation in the spatial-hub based IoE. Two heuristic registering strategies for contact plan configuration are proposed by exhaustively considering the time-fluctuating geography, the discontinuous availability, and the versatile transmission in various climate conditions, which are named Contact Plan Design-Particle Swarm Optimization (CPD-PSO) and Contact Plan Design-Greedy calculation with the Minimum Delivery Time (CPD-GMDT) independently. For the populace based calculation, CPD-PSO not just tackles the CPD issue with a restricted asset condition, yet additionally progressively changes the hunt extension to guarantee the nonstop looking through capacity of the calculation (Dai & Song, 2019). For the CPD-GMDT that settles on CP choices dependent on the present status, the calculation utilizes the possibility of eager calculation to plan Satellite-Platform Links (SPLs) and Inter Satellite Links (ISLs) separately utilizing the procedures of ideal coordinating and burden adjusting. The reenactment results show that the proposed CPD-PSO beats Contact Plan Design-Genetic Algorithm (CPD-GA) regarding wellness and conveyance time, and CPD-GMDT presents preferred in general postponement over Fair Contact Plan (FCP).

The Author M. Sergey, et. Al in the paper **"Cyber security concept for Internet of Everything (IoE)," 2017 Systems of Signal Synchronization, Generating and Processing in Telecommunications** stated that In the article portrays the primary point of view headings of advancement of Worldwide system the Internet uncover: Internet of things, Industrial Internet of things, material Internet of things. These bearings it is wanted to join in the overall idea of Internet of with the essential guideline "Consistently in contact". Conceivably it implies increment number of associations with the Internet to 70 trillion by 2025, remaking and modernization of current correspondence systems and new way to deal with guaranteeing data security. Data security turns into a foundation of formation of correspondence systems of people in the future and how information and correspondence systems will be ensured wellbeing of Society and State will depend. In the event that today questions, conceivably helpless from the Internet, are PCs and the greatest damage which programmer assault can cause is an impermanent suspension of work of robotized control frameworks and admittance to data, in systems of the Industrial Internet of things any component purported "Advanced economy" can become object of assault (Sergey et al., 2017). It is essential for counteraction of possible dangers: to group these dangers; to have the uniform proper portrayal of dangers and the admonition and remedying impact; to have the uniform idea of the association of data security. This article raises addresses which formation of the uniform idea of data security of Russia with the reason to limit likely threat of unsafe effect on noteworthy objects of insurance needs to shape the premise and to prohibit plausibility of system assaults to basic items.

The Author A. Raj, et.al in the paper **"Internet of Everything: A survey based on Architecture, Issues and Challenges,"** stated that Internet of Everything (IoE) is a superset of the Internet of thing (IoT) which implies an association among individuals, cycle, information and things. It interfaces every one of these ideas into one firm world. Essentially, Internet of Everything (IoE) expands on the mainstays of Internet of thing which incorporate system smart framework. Numerous advancements have developed another example for setting up the Internet of Everything (IoE). Internet of Everything is the worldwide system through which individuals, things, keen gadgets are associated with one another and can share data and administrations. This paper chiefly accentuation on the troublesome design of Internet of Everything (loE), difficulties and its related issues (Raj & Prakash, 2018). Correlation between late advances and its particular components are likewise examined. It recommends the powerful exploration course to the specialists in this wide space.

The Author J. Fiaidhi, et.al in the paper **"Internet of Everything as a Platform for Extreme Automation,"** stated that Reports on the idea of the Internet of Everything (IoE). IoE is an idea for wisely associating individuals, cycles, and information in one uniform way, empowering correspondences between machines (M2M), machine-topeople and innovation helped peopleto-individuals cooperations. IoE is relied upon to rethink the business and the computerization wheel all-together. From measures, models to business and assembling structures everything is relied upon to change with the adjustment in information accessible and the savvy availability among individuals and machines for basic dynamic. It is carrying efficiency and seriousness to more elevated levels alongside opening up numerous ways to new and energizing chances (Fiaidhi & Mohammed, 2019). IoE develops the idea of the "Internet of Things" by interfacing gadgets and individuals in a single system. This association goes past the fundamental M2Mcommunications to empower a democratization of aptitude and how it is being conveyed universally. An indispensable aspect of this is to have the option to send contact in apparent genuine time, which is empowered by appropriate mechanical technology and haptics hardware at the edges, alongside an uncommon correspondences organize capacities.

WHY IOE?

IoE is a significant bit of innovation that is set to improve extraordinarily after some time. There are numerous favourable circumstances of having things associated with one another. Here are a couple of the advantages:

- **More information implies better choices**

With included sensors, these gadgets can gather a lot of information on a wide range of zones.

For instance, notwithstanding the useful components of having the option to know which nourishments are leaving date in your brilliant fridge, this upgraded family unit thing will have the option to give you extra data on its capacity utilization, temperature, normal time of the entryway spent open and considerably more.

A more noteworthy progression of data implies that organization behind the gadget can examine enormous patterns in the information to more readily improve the highlights of the gadget. Numerous organizations are understanding the intensity of this innovation and it is prompting an enormous increment in the market (Evans, 2012).

- **Ability to track and screen things**

Just as tracing information for an organization to utilize, it additionally extraordinarily benefits the client.

These gadgets would be able to look out on the current nature of merchandise at home. Knowing the condition of your things will permit a property holder to know when they have to supplant a thing, without them having to reliably check the quality themselves.

- **Lighten the amount of work with automation**

Having a gadget accomplishing most the work done implies that people can spare additional time and cost. It additionally brings about gadgets being made that need almost no human intercession, permitting them to work totally all alone.

- **Increases effectiveness by setting aside cash and assets**

Just as sparing time for the gadget proprietor, it can likewise bring about cost reserve funds. As should be obvious, associated gadgets can give numerous helpful usage. The IoE framework urges Machine to Machine (M2M) correspondence bringing about expanded long haul productivity for both the organization and client.

- **Better personal satisfaction**

At long last, all the advantages lead to an expanded personal satisfaction. Having gadgets track and request things for the user, turn light switches off for the user, and help oversee significant assignments that user might not have the opportunity to do themselves absolutely removes a great deal of pressure. There is no questioning that individuals are for the most part getting busier as the years pass by. With such a significant number of gadgets being made and new innovation being executed, it's difficult to monitor everything. It's extraordinary to have the option to have the option to do the things you appreciate and have a PC deal with the commonplace things realize that need will generally be finished.

Enhancements to the way of life, medical advantages and improved health are likewise part of the IoE future. For instance, those that activity consistently can use wearable innovation to assist them with following their heart rate, body temperature, hydration to remain fit as a fiddle and screen their wellbeing.

Figure 1.

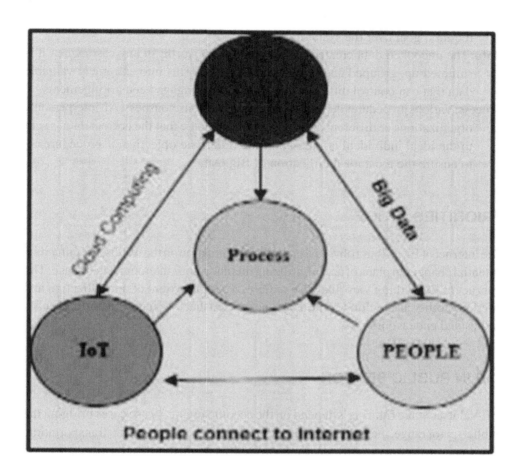

TERMS CONNECTED WITH IOE

Key segments of the IoE showcase are equipment, programming and administrations. With respect to constituent components of the Internet of Everything (Evans, 2013), there are four of them. The fig. 1 illustrates the terms connected with IoE.

People: People give their own bits of knowledge by means of sites, applications or associated gadgets they use, (for example, interpersonal organizations, medicinal services sensors and wellness trackers); AI calculations and other shrewd advances break down this information to "comprehend" human issues and convey important substance as indicated by their own or business needs that encourages them rapidly explain issues or decide.

Things: Here comes the complete IoT idea. Different physical things implanted with sensors and actuators produce information on their status and send it to the required goal over the system.

Data: The uncooked data created by gadgets has no worth. In any case, when it is summed up, grouped and broke down, it transforms into extremely valuable data that can control different frameworks and engage keen arrangements.

Process: Various procedures dependent on man-made consciousness, AI, interpersonal organizations or different advancements guarantee that the correct data is sent to the ideal individual at the opportune time. The objective of procedures is to ensure the most ideal utilization of Big Data.

PRIORITIES OF IOE

The Internet of Everything obviously puts the accentuation on the results, the numerous potential changes in plans of action, utilizing this enormous interconnected space. The Internet of Everything view likewise requires a serious extent of normalization and interoperability. It shouldn't come as an unexpected that is dynamic in normalization bodies and endeavours.

IOE IN PUBLIC SECTOR

IoE Value at Stake figuring's depend on the accompanying 40 use cases bridging the public-sector range, incorporating education, culture & entertainment, transportation, safety and justice, energy & environment, healthcare, defence, and next-generation work and operations (Zielinski, 2015):

Sector-Specific Use Cases

- **Education**
  - Associated learning
  - Smart assessments
- **Culture & Entertainment**
  - Smart game of chance
  - Associated museum
- **Transportation**
  - Smart vehicle parking
  - Public transportation
  - Smart toll gate

- ◦ Road pricing
- ◦ Bridge maintenance
- ◦ Passageway train control
- ◦ Smart street lighting
- **Safety & Justice**
  - ◦ Disaster response
  - ◦ Wildfire suppression
  - ◦ Improvement visits
  - ◦ Video surveillance
  - ◦ Associated offender transport
- **Energy & Environment**
  - ◦ Water administration
  - ◦ Smart grid
  - ◦ Waste administration
  - ◦ Airintensive care

THE ENORMOUS SETTING OF HEALTHCARE STAKEHOLDERS AND IOE POSSIBILITIES

To catch more an incentive in the IoE Economy, associations must adopt a key strategy that includes:

1) Putting resources into great innovation framework and devices
2) Embracing and following comprehensive practices
3) Creating compelling data the executives rehearses.

Public-sector leaders have a one of a kind chance to "act" as opposed to "respond" to the IoE opportunity. The fig 2 represents IoE in healthcare. To begin, public sector pioneers should:

- Determine which IoE abilities their associations have today
- Harness the correlative bits of knowledge of both assistance and IT pioneers
- Identify major IoE opportunity regions and set up an IoE vision
- Reach out to different associations to share the advantages of IoE stages
- Build an "IoE culture" by helping representatives envision the potential outcomes of interfacing the detached

Figure 2.

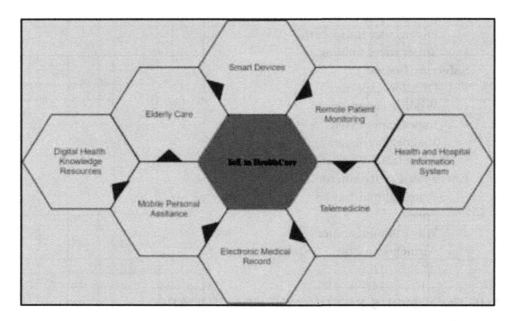

IoE Enabled Healthcare 4.0 System Applications

The Internet of Everything (IoE) has opened up a universe of potential outcomes in medication: when associated with the web, conventional clinical gadgets can gather priceless extra information, give additional knowledge into manifestations and patterns, empower far off consideration, and by and large give patients more authority over their lives and treatment.

Voice Operated Autonomous Wheel Chair

The Fig 3 represents the working of the wheelchair; the mike will get an input from the patient it converted into audio signal. The signal is then passed into the IOT, a program for rotating the wheel chair is fed into the IOT controller (Sangeetha et al., 2019). Then the signal is passed to the motor according to the instruction given by the user or the patient. The command used here is right on, left on, stop, move front and move back. Then sensors are connected to the IoT controller, the sensors used in it are GY87, GY527. The buzzer is also connected to it. This project is about when the person falls from the wheelchair if guardian is not near them, a call is automatically send to the guardian. For that case GY 87 is used, it senses the path of the wheel chair when the wheelchair deviates from the normal path or the chair get disturbed or an obstacle occur it senses and give an instruction to the IoT. This IoT will generate the call to the guardian, the work of the GY 257 is also similar. This will sense the vibration of the patient it is fixed in the wheelchair so that when the seizure occurs to the patient it will indicate or senses by the gyro and gives the instruction to the IoT controller, this IoT makes the call. The program for controlling the wheelchair and the program for making a call for the guardian for the above cases is already programed to the chip. The battery is connected to the motor and a relay is present next to that because replay controls the flow of current. The IoT require only 5 volts, when more voltage is given the components inside the IoT will get damaged and it can be destroyed and misleads the wheelchair. So the voltage is controlled by the relay in this 2 replay is used for the 2 motors. The buzzer is used here for the remainder; an alarm is created according to the time interval. A program, is fed for that, when a patient has to take tablet an alarm is created or generated for the convenience of the patient.

Figure 3.

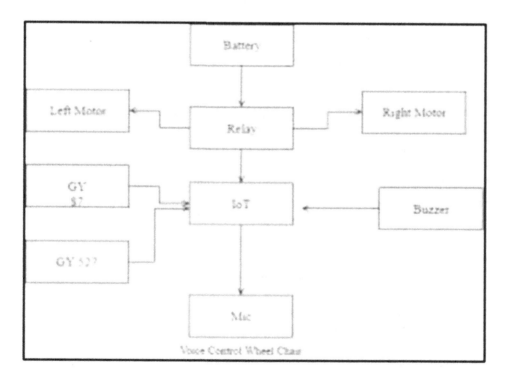

Comprehend Medical

Comprehend Medical is a natural language processing administration that makes it simple to utilize AI to separate applicable clinical data from unstructured content. Utilizing Comprehend Medical, one can rapidly and precisely assemble data, for example, ailment, prescription, dose, quality, and recurrence from an assortment of sources like specialists' notes, clinical preliminary reports, and patient wellbeing records. Comprehend Medical can likewise connect the recognized data to clinical ontologies, for example, ICD-10-CM or RxNorm so it very well may be utilized effectively by downstream social insurance applications.

One of the significant approaches to improve persistent mind and quicken clinical examination is by comprehension and breaking down the bits of knowledge and connections that are "caught" in freestyle clinical content, including emergency clinic confirmation notes and a patient's clinical history.

Comprehend Medical recognizes helpful data in unstructured clinical content. As much as 75% of all wellbeing record information is found in unstructured content, for example, doctor's notes, release synopses, test results, and case notes. Comprehend Medical uses Natural Language Processing (NLP) models to figure out content for important data.

The following accompanying models show how Comprehend Medical can be utilized in human services applications:

Instance 1: Patient care management and outcome

Specialists and medicinal services suppliers can oversee and effectively get to clinical data that doesn't effortlessly fit into customary structures. By examining case notes, suppliers can recognize possibility for early screening of ailments before the condition turns out to be progressively troublesome and costly to treat. It permits patients to report their wellbeing worries in a story that can give more data than basic configurations. The accounts are then effectively accessible to suppliers, permitting progressively precise analysis of ailments.

Instance 2: Clinical research

Life sciences and examination associations can:

- Optimize the coordinating procedure for enlisting patients into clinical preliminaries utilizing data from unstructured clinical writings, for example, case notes and test outcomes. For example, for a clinical preliminary of another heart medication, it empowers straightforward investigation of text for explicit data about cardiovascular breakdown patients.

- Improve pharma covigilance and post-advertise observation to screen antagonistic medication occasions by utilizing Comprehend Medical to recognize relevant data in clinical content.
- Assess helpful viability by effectively distinguishing imperative data in follow-up notes and other clinical writings. For example, it tends to be simpler and increasingly viable to screen how patients react to specific treatments by dissecting their accounts.

Overview therapeutic ampleness by adequately perceiving basic information in follow-up notes and other clinical compositions. For instance, it might be less complex and continuously suitable to screen how patients respond to explicit medicines by separating their accounts.

Instance 3: Medical billing and healthcare revenue cycle management

Payors can extend their investigation to incorporate unstructured archives, for example, clinical notes. More data about a determination can be investigated and used to help decide suitable charging codes from unstructured archives. Characteristic language preparing (NLP) is the most basic segment of PC helped coding (CAC). Comprehend Medical uses the most recent advances in NLP to break down clinical content, assisting with diminishing chance to income and improve repayment exactness.

Smart Monitoring System for Cancer Treatment

The IoE innovation can be applied in cancer care treatment by consistent and secure incorporation of remote innovations for clinical strategies, including chemotherapy medicines, checking, cautioning, and following-up (Miraz et al., 2015). Malignancy medicines can be upgraded by appending WSNs to patients with the end goal that the wellbeing specialists can be alarmed of any changes, difficulties, unfriendly medication impacts and hypersensitivities, missed meds, haemoglobin level detecting and observing, sedate unfavourably susceptible recognition, tranquilize connection checking, and so on. The remote sensors recognize mechanized alarms and squares for off base solutions, and furthermore naturally screen and deal with the creatinine esteem as utilized in the calculation of Glomerular Filtration Rate (GFR) utilized in dosing for certain chemotherapy treatment. It is likewise practicable to screen malignant growth patients distantly by guardians and families through WSNs. The malignant growth care administrations join clinical gadgets that give help to disease patients in case of any issues or entanglements through procedure or methodology robotization, distant checking, correspondence cautions, furthermore, investigation dependent on IoE advances. As identified with the radiation oncology treatment, the direct quickening agents for radiation treatment can likewise be observed by IoE associated gadgets. The Health Level-7 (HL7) availability is outfitted with HL7 interface dependent on semantics and XML innovation for information definition and message trading, sharing and reusing inside and between lab focuses, emergency clinics, and wellbeing locales, which interoperates at least two frameworks for data trade and use. The Digital Imaging and Communications in Medicine (DICOM) availability, then again, encourages association between the radiology focuses to help speed up conclusion and treatment, accordingly connecting systems together for demonstrative picture transmission. The disease care administrations through electronic clinical record and inserted frameworks, for example, Laboratory Interface System (LIS), Pathology Interface System (PIS) and Radiology Interface System (RIS), serve as passageways for the wellbeing suppliers to get to understanding data identifying with lab results, danger or strange (pathology) results, and radiology results. The RIS interfaces with the DICOM availability for the exchange or trade of analytic imaging results from radiology focuses while the LIS and PIS interface with the HL7 network for the exchange or trade of lab and pathology results from the lab administrations. Every one of these frameworks alongside the drug store, clinical oncology, and radiation oncology servers permit access to exhaustive patient diagram data from any gadget, either at the clinic(s) or by means of far off VPN access from outside the clinic(s).

SMART CONTINUOUS GLUCOSE MONITORING (CGM) AND INSULIN PENS

Continuous Glucose Monitoring

Continuous Glucose Monitoring naturally tracks blood glucose levels, additionally called glucose, for the duration of the day and night. Any person can view their glucose level whenever required. Likewise patient can survey their own glucose level changes over a couple of hours or days to see patterns. Seeing glucose levels progressively can assist with settling on increasingly educated choices for the duration of the day about how to adjust the diet physical movement, and medications.

How CGM Works?

A CGM works through a small sensor embedded under the skin, normally on the stomach or arm. The sensor gauges the interstitial glucose level, which is the glucose found in the liquid between the cells. The sensor tests glucose like clockwork. A transmitter remotely sends the data to a screen. The screen might be a piece of an insulin siphon or a different gadget, which may convey in a pocket or satchel. Some CGMs send data legitimately to a cell phone or tablet.

Special features of CGM

- A caution can sound when your glucose level goes excessively low or excessively high.
- Patient can take note of their dinners, physical action, and meds in a CGM gadget, as well, close by their glucose levels.
- Patient can download information to a PC or smart gadget to all the more effectively observe your glucose patterns.

A few models can send data immediately to a second individual's cell phone—maybe a parent, accomplice, or guardian. For instance, if a kid's glucose drops hazardously low for the time being, the CGM could be set to wake a parent in the following room.

Benefits of CGM

Contrasted and a standard blood glucose meter, utilizing a CGM framework can support

- Better deal with glucose levels each day
- Have less low blood glucose crises
- Need less finger sticks

A realistic on the CGM screen shows whether the glucose is rising or dropping - and how rapidly-so a patient can pick the most ideal approach to arrive at objective glucose level.

After some time, great administration of glucose incredibly helps individuals with diabetes remain sound and forestall confusions of the infection. Individuals who gain the biggest profit by a CGM are the individuals who use it consistently or almost consistently.

HoloLens Headset

HoloLens headset that changes over the information from the catheters nurtured into the patient's heart into a geometrical holographic picture that drifts over the patient. The headset, which weighs about a pound, permits the doctor to assume responsibility for the strategy by utilizing their appearance to direct the controls and to keep hands free and sterile. This framework, Enhanced Electrophysiology

Visualization and Interaction System (ĒLVIS), gives a 3D computerized picture of the patient's electro anatomic maps that give an image of within the heart, which they can gauge and control during the strategy. The headset permits the client to see their entire condition, including the patient, in contrast to augmented reality, which remove a client totally from their condition.

Automated Medical Dispenser

Automated Medical Dispenser (AMD) consists of the following three components:

1. Medication Dispenser – A container that can apportion meds to the patients, in light of the medicines proposed by the specialist made sure about by individual standardized tags. These allocators are to be possessed by the drug stores and to be loaded up with meds on the hour of necessity (like ATM machines). Clients of Online Health Communities are the objective clients of these machines who can get suitable proposals from the specialists related with a similar gathering (Suganya & Mariappan, 2019).
2. Datastore – cloud based datastore is required to store the particulars of OHC clients alongside their history of prescription and the grouping of drugs they had and so forth., Firebase is utilized for model demonstrating that can be supplanted with fitting cloud infra.
3. User Interface – an android application that can be utilized by specialists to make solutions for patients enlisted in OHC details.

Working Flow of Medical Dispenser

- Clients of OHC should enroll themselves in the entryway and will be related to a remarkable ID for recognizable proof. Email id is utilized as a methods for distinguishing proof as it is novel.
- Clients can pick their primary care physicians for conversation and counsel through the entryway dependent on the arrangement of discussions and different boundaries like rating and remarks by other network clients.
- Clients can post their issues, which will be labelled with inquiry ID to explicit specialists through the private talk gave in the application.
- The specialists would then be able to see the patient's history, in the event that they are enlisted with the specialist and can recommend suitable meds to the patients.
- A standardized tag will be created combined with special ID of patient and will be sent to patient's login.

- The patient has the adaptability to see solutions all things considered and can pick as per his/her inclination.
- The patient can visit the programmed medication distributor close by and can filter the standardized identification.
- In light of the legitimacy of standardized identification and left-out remedies, the container will apportion the drugs that can be gathered through the vent gave in the gadget.
- The allocator will run consecutively for the same number of quantities of drugs as expressed in the remedy.
- The conveyance status of medicine will at that point be set to be "conveyed" and henceforth the patient can't reuse the medicine to take out the drugs without specialist's conference.
- On the off chance that the patient is conveyed with the meds, all the remedies comparing to the question ID will be bolted to guarantee different conveyances of meds.
- All the information are put away utilizing cloud as a stage to help SaaS (Storage as a Service).

Connected Hospital and Patient Monitoring Facility

The main purpose of this area talks about the framework and the advantages of the IoE equipped an emergency clinic for the condition and the subsequent sub-point covers understanding consideration the board and advantages to the patient (Anitha Kunari et al., 2016).

- **Infrastructure:** While developing the IoE enabled medical clinic, sensors are put in different spots for the executives. Every sensor has a battery and a remote transmitting gadget to caution the support engineer. A model structure of IoE enabled medical clinic is shown in Figure 4.
- **Environment supervision:** Sensors fixed in the structure during development, give information identified with the air quality, temperature, dampness, light level, tremor recognition, and so on., that are additionally handled to change over the information into significant data
- **Water supervision:** The sensors help in improving the effectiveness of the water appropriation system of the emergency clinic. They help in decreasing the wastage of water because of spillage through early expectation.
- **Garbage supervision:** Smart trash observing framework is utilized in each room. The sensor on the head of the dustbin cautions the trash gathering colleague or the nursing station partner when it turns out to be full and the right hand gathers the trash. This diminishes the human endeavours of

checking the dustbin over and over. The tidiness and cleanliness are kept up utilizing this shrewd trash observing framework (Kakkar & Shaurya, 2019).

- **Intelligent wheelchairs and cots:** When a harmed individual shows up at the emergency clinic, a cot prepared with body sensors are utilized to think about the individual's condition en route to his treatment. This spares the time of the specialist from testing his condition first and afterward doing the treatment. Savvy wheelchairs are likewise utilized tomonitor the patient's development inside the premises

- **Telemedicine rescue vehicle:** If the state of the individual is not good enough to be treated in this emergency clinic, he is then sentto an emergency clinic furnished with cutting edge clinical offices through telemedicine rescue vehicle. This emergency vehicle is outfitted with clinical gear that helps in the fundamental treatment of the patient while in transit to the hospital. The individual offering support inside the rescue vehicle is consistently associated with the authorities in the emergency clinic

- **RFID innovation:** RFID perusers are introduced at different places, for example, the passage of the patient room, the room where medications are kept, and so on for wellbeing purposes. Specialists, medical caretakers and other staff individuals are given with RFID labels that are perused while going into a room and the information is sent to the individual database. This aides in keeping up a sheltered and secure spot for the patient

- **WBLC:** Wireless Body lighting control is utilized to control the light serious in the space for the patient's accommodation and force sparing. After a fixed time, the lights go diminish and after some time they are turned off in the medical clinic with the goal that patient can rest calmly

- **Patient care management:** All the advances utilized are associated over the web. The information gathered through the sensors and different advancements are sent to the doctors just as the clinical colleagues, who screen the patient and nature. The doctor, in the wake of examining the data got, sends criticism. Doctors utilize the android application on their cell phone to screen the patient. In the event that any unusual change in the wellbeing of the patient is seen, the doctor is cautioned furthermore, he visits the patient for a registration. All the information is transferred and put away on the distributed storage from where the senior specialists can screen the patients.

- Swasthya record: Swasthya implies wellbeing, sufficiency, and prosperity. The essential tests are done through Swasthya record. It gives moment results and exhortation, which helps in better and quick treatment

- RFID innovation and EMR: Integration of RFID innovation and EMR is utilized to keep the information of a patient at one spot. The convenient accessibility of the patient's record helps in improving the nature of wellbeing conveyance

- Information framework: Information framework is utilized to record information identified with the patient's confirmation, enlistment, installments, quiet consideration the board and dealing with the reports.

Figure 4.

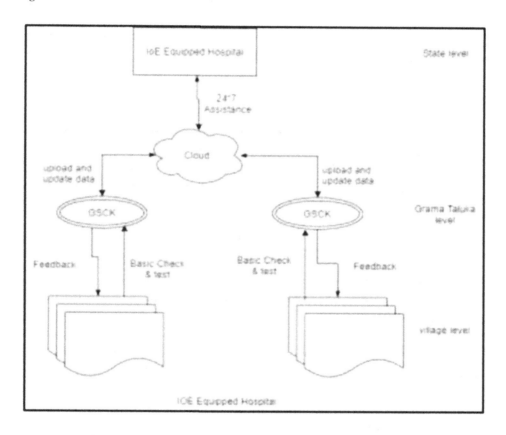

Ingestible Sensors

Ingestible electronic systems have capability of embedded sensing. This is particularly used within the Gastrointestinal (GI) tract and its accessory organs. They have the potential to screen diseases that are difficult, and are impossible to detect at an early stage using other methodologies. On the other hand, these devices have potential to reduce human resource and facility costs for a lot of procedures.

From the digestive system, these ingestibles could sense and then transmit mechanical movements of the gastro-intestinal tract, electrical stimuli which govern the muscle contractions and chemical processes, involving hormones and enzymes, that breaks down the food. These data could then be transmitted to a wearable device, smartphones and healthcare systems. This requires fundamental innovations like,

❖ Miniature electro-chemical sensors
❖ Ultra-low-power miniature interfaces and signal processing electronics, that can coexist with sensors
❖ Volume-constrained wireless power and data communication technologies
❖ Biocompatible thin and safe packaging

Figure 5.

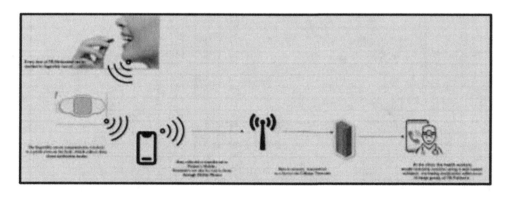

According to a study by the World Health Organisation (WHO) in 2003, 50% of medicines are not taken as directed by the physician. Proteus' system company has created pills which dissolve in the stomach and then send a signal to a sensor worn by the patient. This data is then relayed to a smartphone app, which confirms that the patient has taken their medication as directed.

Proteus has tested the system with pills for treating uncontrolled hypertension, Type 2 Diabetes and antipsychotic medication. In 2017, ABILIFY MYCITE – an antipsychotic medication created by Proteus and Otsuka Pharmaceutical Co. became the first Food and Drug Administration, FDA-approved drug with a digital tracking system. This is allowing the patients to have more informed dialogue with the physician about their treatments. The figure 5 illustrates a scenario of ingestible sensor.

Researchers from Australia have conducted trials using ingestible smart pills for identifying and learning of the gasses in the stomach. They were also able to explore the impact fibre diets have digestion. Tuberculosis (TB) treatment adherence using ingestible sensors administered with TB medications is also an important research factor. A recent cost-analysis that modeled Wirelessly Observed Therapy (WOT) would cost less for TB control programs than the present Directly Observed Therapy (DOT). In the future this system shall allow more efficient use of resources, especially personnel, and facilitate the expansion of monitored TB treatment (DOT) into more distant and difficult to reach remote populations across the globe. The success of DOT programs depends upon prompt identification and intervening when poor adherence to medication is identified with the patients.

WATCH APP THAT MONITORS DEPRESSION

Data says, depression affects about 3 million US teens and these rates have climbed in the past decade. As per U.S. government data 13% of 12 to 17 year olds had depression in 2017, which is up from 8 percent in 2010. This means one in 10 college-aged Americans is affected.

Takeda Pharmaceuticals United States of America (U.S.A.) and Cognition Kit Limited, a platform for measuring cognitive health, collaborated in 2017 to explore the use of an Apple Watch app for monitoring and assessing patients with Major Depressive Disorder (MDD). The results from this exploratory study were p resented in November 2017 at the pharma and biotech conference central nervous system (CNS) Summit.

The study has found that the data from the app has a very high level of matching with participants' mood and cognition. The app's daily assessments were also found to correspond with more in-depth and objective cognition tests. Further, the patients reported outcomes, showing that cognitive tests delivered via an app are robust and reliable. While the study was only an exploratory pilot, it has demonstrated the potential for wearable technologies and can be used to assess the effects of depression in real-time. Like other smart medical devices that gather data, the Apple Watch app could also give patients and healthcare professionals more insight on their condition, which enables more informed conversations about health.

There are many IoE applications in mental health focused on alleviating depression and anxiety. One such concept idea is a wristband that can monitor for the symptoms of a panic attack. When an imminent attack is detected, the 'Breathe Watch' alerts the wearer and/or their carriers, and can also provide calming techniques such as breathing exercises and verbal walk-throughs to provide early relief. Similarly, Alexa and Google Assistant can help people to detect potential mental health difficulties and provide assistance. They can do basic diagnosis by asking users how well they are sleeping, eating, working and so forth. Based on the answers, the device shall recommend specific advice to improve sleeping patterns, for example tell someone to visit their physician. Of course, none of these IoE applications are designed to fully replace doctors and psychologists. The aim of it has to make services more accessible and provide hands when other solutions aren't forthcoming.

An app co-developed by Takeda and Cambridge, UK-based Cognition Kit has impressed a pilot observational study that monitors depression. The Apple Watch app, currently dubbed Major Depressive Disorder (MDD-5003), that seeks to improve patient monitoring and patient recorded assessments for people diagnosed with MDD. According to the previous research, many of the symptoms of MDD are unrecognised by doctors while the condition has affected around 350 million people worldwide and is the leading cause of disability across the globe. To achieve better patient monitoring, app users have to complete cognitive tests that are aimed at measuring attention, memory and reaction speed throughout the day. When this is combined with other Apple Watch data gleaned from its various sensors it is intended to present a complete view of the user's mental health. The study initiated earlier in 2017, tested the app in regards to its feasibility, compliance and functionality in a cohort of 30 people with mild to moderate depression who has already been prescribed an antidepressant for MDD.

It is believed that measures of mood and cognition were compared with traditional neuropsychological testing and patients reported outcomes regarding symptoms at six weeks. The app has achieved great results: 95% of users were compliant and used the device daily to evaluate mood, and 96% used it to measure cognition. The app's daily tests corresponded with objective cognitive tests (Cambridge Neuropsychological Test Automated Battery) and patient-reported outcomes Patient Health Questionnaire (PHQ-9) and Perceived Deficits Questionnaire - Depression (PDQ-D) measures. So far no adverse events were reported.

COAGULATION TESTING

Blood clot level plays a crucial role in the human body, as this is used in treatment of multiple diseases such as stroke, diabetes and others. IoE enabled healthcare devices have the ability of real time monitoring of blood coagulation; this helps to keep the patient's activity under the therapeutic range with increased reduction of risk factor. Key advantage of these devices is that it helps the patient and physician to quickly monitor blood clots. It also lowers the risk of bleeding problems for diabetic patients. This IoE enabled application has a facility to remind patients to test their clot level, thereby reduction in risk factors. These coagulation testing market trends are anticipated to create lucrative opportunities for the growth of the global coagulation testing industry. The Fig 6 provides the attractive market share for coagulation testing.

Figure 6.

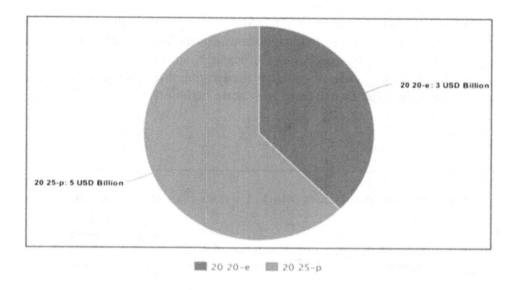

In healthcare, IoE is known for coagulation testing, that helps people treat cancer and diabetes, etc.In 2016, Roche launched a Bluetooth-enabled coagulation system that allows patients to check how quickly the blood can clot. This is known to be the first device of its kind for anticoagulated patients. This enables self-testing to help patients stay within their therapeutic range and lower the risk of stroke or bleeding. As this can transmit results to healthcare providers which means fewer visits to the clinic. The device also allows patients to add comments to their results, send reminders for tests, and flags the results in relation to the target range.

It is projected that the global coagulation analyzers market can reach USD 5.0 billion by 2025 from its current valuation of USD 3.8 billion in 2020; fig.7 illustrates that further this has a Compound Annual Growth Rate (CAGR) of 5.7% between 2020 and 2025. Emerging economies such as India, China, and Brazil are expected to provide a wide range of opportunities for players in this industry. Furthermore, the increasing prevalence of cardiovascular diseases, blood disorders and the rising geriatric population expects these technologies to solve the next generation health care sector.

The prothrombin time testing segment accounted for the largest share of the coagulation analyzers market in the year 2019. Growth in this market segment can be attributed to the high usage of prothrombin time tests that measure the time it takes for blood to clot. These tests can be used to monitor patients implanted with mechanical heart valves, ventricular assist devices, chronic atrial fibrillation, venous embolism and thrombosis of deep vessels of lower extremities, deep venous thrombosis, and pulmonary embolism.

Clinical laboratories segment dominated the coagulation analyzers market in 2019. On the basis of end users, the coagulation analyzers market can be segmented into 3 segments such as clinical laboratories, hospitals, and other end users. This can be attributed to the large volume of coagulation testing that is being performed at these facilities. Asia Pacific market to grow at the highest rate from 2020 to 2025.

Figure 7.

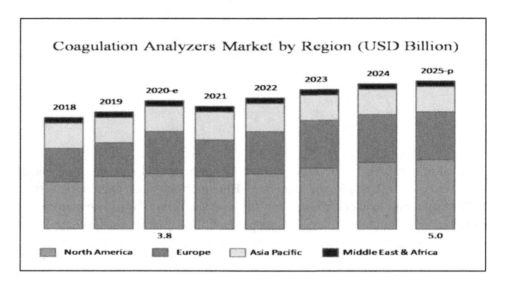

The coagulation analyzers market in the Asia Pacific expected to grow at a high CAGR in the coming years. The major players operating in the coagulation analyzers market are Abbott Laboratories (US), Danaher (US), Siemens Healthineers Group (Germany), Sysmex Group (US), Thermo Fisher Scientific (US), Horiba (Japan), Nihon Kohden (Japan), Roche Diagnostics (Switzerland), Maccura Biotechnology Co. Ltd. (China), Bio Group Medical System (Italy), Genrui Biotech Inc. (China), A&T Corporation (Japan), Beijing Succeeder Technology Inc. (China), Diagnostica Stago SAS (France), Helena Laboratories (US), Hycel (Austria), Eurolyser (Austria), Bpc Biosed Srl (Italy), Robimes India Pvt. Ltd (India), Meril Life Sciences (India), ERBA Diagnostics, Inc. (US), Sclavo Diagnostics International S.r.l (Italy), Haematonics (US), Biosystems S.A. (Spain), and ACON (US).

Pre and Post COVID-19 impact on Coagulation Testing Market and its Key Highlights

Coagulation test is carried out with the coagulometer that detects blood clotting time and blood's ability to clot. As per the study of Research Dive, coagulation testing market forecast a revenue of $3,566.0 million in the year 2026 growing a healthy CAGR of 5.9%. The growing prevalence of various blood clotting disorders, such as deep vein thrombosis (DVT), and hemophilia along with the rise in the aging population across the globe are the significant factors for the coagulation testing.

Coagulation Testing Market Segmentation by Product Type is as follow

❖ Instruments
❖ Consumables

Coagulation Testing Market Segmentation by Application is as follow

❖ Prothrombin Time
❖ Activated Partial Thromboplastin Time
❖ Thrombin Time
❖ Activated Clotting Time

On the other hand, factors such as lack of expertise in this field and higher costs of coagulation test devices are expected to slow down the growth of the coagulation testing industry.

Coagulation Testing Market Segmentation by End-Use

❖ Hospitals
❖ Clinical Laboratories
❖ Point-of-Care Testing
❖ Others

Remarkable advances and vast research and development (R&D) efforts from manufacturers result in improvisation of reliable analyzers. Demand for high precision and advanced coagulation analyzers are expected to drive the growth of the global market. Furthermore, these analyzers are fully automated, and also can perform immunologic and chromogenic assays.

Key Companies Profiled under this development includes

• Thermo Fisher Scientific Inc. (NYSE: TMO)
• Medtronic (NYSE: MDT)

- Abbott. (NYSE: ABT)
- Danaher (NYSE: DHR)
- Helena Laboratories Corporation.
- Micropoint Biosciences
- F. Hoffmann-La Roche Ltd
- NIHON KOHDEN CORPORATION.
- Sysmex Corporation ● BD.

Market players are focusing more on the innovations in the coagulation tests and devices, for example, Japan based company, Sysmex launched new Products called Automated Blood Coagulation Analyzers CN-3000 and CN-6000. This device offers enhanced levels of reliability and productivity, in turn responding to various customer needs and advanced quality in the field of hemostasis, a process to prevent and stop bleeding; these advances in technology are projected to augment the growth of Asian market. The Europe region is focusing more on recent innovation and excellent strategies are anticipated to drive the European Market growth. Since the past 25 years, the number of Cardiovascular disease (CVD) cases has increased in Europe. This is mainly due to rise in fat consumption. In addition, levels of obesity are high across Europe in both adults and children. These health issues are projected to augment the growth of the market of Europe region.

ADAMM Asthma Monitor

The World Health Organisation (WHO) predicts that the asthma illness will become the third leading cause of death worldwide by 2030 due to the rise of air pollution, and the persistent habit of smoking. A ccording to WHO estimates, 235 million people suffer from asthma, the chronic disease characterized by recurrent attacks of breathlessness and wheezing. About 300,000 new patients are diagnosed with asthma annually, and nearly 250,000 people die prematurely each year due to the condition. Asthma is living with a condition that restricts breathing which is like living with a condition that threatens the very essence of our lives.

A team of educated professionals at Health Care Originals (HCO) has a mission to make living with asthma better. In fact, they've recently released a powerful tool for managing it. Adhesive Dermally Applied Microarray (ADAMM) is a wearable smart asthma monitor. It purports to detect the symptoms of an asthma attack before its onset, thereby allowing the wearer to manage it before the attack gets worse. It vibrates to notify the person wearing it of an impending asthma attack; it can also send a text message to a designated carer in such situations. Other features of the device include inhaler detection; i.e., the device can detect and track inhaler use. if

230

the patient can't remember whether they've used one and voice journaling to record things like changes, feelings and behaviours.

The first device got FDA clearance in September 2019. These devices can take a long time to come to market even once developed. It even works with children. It also has an algorithm technology that makes it personalized to the wearer. It learns and adapts to the wearer over time, allowing it to better understand when something has changed, the so called outliers. ADAMM can work in conjunction with an app and web portal. It helps asthma patients to set medication reminders, view data from the device anywhere anytime; they have capability to remind / advise their treatment plans. ADAMM will track coughing counts, respiration, wheezing and heart rate. Users can put it on the charger while they sleep; and the beauty is it can still monitor coughing while it's under charge. The device can provide notifications, detects inhalers, and allows voice journaling. The best part is it does not necessarily require a smart device to connect, which makes perfect for children.

ADAMM shall establish a baseline by monitoring the patients activity. Once it has your normative symptoms, it will notify you when they deviate from the baseline. There is a voice journaling feature, where users can log verbal entries of data. Along with other data, these voice journals roll up into long-term records. Over time, the user can see how they are progressing against that baseline. This acts as a measure of improvement in the condition of asthma patients.

The data collected and stored by ADAMM is Health Insurance Portability and Accountability Act (HIPAA) compliant data. The user or the doctors can access this information over smart devices or on the world wide web (WWW).

USE CASES

IoT Greengrass

Amazon Web Services (AWS) IoE Greengrass lets devices process the data they generate locally, while still taking advantage of AWS services when an internet connection is available. Many devices mentioned above ingest huge amounts of data. Processing them and getting insights out of them is a real challenge. AWS Greengrass, can play a key role in gathering and pre-processing those data from IoE devices. Furthermore, due to the widely known availability factor or AWS across the globe, it can be easily integrated.

AWS IoT SiteWise

With the help of AWS IoT SiteWise, we can easily gather data reliably from multiple facilities, structure them, and make them accessible and understandable without any additional software development. We can easily index information and metrics about equipment or processes across multiple facilities, so it's readily available for applications. This means any analytics on data over the information gathered from the smart devices can be pre-processed and visually represented over WWW. So, Researchers can invest development resources on new applications that help them learn more from the data.

Visibility across industrial facilities allows the sector to streamline operations, as well as identify gaps in production and waste. With IoT SiteWise, Users can create models of industrial processes and equipment across multiple facilities, and then automatically discover and visualize live and historical asset data through customizable charts and dashboards. Through AWS SiteWise Monitor, we have the ability to launch a web application with asset data in minutes and give hospitals the visibility to react to issues or identify differences across facilities.

CONCLUSION

Smart gadgets are in use all over the world anywhere and everywhere. The IoE period has emerged into the world. This new period of IoT and IoE is generally new. In the occasion that recollect only 20 years earlier, most of Internet-associated gadgets were work area PCs and other stationary equipment. At that point, huge cell phones began to be presented. From here, a wide range of regular "things" became, and are turning out to be, Internet-associated. These contraptions are agreeably both aided by practicality data and help create AI with a lot of data that customers are making. These IoT devices, for instance, vehicles, wearables, devices, and anything is possible from that point, wound up embedded with sensors, control systems, and processors in order to enable level correspondence all through an open, multinode orchestrate. Today, IoE is viewed as a superset of IoT. Internet of Everything, acknowledges that this method brings people, data, and things together to make sorted out affiliations progressively relevant and significant. With this, the goal is to have "new limits, increasingly luxurious experiences, and remarkable budgetary open entryway for associations, individuals, and countries.

REFERENCES

Anitha Kunari, Sudha, Sadasivam, & Akash. (2016). A secure android application with integration of wearables for healthcare monitoring system using 3D ECCDH PAKE protocol. *Journal of Medical Imaging and Heath Informatics, 6*(6), 1548-1551.

Aruna, S., & Venkataswamy, R. (2018). Academic Workbench for Streetlight Powered by Solar PV System Using Internet of Everything (IoE). *International Conference on Communication, Computing and Internet of Things (IC3IoT)*, 186-190. 10.1109/IC3IoT.2018.8668152

Chauhan & Jain. (2019). A Journey from IoT to IoE. *International Journal of Innovative Technology and Exploring Engineering, 8*(11).

Dai, C., & Song, Q. (2019, March). Heuristic computing methods for contact plan design in the spatial-node-based Internet of Everything. *China Communications, 16*(3), 53–68.

Demir, A. K., & Bilgili, S. (2019). Fine Tuning Distributed Divergecast Scheduling Algorithms in IEEE 802.1S.4e TSCH for Internet of Everything. *2019 International Symposium on Networks, Computers and Communications (ISNCC)*, 1-6. 10.1109/ISNCC.2019.8909093

Evans, D. (2012). *The Internet of Everything How More Relevant and Valuable Connections Will Change the World. Cisco Internet Business Solutions Group.* IBSG.

Evans, D. (2013). *The Internet of Everything Global Public Sector Economic Analysis. Cisco Internet Business Solutions Group.* IBSG.

Fiaidhi, J., & Mohammed, S. (2019, January-February). Internet of Everything as a Platform for Extreme Automation. *IT Professional, 21*(1), 21–25. doi:10.1109/MITP.2018.2876534

Kakkar & Shaurya. (2019). An IoT Equipped Hospital Model: A New Approach for E-governance Healthcare Framework. *International Journal of Medical Research & Health Sciences.*

Lu, H., Su, S., Tian, Z., & Zhu, C. (2019, March). A novel search engine for Internet of Everything based on dynamic prediction. *China Communications, 16*(3), 42–52.

Masoud, Jaradat, Manasrah, & Jannoud. (2019). *Sensors of Smart Devices in Internet of Everything (IoE) Era: Big Opportunities and Massive Doubts.* Research Gate.

Miraz, M. H., Ali, M., Excell, P. S., & Picking, R. (2015). *A review on Internet of Things (IoT), Internet of Everything (IoE) and Internet of Nano Things (IoNT). In 2015 Internet Technologies and Applications.* ITA. doi:10.1109/ITechA.2015.7317398

Raj, A., & Prakash, S. (2018). Internet of Everything: A survey based on Architecture, Issues and Challenges. *5th IEEE Uttar Pradesh Section International Conference on Electrical, Electronics and Computer Engineering (UPCON),* 1-6. 10.1109/UPCON.2018.8596923

Sangeetha, Vigneshwari, Dhinakaran, Prabu, & Karpagam. (2019). Voice Controlled Autonomous Wheelchair Using IoT. *International Journal of Research in Engineering, Science and Management, 2*(10).

Sergey, Nikolay, & Sergey. (2017). Cyber security concept for Internet of Everything (IoE). *Systems of Signal Synchronization, Generating and Processing in Telecommunications (SINKHROINFO),* 1-4. . doi:10.1109/SINKHROINFO.2017.7997540

Suganya & Mariappan. (2019). *IoT based Automated Medicine Dispenser for Online Health Community using Cloud.* Research Gate.

Taştan, M. (2018). IoT Based Wearable Smart Health Monitoring System. *IoT Based Wearable Smart Health Monitoring System,* (September), 343–350. Advance online publication. doi:10.18466/cbayarfbe.451076

Zielinski. (2015). *Internet of Everything (IoE) in Smart Grid.* Research Gate.

Chapter 12
Constructive Solutions for Security and Privacy Issues at the Edge:
Securing Edge Framework – A Healthcare Application Use Case

Indra Priyadharshini S.
R. M. K. College of Engineering and Technology, India

Pradheeba Ulaganathan
R. M. K. College of Engineering and Technology, India

Vigilson Prem M.
R. M. D. Engineering College, India

Yuvaraj B. R.
Anna University, India

EXECUTIVE SUMMARY

The evolution in computing strategies has shown wonders in reducing the reachability issue among different end devices. After centralized approaches, decentralized approaches started to take action, but with the latency in data pre-processing, computing very simple requests was the same as for the larger computations. Now it's time to have a simple decentralized environment called edge that is created very near to the end device. This makes edge location friendly and time friendly to different kinds of devices like smart, sensor, grid, etc. In this chapter, some of the serious and non-discussed security issues and privacy issues available on edge are explained neatly, and for a few of the problems, some solutions are also recommended. At last, a separate case study of edge computing challenges in healthcare is also explored, and solutions to those issues concerning that domain are shown.

DOI: 10.4018/978-1-7998-4873-8.ch012

INTRODUCTION

Edge is only the augmentation of the fog. Edge computing has the accompanying attributes: it ranges to contiguous physical areas; upholds online examination; the administration is given by savvy, yet not ground-breaking gadgets; underpins different interchanges arranges, and is circulated computing The objectives of the edge computing worldview are to diminish the information volume and traffic to fog workers, decline inertness, and improve nature of administration (QoS). Edge computing comprises 3 fundamental parts, (an) IoT nodes, (b) edge nodes, and (c) back-end fog. The principle parts of layer 1 are the IoT gadgets and correspondence joins between them. These gadgets are answerable for detecting and acting in the earth by producing occasions and sending them to higher layers. Layer 2 involves the switches, switches, entryways, and gadgets that encourage the associations between gadgets at the edge of the system and the Internet. This layer mirrors the great definition proposed for Edge computing. At present, the Edge infrastructure idea may likewise remember the gadgets for layer 3. Layer 3 contains the infrastructure for customary Fog computing (elite workers, and server farms with immense capacity and processing limits) (Ren et al., 2019)

Another captivating zone where the modernization has pushed its foundations is IoT. IoT is getting expanding coordinated into our everyday lives. Contemplating this IoT can be utilized to give a skilled and sorted out way to deal with and improve the healthcare of humankind. By utilizing these smart articles, they can be coordinated into healthcare to offer wise types of assistance for far off observing the wellbeing and prosperity of patients. By utilizing this it could help manage staff deficiencies and reaction times inside healthcare. As IoT has the attribute of pervasiveness the frameworks associated with healthcare (medication, apparatuses, and people) can permit the ceaseless observing and the board of these substances. Along these lines, the expense and nature of the healthcare offered can be improved via robotizing processes that were recently directed by people. How IoT and Edge go connected at the hip?

Edge computing gives calculation, stockpiling, and systems administration administrations between end gadgets (Things) and customary fog computing server farms. Edge computing stage is ordinarily situated at the edge of the system; here and there the expression "edge" is utilized reciprocally with the expression "edge". It gives low inertness, area mindfulness and improves Quality of Service (QoS) and Quality of Experience (QoE) for healthcare administrations by diminishing idleness and expanding its consistency when contrasted with the fog. Despite edge computing being a promising new turn of events, to serve IoT Things and applications effectively, there are various explorations provokes that should be thought of. Inside edge computing which can comprise of different gadgets in the system (switches, switches, and so on.) and end gadgets or potentially things (smartphones, wearable gadgets, and virtual sensor nodes that could be utilized inside healthcare frameworks)? Consequently having the option to gather, configuration, and process this heterogeneous information just as the capacity of correspondence among various gadgets is as yet an open examination challenge.

Considering that edge devices work at the edge of networks, edge faces new security also, security challenges on the head of those inherited from fog computing. Assault vectors, for example, man-in-the-middle have the potential to become an ordinary assault in Edge computing. Edge computing is a promising answer for help data fusion, filtering, and investigation in e-healthcare systems since it extends data computing from fog to the edge of a network and is more intelligent and powerful than e-healthcare devices. Without appropriate security and protection protections for underlying connected health systems, providers and patients need trust in the arrangements. News about the absence of security of IoT devices and unethical practices of some companies that gather and abuse personal data from owners of connected devices have made consumers care about the technology and more proactive in protecting personal data. Even when the IoT health care system itself isn't compromised, the care receivers can be the casualties of overzealous enterprises that have questionable use of patient data with potential legal ramifications, as medical data in numerous countries is protected by law.

In the customary edge-assisted data sharing scheme the edge node is integrated to process and re-encrypt the shared data for efficient medical examination. Privacy leakage and security threats may happen during data partaking in edge-assisted e-healthcare systems. Initially, personal privacy may be disclosed during data sharing. Unauthorized users may access the shared data collected from patients. For example, some corrupt pharmaceutical companies may analyze the health data and get patients' health status to spread advertisements and medication advancements. The shared health data might be tampered with during data transmission from data collection to storage. For instance, the blood glucose of patients might be altered when it is delivered to healthcare centers, leading to incorrect healthcare treatments. To protect the shared data against privacy leakage, unauthorized data access, and data tampering, Ciphertext-Policy Attribute-Based Encryption (CP-ABE)(Tang et al., 2019) is widely proposed for health data sharing through the fog, because it can uphold multiple data accessing standards with data confidentiality preservation. Patients define access policies to encrypt their shared data and send the ciphertext to the fog server. Data users access the shared data and decrypt the ciphertext just if their attributes fulfill access policies. But the same level of protection can't be given to the edge side, as they are different devices in nature. Some of the popular research articles give solutions to general issues like data accumulation, latency, preliminary security for transferring data, etc., However, the accompanying issues despite everything remain unaddressed. (1) How would we pre-process health data on the edge node for efficient data use? (2) How would patients be able to retrieve and decrypt their health data after the edge node encrypts them? (3) How would we be able to guarantee patient privacy when the shared data are re-encrypted? by the semi-trusted edge node? (4) How would we prevent unauthorized data access if the edge node collides with other entities for the shared plaintext?

With these brief introductions, this chapter is organized as follows: the immediate next topic briefs the reason for the evolution of edge computing from fog (along with issues in fog), then a general architecture of edge with obligatory working details, attacks &threats, Cryptographic techniques, authentication and access control policies and a case study of edge based healthcare framework with specific security issues, solutions and recommendations is explained.

NECESSITY OF EDGE COMPUTING – FROM THE PERSPECTIVE OF SECURITY AND PRIVACY

Before getting into the necessity of Edge, one ought to get into the real difference between fog and Edge. Some of the key features which make both of these computing ends differently are, Fog architecture is centralized and comprises large data centers that can be located the world over, a thousand miles from client devices. Edge architecture is distributed and comprises a large number of little nodes located as close to client devices as could be expected under the circumstances. Edge goes about as a mediator between data centers and hardware(Ren et al., 2017), and hence it is closer to end-users. On the off chance that there is no edge layer, the fog communicates with devices directly, which is time-expending. In fog computing, data processing takes place in remote data centers. Edge processing and storage are done on the edge of the network close to the source of data, which is critical for real-time control. Fog is more powerful than an edge regarding computing capabilities and storage limits. The fog comprises a few large server nodes. Edge includes a huge number of little nodes. Edge performs momentary edge examination due to moment responsiveness, while the fog focuses on long haul deep investigation due to slower responsiveness. Edge provides low latency; fog — high latency.

A fog system collapses without an Internet connection. Edge computing uses different conventions and standards, so the danger of failure is a lot of lower. Edge is a more secure system than the fog due to its distributed architecture(Dimitrievski et al., 2019). Like Fog systems, an Edge system is composed of IaaS, PaaS, and SaaS respectively, alongside the expansion of Data services. The Edge IaaS stage is created utilizing Cisco IOx API, which includes a Linux and CISCO IOS networking operating system. Any device, for example, switches, routers, servers, and even cameras can become an Edge node that has computing, storage, and network connectivity. Edge nodes collaborate among themselves with either a Peer-to-Peer network, Master-Slave architecture, or by framing a Cluster. The Cisco IOx APIs enable Edge applications(Wang et al., 2014) to communicate with IoT devices and Fog systems by any user-defined convention. It provides simplified management of utilizations, automates policy enforcement, and supports multiple development environments and programming languages. The data service decides the suitable place (Fog or Edge) for data examination identifies which data. Numerous researchers are embracing a security-centric or secure by design reasoning for creating such distributed systems. Yet, this viewpoint is still in its outset and needs a comprehensive understanding of the security threats and challenges confronting an Edge infrastructure. This chapter provides a systematic review of Edge stage applications, determines their possible security holes, analyses existing security arrangements, and then advances a rundown of comprehensive security arrangements that can eliminate numerous potential security flaws of Edge-based systems.

Fog Security Alliance(Waters & Encryption, 2011) has identified five basic security issues and these issues directly sway the distributed, shared, and on-demand nature of fog computing. Being a virtualized environment like Fog, the Edge stage can likewise be affected by the same threats however there are very solid security mechanisms that could easily get integrated with edge architecture.

1. Authentication and Trust issues
2. Privacy
3. Security
4. Fog Servers
5. Energy consumption

Details about the above sorts of threats are explained in (Curtis, 2020). However, the betterment over the fog stage can be discussed as follows. The accompanying rundown details three such technologies, including some of their key differences with Edge systems. Edge Computing performs localized processing on the device utilizing Programmable Automation Controllers (PAC), which can handle data processing, storage, and correspondence. It poses an advantage over Edge computing as it reduces the purposes of failure and makes each device more independent. However, the same feature makes it hard to manage and accumulate data on large scale networks. Foglet is a middle piece of the 3-tier hierarchy "mobile device - foglet - fog". There are four significant attributes of Foglet: entirely self-overseeing possesses enough compute power, low end-to-end latency, and expands on standard Fog technology. Foglet differs from fog computing as application virtualization isn't suitable for the environment, consumes more resources, and can't work in offline mode. A miniaturized scale data center is a little and completely useful data center containing multiple servers and is capable of provisioning numerous virtual machines. Numerous technologies, including Edge computing, can benefit from Microdata centers as it reduces latency, enhances reliability, is relatively portable, has underlying security conventions(Yang et al., 2015), saves bandwidth utilization by compression, and can accommodate numerous new services. So on the whole the accompanying attributes make the edge it gets different from the fog and makes it better than the above.

An Edge framework will have moderately small registering assets (memory, preparing, and capacity) when contrasted with a Fog framework, notwithstanding, the assets can be expanded on-request; They can process data generated from a diverse set of devices; They can be both dense and sparsely distributed based on the geographical area; They uphold Machine-to-Machine correspondence and wireless connectivity; an Edge system can be installed on low specification devices like switches and IP cameras, and One of their principal uses is currently for mobile and portable devices. On the whole, these are the main differences between fog and edge because of which edge has become flexible to most of the devices. So it's time to learn some problems that are available with edge and to know some common solutions to those problems.

GENERAL EDGE ARCHITECTURE

The physical distance to the Cloud and the available resources inside the infrastructure increases the latency and reduce the Quality of Service (QoS). One of the recent standards in this area to solve issues of Cloud Computing is Edge Computing. Even though there are several naming for Edge computing, for example, Fog Computing and Cloudlets, inside this paper, just the term Edge Computing will be used. Figure 1 shows how the layered architecture can be the plot in between Cloud, Fog, and Edge Computing. Edge Computing combines multiple technologies, for example, Cloud Computing, Grid Computing, and IoT. It includes an extra tier between the Cloud and the end-devices and moves computational power to the end-device as close as could be expected under the circumstances. This means that, in the need of more computational resources by the end-device or a system, the errand can be offloaded to an Edge Server instead of the Cloud. Edge Computing is expected to reduce the latency and increase the QoS for errands which can't be handled by these devices. These undertakings are normally computationally heavy, for example, enormous data processing, video processing, computerized reasoning, or time-sensitive. On the off chance that the calculation must be done in real-time, usage of Cloud is not feasible since Cloud and Internet offer just best-effort service and delivery. Devices with limited computing limits may likewise have basic deadlines for their essential errand. In these circumstances, the errand can be offloaded to an Edge Server utilizing the same imperatives and can be accomplished at this level. Depending on the outcome of the undertaking, the system reacts to the result, e.g., sends the data back to the end-device. The Edge Servers can likewise offload the errands to other Edge Servers by considering the available resources, network, and calculation delays. One of the principle objectives of Edge Computing is to reduce latency and to keep the QoS as high as could reasonably be expected. Edge Computing intends to solve the issues of Cloud Computing or IoT by including an extra tier between the IoT devices and back-end infrastructure for computing and correspondence purposes. As this tier additionally have intermediate components for the primary gathering, investigation, calculation of the data. These intermediate components are called Edge Servers. Edge Server is definitely not a complete replacement of the Cloud with respect to its functionalities. Even though its available resources are higher than the end-devices, they are lower than the Cloud. Instead, exceptionally repeated errands, or undertakings that require in time response are preferred to be executed in an Edge Server. The proposed architecture for Edge Computing comprises of Cloud Tier, Edge Tier, and Device Tier. In the Device Tier, there are end-user devices. The green squares in the Edge Tier are Edge Servers. These servers gather, aggregate, analyze, and process the data before offloading them to the Cloud Tier or send back to the devices. The end devices can be in the same physical area, or in different areas as depicted in the figure. When an end-device needs to communicate with the Cloud, first, the request is sent to then, if the Edge Server is capable of completing the assignment without anyone else, it naturally handles the data and responds to the end-device with the result. If not, the data is offloaded to another server in the same tier provided that it exists. Otherwise, the data is offloaded to the Cloud. Edge Computing is a worldview which uses Cloud Computing technologies and gives more responsibilities to the Edge tier. These responsibilities are namely, computing offload data reserving/storage, data processing, service appropriation, IoT management, security, and privacy protection. Edge Computing is a worldview which uses Cloud Computing technologies and gives more responsibilities to the Edge tier. These responsibilities are namely, computing offload data reserving/ storage, data processing, service appropriation, IoT management, security, and privacy protection Without restricting the Cloud Computing features, Edge Computing needs to have the accompanying requirements, some of which are likewise defined for Cloud Computing: Interoperability, Scalability, Extensibility, Abstraction, Time sensitiveness, Security & Privacy, Reliability

Edge arrangements are typically multi-layered disseminated models incorporating and adjusting the remaining task at hand between the Edge layer, the Edge cloud or Edge organization, and the Enterprise layer(Li et al., 2018). Moreover, when we talk about the Edge, there are the Edge gadgets and the neighborhood Edge workers. It should be noted that Edge processing structures are an extension of IoT (Internet of Things) models and use terms like OT for operational innovation. The change and union of IT and OT advancements can convey colossal incentive throughout the following decade. Brief flow of computing in the edge environment is shown in Figure 2.

Figure 1. Layered Architecture of Edge with Fog and Cloud Layers

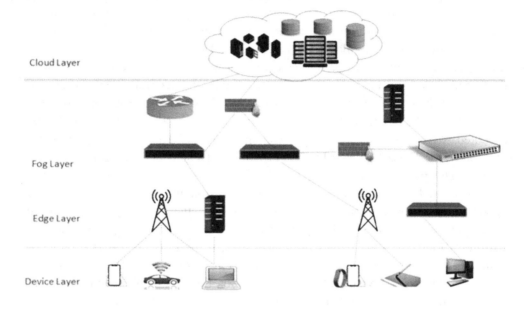

Figure 2. Edge Computing Device Hierarchy

From a systematic perspective, edge networks provide a distributed computing system with hierarchical geography. Edge networks target meeting stringent latency requirements, reducing power utilization of end devices, giving real-time data processing and control with localized computing resources, and decreasing the burden of backhaul traffic to centralized data centers. And of course, excellent network security, reliability, and accessibility must be inherent in edge networks. Edge Computing utilizes wide scope of advancements and unites them. Inside this area, Edge Computing uses numerous innovations, for example, remote sensor organizations (WSN), portable information securing, versatile mark examination, Fog/ Grid Computing, disseminated information activities, distant Cloud administrations, and so forth. Also, it consolidates the accompanying conventions and terms:

1) **5G correspondence**: It is the fifth era remote framework that focuses on the higher limit, lower power utilization, and lower dormancy contrasted with the past ages. Because of the expanded measure of information between the information, 5G is required to understand traffic issues that emerged with the expanded number of associated gadgets.

2) **PLC conventions**: Object Linking and Embedding for Process Control Unified Architecture (OPC-UA) is a convention created for mechanical computerization. Because of its transparency and strength, it is broadly utilized by ventures in the region of oil and gas, drug, advanced mechanics, and assembling.

3) **Message line specialist**: MQTT and TCP/IP are famous message conventions of savvy sensors and IoT gadgets. Supporting these message intermediaries, Edge Computing expands the gadget check that it interfaces. For the issue of MQTT security, AMQP is helpful in the correspondence with Cloud Computing worker.

4) **Event processor**: After messages of IoT show up in the Edge worker, occasion processor investigations those messages and makes semantic occasions utilizing pre-characterized rules. EsperNet, Apache Spark, and Flink are a few models for this empowering influence.

5) **Virtualisation**: Cloud administrations are conveyed as virtual machines on a Cloud worker or bunches. Utilizing virtual machines permit running different examples of working frameworks (OS) on a similar worker.

6) **Hypervisor**: As well as a virtual machine, execution assessment and information dealing with are required and acknowledged by the hypervisor to control virtual machines in the host PC.

7) **OpenStack**: Managing numerous assets could be testing. OpenStack is a Cloud working framework that makes a difference control of pools of processing and capacity assets quiet through a control board and observing devices.

8) **AI stage**: Rule-based motor and Machine learning stage upholds information investigation in neighborhood level. As expressed in

Segment III-A, this is very critical to arrive at one of the objectives of Edge Computing which is to assemble, break down, and play out the first sifting of the information.

9) **Docker**: Virtual machines work with establishment of working frameworks. In contrast to virtual machines, Docker is a Container as a Service (CaaS), which can utilize a solitary shared working framework and run programming in detached condition. It just requires the libraries of the product which makes it a lightweight framework without agonizing over where the product is conveyed.

That is about the prologue to edge design with every minor detail. We should save this one as the base for comprehension for investigating the security issues and their proposals which can be application explicit.

GENERAL ISSUES IN EDGE ARCHITECTURE

Web Advancement

What's more, edge nodes can recognize users based on MAC addresses or cookies, track user requests, cache files, determine nearby network conditions. It is additionally possible to embed feedback contents inside a web page to measure the user browser's rendering speed. The feedback content reports directly to the Edge nodes and illuminates the user's graphical resolution, current area reception (if wireless), and network congestion. In another comparable paper, Edge computing altogether reduced the response time of a Fog-based temperature prediction system. Due to Edge systems, the prediction latency was decreased from 5 to 1.5 s, web-page show latency from 8 to 3 s and internet traffic throughput from 75 to 10 Kbps. Utilizing Edge stages for upgrading web-services will likewise introduce web security issues. For example, if user input isn't properly validated, the application becomes vulnerable to the code injection assaults, SQL injection, where SQL code provided by the user is consequently executed resulting in the potential for unauthorized data access and change. This could result in the compromise of the entire Edge system's database or the sending of modified data to a central server. Additionally, due to insecure web APIs, assaults like a session and cookie hijacking (acting as a legitimate user), insecure direct object references for illegal data access, pernicious re-directions, and drive-by assaults could force an Edge stage to expose itself and the attached users.

Reconnaissance Video Transfer Preparing

A video data stream generated by camera sensors is sent to the respective Edge nodes, where it is stored and processed. The privacy of the stream ought to be maintained as it contains sound and visual data, which are transmitted to heterogeneous clients. Here, not exclusively is the security of Edge node is significant, yet the network and all end-user devices involved in the transmission ought to likewise be considered, especially against APTs. On the off chance that an Edge stage or network contains any bugs due to the absence of diligence, the critical video stream may be viewed, altered, and even destroyed. It is significant that the Edge node ensures a secure connection between all imparting devices and protects multi-media content by obscurity techniques, fine-grained access control, generating a new connection for the video stream, selective encryption, and restricting the number of connections.

Sparing Energy in Edge Computing

This specific application encourages the use of Edge stages in putting away and processing specific (user-defined) sorts of the (private) data locally in the Edge nodes, reducing the correspondence cost and delay. However, the presence of such private data places the Edge stage in a sensitive position(Merlino et al., 2019). As previously mentioned there are numerous threats, which are capable of bargaining the CIA of data, for example, noxious insiders can read, alter, and delete data. These issues can be resolved using encryption, authentication (uniquely approving and verifying each user), data characterization based on sensitivity, checking, and data coverage.

Catastrophe Reaction and Antagonistic Situations

Disaster recovery is a sensitive area whereby Edge systems and connected devices are supposed to work in extreme circumstances. In this case, the integrity and accessibility of the system are more significant than confidentiality. Wireless security conventions can do checksum (detect data errors), encrypt packets with negligible resources, and arrange fine-grained access control to carefully validate users (terminating unwanted connections(Glikson et al., 2017)). Furthermore, in case of emergency and key management to prevent losing decryption keys, these mechanisms ought to be considered to retain accessibility and integrity without trading off the overall performance of the system.

SECURITY AND PRIVACY ISSUES IN EDGE COMPUTING

Edge Computing facilitates the shift of storage and computation jobs from execution in cloud environments to the edge of the network. But this comfort comes with the confront questions in Privacy and security. The integration of emerging technologies such as Cloud or Edge computing, IoT, Artificial Intelligence, Machine Learning, Big Data Analytics is bringing enormous outcomes in various domains like Finance, Health, Education, E-commerce, etc., (Alabdulatif et al., 2019) The characteristics of Edge computing gives an easy way for lightweight devices to efficiently perform the complex processing tasks in the network edge itself. The Healthcare industry is also undergoing a huge paradigm shift from its traditional working model to digital services. The rapid advancement of this digitization of health records, IoT devices, and edge computing all together is transforming the healthcare industry.

The wide use of smart IoT devices, attached to networking technologies these days have improved less expensive and more reasonable medical systems. IoT has become a significant factor in the development of these health frameworks, giving (cheap cost) sensors to monitor the status of patient life. Health Frameworks based on Edge computing consists of sensitive patient data which has to be protected from unauthorized access (Alabdulatif et al., 2019). The electronic health records stored should be anonymous in such a way that the patient's identity should not be revealed, as the privacy of the patients has to be preserved. Sensitive patient health records should maintain the integrity and must be available with no delay. Hence security and privacy of outsourced patient's sensitive data is a challenging problem in the health frameworks built on Edge Computing.

Where to Enforce Security?

Security procedures are not confined to the basic networking level and can likewise be significant at much higher abstractions, for instance, at the service provisioning level. As services become more distributed, data such as service type and interface, device hostname, and possession might be viewed as delicate and require protection. Huge consideration has been devoted to the design of protocols for private (as in privacy-preserving) service discovery over the network (Khan et al., 2017). Unfortunately, a significant number of these conventions were proposed as of late and have not been completely investigated concerning security, performance, or simplicity of deployment, which adds up to interesting research challenges.

1)   **Cloud Data Center – Top Layer**:

It is important to indicate that, all edge paradigms might be supported by many infrastructures like centralized cloud service and the administration frameworks, core infrastructures are managed by similar third party providers such as mobile network operators. This would raise tremendous difficulties, for example, privacy leakage, data altering; denial of service attacks and service control, given these core infrastructures might be semi-trusted or totally untrusted. This results in challenges of privacy disclosure and damage to data integrity.

2)   Distributed Edge Nodes:

As previously mentioned, edge computing understands the interconnection of IoT devices and sensors by the combination of various communications, for example, mobile core network, wireless network, and the Internet, which raise many network security difficulties of these communication infrastructures. By utilizing the servers at the edge of the network, the conventional network attacks, such as denial of service (DOS) and distributed denial of service (DDOS) attacks, can be restricted efficiently. Such attacks will just upset the vicinity of the edge networks and have very little impact on the core network; additionally, the DOS or DDOS attacks happening in core networks may not truly interfere with the security of the edge data centers..

3)   IoT Devices on the Edge:

In edge computing, the edge devices dynamically played as an active participant in the distributed edge network at different layers, so that even a small loophole in the security aspect of edge devices may lead to dangerous outcomes for the whole edge ecosystem. For example, any devices controlled by an adversary can endeavor to agitate the services with a mixture of false information or intrude the system with some malicious actions. Likewise, malicious devices can control services in some particular circumstances, where the malicious enemies have captured the control advantage of one of these devices.

ATTACKS AND THREATS

The following list shows the predominant threats and attacks that are encountered by the edge computing frameworks in various application domains (Xiao et al., 2019). These types of threats are usually caused because of the weak framework design or flaws in the design, security misconfigurations and errors due to the implementation.The protective mechanisms deals with detection of such loopholes in the system which acts as an entry point for the attacks or preventing the attacks from happening through blocking the unusual activities.

1)   Distributed Denial of Service Attacks (DDoS)

DDoS is the attack which disturbs the services given by a single or set of servers by using botnets i.e. by compromising a cluster of edge devices and sending continuous requests to the server. This attack is a dangerous attack as it blocks the service of authorised users through bogus requests pretending as legitimate requests.

A conventional DDos attack happens when the attacker continuously sends many request packets to the server from the compromised devices in the distributed network. The server's hardware resources gets exhausted servicing these bogus requests persistently thereby leaving the legitimate requests unserviced. DDos attacks are more troublesome in case of edge servers because they are computationally less capable to defend themselves when compared to cloud servers. These bogus requests might confuse the edge server to decide that all its communication channels and hardware resources are busy. Edge servers provide services to the edge devices connected to them. In general, these edge devices are weak with respect to security because they have limited hardware resources and multiplatform software. Attackers utilize this and attack the edge devices first and then they use these compromised edge devices to attack the edge server. A notorious example is the 'Mirai' botnet where the attacker compromised 65000 IOT devices and these devices are used to initiate a DDoS attack to attack the servers like Kerbs and Dyn.

Figure 3. DDoS attack on Edge Server

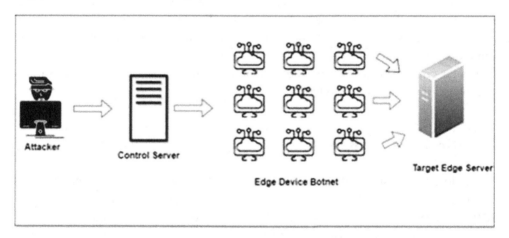

The Figure 3 depicts an example DDoS attack on Edge Server. DDoS attacks can be categorized into flooding attacks and zero day attacks.

a.   Flooding Attacks:

This attack is a common type of DDoS attack which stops or limits the service of a server by flooding huge numbers of bogus or malicious packets. The different kinds of flooding attacks are as follows,

i.   i) UDP Flooding:

ii.   The attacker persistently floods many UDP packets to the victim edge server resulting in the failure of the victim edge server where it can't service the legitimate UDP packets and leads to disturbed UDP services from the edge server.

iii. ii) CMP Flooding:

iv.   This attack makes use of ICMP protocol and sends a huge number of ICMP request packets continuously not even bothering about the reply messages. This makes the victim edge server suffer on the two way communication channel receiving the ICMP echo request and sending the reply messages which slowly turns the server incapable.

v.   iii) SYN Flooding:

vi.   The three way handshake protocol of TCP is utilized by this attack. The attacker sends a lot of SYN requests with spoofed IP addresses continuously and the victim servers respond with SYN+ACK messages to the spoofed IP addresses, waiting for the reply ACK messages which would never come from the spoofed IP addresses.

vii. iv) Ping of Death (PoD):

viii. This attack exploits the maximum size of an IP packet which is 65535 bytes. The attacker creates an intended IP packet with malicious content which is more than the maximum number of bytes. so the IP packet is splitted into fragments. These segmented packets are again reassembled at the edge server again. If an attacker keeps on sending such large packets, the victim edge server is kept busy and all its resources are utilized in the fragmentation and reassembly process.

ix.   v) HTTP Flooding Attack:

x.   This type of attack generates many standard requests like HTTP GET, PUT, POST and sends them as legitimate requests to the target edge server. This results in the choking of edge server as it becomes busy serving bogus requests and it runs out of computational resources to resolve the real legitimate requests.

      vi)   Slowloris Attack:

In this type of attack, the attacker initiates a number of incomplete HTTP connections resulting in keeping the target server maintaining these partial HTTP connections in parallel till it reaches the maximum pool size after which the server crashes. Incomplete HTTP connections are created by sending only the HTTP headers and not the subsequent messages.

b. **Zero-day DDoS attacks**:

This attack is usually launched by an experienced attacker where he finds an unknown vulnerability in the application code or operating system running on the target server. This unknown vulnerability found is called zero-day vulnerability, which is exploited and attack is made with a relevant payload causing serious damage in memory or computing ability leading to server crash. These attacks cause serious damage and it is difficult to detect and defend because it utilizes the zero-day vulnerability which is not known before.

2) Side Channel Attacks:

The escape characters are not filtered in SQL queries when it is processed in database management systems. Attackers make use of this loophole and attempt to do SQL injection attacks resulting in loss of data confidentiality and integrity. In addition, a more serious problem is that attackers can inject malicious scripts or malwares through SQL select statements. Consider this scenario, when an edge server gets service from other cloud servers or edge servers, it visits them as a client and accesses the services. If an attacker tries to perform an XSS attack now, it is a client side attack which injects malicious javascript codes into the code executed by the target server. The client is the edge server which gets the service and the target server is the edge or cloud server which provides the service. Unlike conventional client -server systems, XSS attacks can happen in edge servers in edge computing model.

The technique of compromising security and privacy through publicly available information is called side channel attacks. This kind of public information which need not be privacy-sensitive is called side channel information.Such side channel information related to secret private data must be protected. Side channel attacks are more prevalent in edge computing systems. Because there are lot of side channels in edge computing systems like communication paths, power consumption by edge devices, /proc file system used by smartphones, sensors etc., Consider the following scenario, when an attacker compromises an edge framework by collecting particular side channel information (for example, accessing the data from /proc file of mobile phones) and the obtained information is given as input to particular machine learning models, a lot of sensitive inferences can be obtained as output.

a) Communication Channel attacks:

Utilizing the communication channels in the edge computing system is the easiest way to initiate the attack and also an effective way to steal the sensitive information. Because the attacker need not be an edge device or an edge server to monitor the communication channel, he can be any malicious node on the network who passively sits and eavesdrops the communication channel to pull out the sensitive information from it. Communication channel attacks can be categorized into two kinds i) Analyzing the packet streams in channel and ii) Analyzing the wave signals in channel.

b) Attacks based on Power Consumption:

Attacks based on the analysis of power consumption of various devices on the edge system reveals the information about the devices itself through the power consumption profiles.The consumption of power is based on the strength of computations of a process. so this might give a lead to explore its relationship with sensitive data. This attack can be categorized into i) attacks based on power consumption measured by meters ii) attacks based on power consumption measured by oscilloscopes.

i) Attacks based on power consumption measured by meters:

Nowadays smart electric meters are available which precisely calculates the power consumption of households. In the era of IoT and Cloud, smart homes are implemented where everything is connected. Therefore analysing the power consumption data of smart home appliances, sensitive activities at home can be detected.

ii) Attacks based on power consumption measured by oscilloscopes:

In embedded systems, security is achieved by implementing the cryptographic algorithms in a chip. The power consumption of a hardware device can be measured by an instrument called an oscillator. Researchers have proved that the key to break the algorithm can be guessed by analysing the power consumption of hardware. however such power analysis attacks can be done only when the attacker is able to access the target device physically or gets access to the target device through some malicious applications.

c) Attacks based on smartphone communication channels:

Smartphones play a key role in edge based systems. In addition to IoT devices, smartphones also act as edge devices in the system. They are more advanced than IoT devices as well as more prone to attacking. Attacks on smartphones can be done in two ways.i) attacks on the /proc file system and ii) attacks on the sensors embedded in smartphones

3) Malware Injection Attacks

The process of injecting malicious code or malwares into computers is termed as malware injection attacks. The conventional computer networks have strong attack defence systems to enforce security and maintain data integrity like firewalls, Intrusion Detection Systems etc., But edge based systems have less computational power devices and minimally configured edge servers. so they may not have strong defence mechanisms and are prone to these injection attacks. Figure 4 shows the architecture of malware injection attacks in edge computing systems.

As shown in the architecture diagram above, the malwares are injected to both edge server and edge devices to steal sensitive information.

Figure 4. Malware Injection attacks in Edge systems

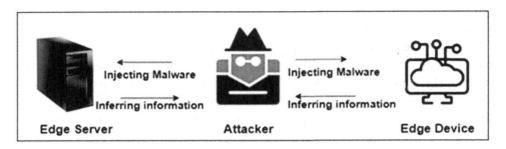

i) Injection on Edge Server

In edge based frameworks, injection attacks primarily focus on the edge servers. Popular injection attacks which gets placed in OWASP top 10 releases include XSS - cross site scripting, CSRF- Cross-site Request Forgery and XML based attacks. SQL injection attacks utilizes the loophole of SQL's nature of not filtering the escape characters in the user constructed sql queries. Authorized users may construct sql queries with columns they are allowed to access but the attacker constructs SQL queries inserting escape characters like quotation marks and tries to access the unauthorized data.

XSS attacks tries to include malicious client side scripts in the web data content which is automatically executed by the server. CSRF is a similar attack where an edge server is tricked to execute malicious code through web applications. When edge based frameworks use Simple Object Access Protocol (SOAP) for communication, XML based attacks can be easily deployed because SOAP exchanges messages in XML format.

ii) Injection on Edge Device

IoT devices are lightweight and heterogeneous in nature of both hardware and firmware. If any zero-day vulnerabilities are found by attackers in firmware, malwares can be injected to gain the command and control of edge devices.

CRYPTOGRAPHIC TECHNIQUES TO ENFORCE SECURITY

In the edge computing paradigm, the edge devices are more reliable and have incredible performance than cloud computing terminals, they are data owners, yet in addition they also play the job of data producers. For an edge user, the advantages from edge thing are as per the following: processing offload, caching the data, storage ability and processing, decreased maintenance cost, minimal transmission consumption and response time, and also the distributed request and service delivery from edge things, brings about a more elevated level of utilization of resources, and along these lines, forces little power cost to service providers (Alabdulatif et al., 2019). Despite the fact that the edge computing model has many advantages contrasted with conventional cloud computing model, there are still security concerns that developed as a hitch to acquisition of edge computing model.

1) Symmetric key Encryption

Symmetric encryption algorithms can be grouped into stream ciphers and block ciphers where the plain text bits are encoded individually in stream ciphers and using blocks of bits in block ciphers. Despite the fact that block ciphers require more hardware and memory, their performance is commonly better than stream ciphers since they have a permutation stage and also a substitution stage. As recommended by Shannon, plaintext must be prepared by two primary substitution and permutation stages to achieve the confusion and diffusion properties.

2) Public Key Encryption

Symmetric key encryption or public key encryption is utilized to solve the issue of key circulation. In Asymmetric keys, two keys are utilized; private and public keys. Public key is utilized for encryption and private key is utilized for decryption (E.g. RSA and Digital Signatures). Since users will in general utilize two keys: public key, which is known to the public and private key which is known uniquely to the user[2]. There is no requirement for conveying them preceding transmission. In any case, public key encryption depends on mathematical functions, computationally intensive and isn't exceptionally effective for small mobile devices. (Curtis, 2020). Asymmetric encryption strategies are very nearly 1000 times more slow than Symmetric methods, since they require more computational processing power.

3) Attribute Based Encryption

Attribute-based encryption (ABE) is a basic cryptographic technique to control the decryption capacity of the data owner over the encrypted data. An attribute-based access control framework comprises two elements: 1) Trusted authority (TA) who is responsible for distributing attribute keys and dealing with users' attribute set, 2) The user incorporates the message sender and the recipient which relate to the data owner and user. The basic Attribute-Based Encryption (fuzzy IBE) as a modification of IBE scheme in which the identities are replaced with a set of attributes. In ABE algorithm, the attributes of the user is mapped as $Z*p$ by the hash functions, which the ciphertext and private keys are identified with the attributes. Two types of ABE are i) Key Policy based ABE (KP-ABE) and ii) Cipher Text based ABE (CP-ABE).

4) Identity based Encryption

Identity-Based Encryption (IBE) is a public key encryption methodology where a public key is a random string, for example, an email address or a phone number (Patonico et al., 2019). The respective private key in the pair must be produced by a Private Key Generator (PKG) who knows about a master secret. Utilizing this development, anybody can encode messages or validated signatures without prior key distribution past the spread of public boundaries and the public key "strings." This is valuable where the arrangement of a conventional authentication authority-based PKI is badly designed or infeasible, as IBE-based frameworks don't need certificate manager, eliminating the requirement for certificate searches and complex certificate revocation schemes. The main focus of Identity-Based Cryptography is that private keys must be received from the PKG. How one safely and productively acquires this private key is essential to the security of the framework. For instance, how the PKG concludes who has to be given the private key related to an email address is pivotal to maintain the integrity of the system. Another thought is cost: key generation can be computationally costly.

5) Proxy Re-encryption

Proxy Re-encryption (PRE) is the ciphertext switching protocol which converts the ciphertext of one key into ciphertexts of another key by using a proxy element. In other words, a proxy is made to convert the ciphertext encrypted by the data owner's public key into a ciphertext as if it is encrypted by data user's public key with the help of encryption key and also there is an assurance that the proxy may not be able to decrypt the ciphertext. So the PRE scheme is popularly used in cloud based applications for performing data forwarding, data distribution, and data exchange operation in multiuser environments.

6) Homomorphic Encryption

Homomorphic encryption, otherwise called privacy homomorphism, is a cryptography method that permits users to work the ciphertext to perform arbitrary mathematical operations. This means, when we perform one basic mathematical operation, say addition, on the ciphertexts and, at that point when you decrypt, this decryption result is the same as the outcome that we legitimately perform addition on the plaintext. The benefit of this particular encryption form is that the user can perform any operation on the encrypted data with explicit conditions, the encryption strategies with these benefits can improve the effectiveness of data processing, guarantee the protected transmission of data, and also can get the correct decryption results. From this unique computing feature, the homomorphic encryption technique can be broadly utilized in data encryption, preserving the privacy, encrypted querying, and secure multi-party computation, The different types of Homomorphic encryption are as follows,

a. Full Homomorphic Encryption
b. Partial Homomorphic Encryption
c. Somewhat Homomorphic Encryption

7) Searchable Encryption

It is desirable to store data on data storage servers, for example, mail servers and file servers in encrypted form to decrease security and privacy dangers. In any case, this normally infers one needs to forfeit usefulness for security. For instance, if a customer wishes to recover just reports containing certain words, it was not recently realized how to let the data storage server perform the search and answer the question without loss of data classification''. The most immediate arrangements are as per the following: 1) One technique is to download all the ciphertext data to the nearby and decryption, at that point search in plaintext with keywords, however this activity will likewise download the superfluous records that don't contain the specific keywords which may cause the asset squandering of network and storage. Moreover, the decryption and searching activity of superfluous records will cost the enormous computational overhead, and this technique isn't reasonable for low broadband network situations. 2) Another outrageous arrangement is sending the private key and keywords to the storage server, at that point decode the encrypted archives and search on the server. An undeniable downside to this methodology is that the user's private data is re-presented to the server which will be a genuine danger to data security and individual privacy. Two types of searchable encryption are 1) Symmetric searchable encryption and 2) asymmetric searchable encryption.

AUTHENTICATION POLICIES AND ACCESS CONTROL SCHEMES

Access control policies identify authority, that is, power which has been authentically acquired, and to how authority is designated. Access control is related to guarantee that subjects and processes in a system access resources in a controlled and approved way (Moffett, 1994). Resources, for example, files and directories must be shielded from unapproved access and access authorization must be allocated distinctly by subjects or managers with authority to do such tasks. The Figure 5 shown below describes the entities participating in the Access Control Policies.

1)   Attribute based Access Control

Attribute-based control policies (ABAC) is one of the transcendent innovative technologies to control information access in cloud computing, which can be all around applied to the distributed architecture and accomplished fine-grained data access control by setting up the decoding ability based on a user's attributes.

Figure 5. Entities in Access Control Policies

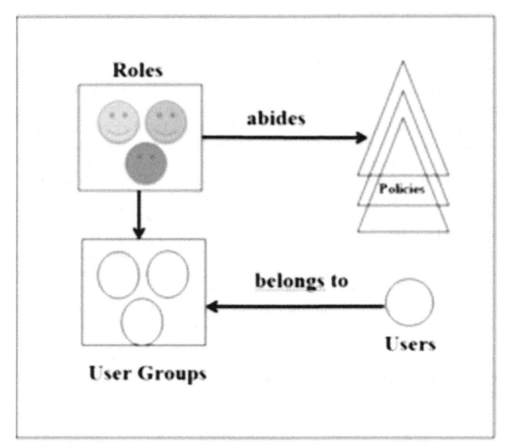

2)   Role-based Access Control

Role Based Access Control (RBAC) can give an adaptable access control and privilege management by users-to-roles and roles-to-objects authority mapping mechanism which implies the RBAC can manage the access of users to resources and applications dependent on recognizing roles and actions of users in the framework(Osborn et al., 2000).

3)   Discretionary Access Control

Discretionary access control policies allow users to assign rights to objects through building rules by subjects. Subjects have the control to decide who can access objects. DAC model is followed by major operating systems to implement file systems (Li & Tripunitara, 2005). For example, sample.txt rwxr-xr-x indicates the owner of sample.txt can read, write and execute the file, the other user groups can execute and read the file but could not write it.

4)   Mandatory Access Control

Mandatory access control (MAC) assigns privileges based on a tree -like structured hierarchical model (Ausanka-Crues, 2001). All users in the system are assigned with a security clearance level. All object resources are assigned with the security label in the hierarchical model. Users can access a resource in the same security level or below level in the hierarchy.

CASE STUDY: HEALTHCARE FRAMEWORK BASED ON EDGE COMPUTING

Introduction

Another use of Edge computing in healthcare includes Electrocardiogram (ECG) feature extraction to diagnose heart diseases. This involves medical sensors communicating data to an Edge layer that stores data in distributed databases, extract ECG features, and giving a graphical interface to show results in real-time.. The detection of a person having a stroke is of key importance as the speed of medical intervention is a life basic. Two fall detection systems have been implemented utilizing the Edge stage, named U-FALL and FAST. The two systems distribute computational errands between Edge and Fog stages to provide an efficient and scalable arrangement, which is essential as it considers a fast detection and notice of a patient fall. Patient health records contain sensitive data and there are multiple focuses in any Edge stage where they can be compromised, for example, by exploiting any system and application vulnerability, unauthorized data access while in storage or during transmission, malignant insiders threat, and while offering data to other systems. Medical sensors are constantly communicating data to Edge stages, through either wired or wireless connection. It is quite possible to compromise patient privacy, data integrity, and system accessibility by exploiting sensors and their underlying correspondence network. Wireless sensors for the most part work in open, unattended, and hostile environments. This ease-of-access can increase the chances of assaults like DoS, report disturbance, and selective sending assaults. What's more, if the Edge node manages sensitive data and needs access control mechanisms, it may leak the data due to account hijacking, unintended access, and other vulnerable purposes of entry. To stay away from such issues, exacting policies ought to be enforced to keep up a significant level of control utilizing multifaceted or shared authentication, private networks, and fractional (selective) encryption.

Requirements of the Edge based HealthCare Framework

The requirements (Zhang et al., 2018) of healthcare framework build using edge computing is as shown in the Figure 6 below.

Figure 6. Security Requirements

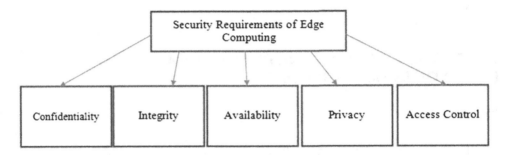

1)   Confidentiality

The basic need of any healthcare framework is to ensure that the EHRs of patients are only accessed by the EHR owner and authorised users, if any. EHRs must not be accessed by unauthorized users when it is being processed or stored in the edge or cloud data centers. In edge computing, the sensitive health data of patients is moved to the edge server and its ownership and control are isolated, which makes users lose their physical authority over the outsourced health data. Moreover, the sensitive health data in the edge servers are prone to data loss, breach of EHRs (Electronic Health Records), illegitimate data access or alterations (for example duplicating or removing the health records, and disclosure or distribution of health records). To address these dangers, a proper data confidentiality scheme has to be prepared to ensure the security of health data moved in the edge servers, which implies the patient's sensitive data has to be encrypted before moving it to the edge servers. At present, to maintain the confidentiality and to secure the patient data, the traditional method is to encrypt the sensitive data, and then it is outsourced to edge servers, after which it is uploaded to the data centers and can be decrypted by any legitimate user on demand.

2) Integrity

This requirement ensures the correctness of the patient's data stored in the edge or cloud. If the integrity of the EHR is not maintained, it may lead to serious problems. Assume if the vital signs of the patient are altered by an intruder, it may result in critical issues even causing the loss of the patient's life. Data integrity is a significant issue for the security of edge computing since the patient's data is moved to the edge servers while the data integrity is questionable during this transit. This leads to the process that the data owners must check the integrity and accessibility of outsourced data to ensure that there are no undetected modifications of data by any illegitimate users or systems. With respect to edge computing, data integrity must be concentrated on the following factors, batch auditing, dynamic auditing, privacy preserving and low complexity.

3) Availability

Health data stored in the system should be made available to the authorised users on demand for quick diagnosis. To maintain the purpose of automated healthcare services the immediate availability of EHRs is very much essential for quick diagnosis of diseases. The shorter the delay in response time and the reliable maintenance makes the automation of healthcare systems more popular.

4) Privacy

Privacy is one of the significant difficulties in other computing standards as the patients' sensitive data and personal data are moved from edge devices to the remote servers. In edge computing, privacy issues are an important issue because there are various honest but curious adversaries, for example, edge data centres, infrastructure service providers, other service providers and even some users. These attackers are generally approved entities whose main objective is to acquire sensitive data that can be utilized in different selfish manners. In this circumstance, it is unacceptable to expect to know whether a service provider is trustworthy in such an open ecosystem with various trust spaces. For instance in smart grid, a considerable amount of private data of a family can be revealed from reading the smart meters or some other IoT gadgets, it implies that regardless of the house is empty or not, if the smart meters were controlled by an adversary, the user's privacy is completely leaked. Specifically, the leakage of private data, for example, data, identification, can lead to dangerous situations.

5)   Access Control

Due to the outsourcing characteristic of edge computing, if there are no proficient authentication policies in that place, any malicious user without an authorized access can misuse the resources in edge or cloud data centers. This presents a major security challenge for the protected access control framework; for instance, the virtualization asset of edge servers can be accessed, misused, and altered by edge devices if they hold any specific privileges. Furthermore, in the distributed edge computing paradigm, there are numerous trust areas by various infrastructures cohabiting in one edge ecosystem, so it is important to build up the fine-grained access control framework in each trust domain. But most of the conventional access control mechanism usually focuses on one trust domain, and not on multiple trust domains in edge computing. There are many cryptography based solutions and policies to enforce access control in edge computing paradigms.

Architecture of the Edge based HealthCare Framework

Here we are representing a sample framework for depicting Healthcare networks with computational ends. Figure 7 shows the flow of processing the healthcare data right from the sensor till the higher end.

Figure 7. Healthcare Framework with Edge Computing

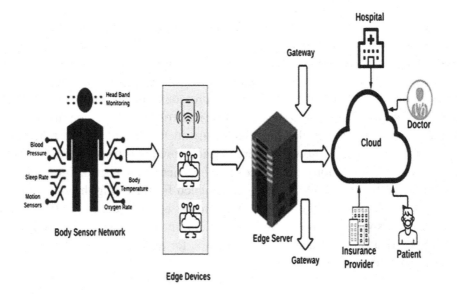

The following scenario in a health cloud environment which uses Proxy Reencryption(PRE) scheme is explained below.

1) Doctor encrypts the EHR of a Patient or the sensor data of patients using his Public Key PU_A - Ciphertext C1 is moved to cloud

2) Re-encryption key is generated to give access to an insurance agent. Doctor generates the re-encryption key encrypting his/her Public Key PU_A with the Insurance agent's public key PU_B and the encryption key $RK_{A->B}$ is transmitted to the cloud.

3) The cloud service provider may act as a proxy and it re-encrypts the Ciphertext C1 with $RK_{A->B}$ - Ciphertext C2

4) The Insurance agent decrypts the re-encrypted ciphertext with his private key PR_B.

The above procedure clearly shows that the intruder or adverse enemy can't decrypt the encrypted text. The disadvantage is that the semi-trusted proxy not only transfers the ciphertext from doctor to insurance agent but also vice-versa, which means it can reversibly converts the ciphertext of insurance agent to doctor without the permission of insurance agent by exploiting the discrete logarithm properties. Another issue with the PRE scheme is that both doctor and proxy can collude and try to deduce the private key of the insurance agent. To solve these problems variants of this scheme are introduced namely Identity based PRE, Conditional PRE etc.

Security Requirements in Edge based HealthCare Framework

Even however each Edge deployment has a different set of security requirements, applications, and sensitivity, the accompanying subsections provide comprehensive, efficient, and applicable security requirements for healthcare systems. They can likewise be used as generic best practice guidelines while developing the Edge software, so the security is enabled from inside the stage. Some of the working arrangements are,

Data Encryption

The data needs to be secured before (at rest in source area), during (moving through the network) and after (at rest in destination area) correspondence among IoT devices, the Edge network, and the Fog stage.

Preventing Cache Assaults

Edge stages maintained for the Cache management system are prone to software cache-based side-channel assaults, for example, exposing cryptographic keys, which may lead toward leaking sensitive data.

Network Checking

Edge systems that are consistently handling private data (e.g. generated by IoT devices) from end-user to Fog stage and vice versa, should screen and detect abnormal action in a network through automated enforcement of correspondence security rules and policies.

Malware Protection

Edge systems ought to protect themselves against both new and existing malware-based assaults, which can happen as infection, Trojan, rootkit, spyware, and worms to keep away from unwanted infection and serious damage.

Wireless Security

The internal and external wireless interchanges of the Edge stage with end-user devices need to minimize packet sniffing, rouge access focuses, and comparative challenges by implementing both encryption and authentication procedures. In Secured vehicular networks, to increase street safety and real-time utilization of vehicular networks(Freedman, 2003), they ought to protect themselves from internal and external security threats.

Secured Multi-tenancy

Edge computing should enable profoundly constrained access control on both data and network, alongside reasonable resource assignment mechanisms to protect confidentiality and integrity inside a multi-user environment.

Backup and Recovery

Depending upon the sort of utilization, Edge stages ought to have a data backup and recovery modules. Such a system should reflect copies of data on location, off-site, or both on a regular premise. It will benefit the two customers and friends to keep the operations running from utilizing previous backups, limiting service interruptions.

Security with Performance

A balanced trade-off between the level of usefulness and integrated security is fundamental for Edge network performance. It will enable completely featured applications meanwhile protecting the CIA of data and networks against internal and external threats.

Security Solutions Recommendations for Edge Based HealthCare Framework

Privacy Safeguarding in Edge Figuring

With regards to medical care, the primary examination gets into safeguarding protection in sensor-edge networks comprises of the accompanying summed up steps to make sure about wellbeing sensor information between end-client gadget and Edge organization: They gather sensor information and concentrate highlights. Fluffing of information by embeddings Gaussian commotion in information at a specific degree of difference to bring down the opportunity of listening in and sniffing assaults; Segregation by parting information into squares and rearranging them to maintain a strategic distance from Man-in-the-Middle (MITM) assaults; Implementing Public Key Infrastructure for encoding every information square; and Transmit isolated information to Edge hub, where information bundles are unscrambled and re-requested. The framework additionally incorporates a component decrease capacity for limiting information correspondence with Edge hubs to help limit hazard. This work is of criticalness as it focussed on safeguarding individual and basic information during transmission. A method can be improved by choosing an encryption and key administration calculation, focussing on those that assume a significant part in keeping up the security of information. Anyway, the necessary computational overheads for performing broad information control (fluffing, isolation, encryption, unscrambling and requesting, reordering) when the correspondence must be investigated before its gets into the real usage of the situation. This could be of essentialness when planning and creating an Edge framework as the necessary calculation overheads probably won't be accessible. Another significant perspective to see here is that sensors send information persistently, perhaps over longer timeframes, stickand the proposed security structure may over-burden or even accident the fundamental Edge framework. That is the place the heap adjusting calculations must be work.

Alleviating Insider Information Burglary

One path for shielding information from malignant insiders any delicate gadget organization, for example, medical services utilizing parts of Edge and Cloud figuring would consolidates conduct profiling and fake ways to deal with alleviate security dangers. On the off chance that any profile shows anomalous conduct, for example, the expansion of getting to various archives at uncommon occasions, the framework will label the entrance as dubious and square the individual client. Fake is a disinformation assault that incorporates counterfeit reports, honeyfiles, honeypots and different sorts of goading information that can be utilized to distinguish, befuddle and get the malevolent insider. This examination space is huge as it exhibits likely adjusting and alleviation strategies to shield against information burglary. All the more explicitly, One can show that the proposed strategy can accurately distinguish unusual conduct with a normal exactness more noteworthy than 90%. For instance, an examination is performed with a restricted measure of information. All the more explicitly, eighteen understudies from a solitary college over the term of four days. Consequently, the outcomes regarding exactness they guarantee may not reproducible or widespread. Their procedure can be improved by expanding the populace size and running the trial over longer stretch of time(Stolfo et al., 2012). Moreover, the computational prerequisites of such a methodology are not referenced. The paper gives no subtleties on the amount of information that is put away, just as the CPU time and memory required during investigation. Such conduct profiling methods are regularly acted in a conventional customer worker engineering where calculation assets are openly accessible. It isn't clear how this strategy can be executed on an Edge hub without having unfriendly effects on center usefulness. The method can be additionally improved through fundamentally breaking down and choosing achievable machines learning procedures and preparing information required for conduct profiling. This conveys more significance because of the presence of an enormous number of patients and records. The conduct profiling, checking and client coordinating cycle would not apply any weight on Cloud assets and forestall real information burglary without uncovering any patient touchy information. As an additional advantage, these tasks will happen on-premise and execute generally quicker because of low transmission capacity idleness.

Strategy Driven Secure Administration of Assets

The following famous issue in medical care is strategy the board system for the assets of Edge registering to upgrade secure collaboration, sharing and interoperability among client mentioned assets. The framework is separated into five significant modules:

1) Policy Decision Engine (PDE) for making a move dependent on pre-characterized strategy rules;
2) Application Administrator (AA) to oversee Edge multi-occupancy;
3) Policy Resolver (PR) for characteristic based validation;
4) Policy Repository (PRep) holding rules and approaches; and
5) Policy Enforcer (PE) to distinguish any inconsistencies in strategy execution.

AA is answerable for characterizing rules and arrangements (put away in PRep) while thinking about different occupants, applications, information sharing and correspondence administrations. At the point when a specific assistance demand is produced using a client, it is sent to a PR that recognizes the client dependent on explicit arrangement of traits and access benefits against a mentioned asset. The client ascribes and their separate authorizations are put away in an information base. PDE takes client data from the PR, separates rules from the PRep, dissect them and authorize through the PE. The eXtensible Access Control Markup Language (XACML) is utilized to make rules and the OpenAZ system for building PDE. Regardless of being in an underlying stage, this strategy structure can possibly turn into a vital piece of constant circulated frameworks in future, where there is a solid requirement for access, personality and asset the executives capacities. Notwithstanding, this structure is restricted to just those frameworks, which can distribute devoted assets inside Edge stages for the greater part of calculations required by different modules to execute the system. Edge stages ought to be fit for dealing with profoundly time-delicate applications, be that as it may, the proposed approval cycle may take more time to decide. Another imperfection in their strategy is that the arrangement itself is characteristically powerless against DoS assaults because of the intricate confirmation measure in PR and PDE. On the off chance that an aggressor sets up a lot of associations all the while, rehashes the 'approval cycle's in a similar association ceaselessly or reacts to the validation convention in a low and moderate way, the Edge assets will get depleted and delivered inaccessible for the proposed clients. In any case, these security concerns can be decreased by building an exhibition model that is gathering estimations of memory, CPU and plate use and occasionally contrasting and assessed values. In the event that the framework recognizes an oddity, the client would be diverted to the Shark Tank group, which is basically an intermediary to intently screen the client however can give full application capacities.

Verification in Edge Stage

Shaky validation conventions between Edge stages And medical care gadgets have been recognized as a fundamental security worry of Edge registering. The case is that that the IoT gadgets, particularly in keen lattices, are inclined to information altering and satirizing assaults and can be forestalled with the assistance of a Public Key Infrastructure (PKI), Diffie-Hellman key trade, Intrusion discovery strategies and observing for changed info esteems. Moreover, effect of MITM assault on Edge processing by dispatching a Stealth assault on video call among 3G and the WLAN clients inside an Edge network didn't cause any noticeable change in memory and CPU utilization of Edge hub, henceforth it is very hard to distinguish what's more, relieve. The proposal is that the danger of such assaults can be forestalled by making sure about correspondence channels between the Edge stage and the client of medical services gadgets to execute validation plans. In view of the present status of validation in wellbeing system Edge stage, they are missing thorough verification and secure correspondence conventions according to their determination and prerequisites. In an Edge stage both security and execution factors are considered related, and systems, for example, the encryption procedures known as completely homomorphic and Fan-Vercauteren to some degree homomorphic can be utilized to make sure about the information. These plans comprises of a half and half of symmetric and public-key encryption calculations, just as different variations of quality based encryption. As homomorphic encryption grants ordinary activities over the records information without decoding the information, the decrease in key dissemination will keep up the protection of information. A framework can perform information collection dependent on the homomorphicPaillier cryptosystem. As the homomorphic capacity of encryption makes it workable for neighborhood network passages to play out a procedure on figure text without decoding, it decreases the confirmation cost (regarding preparing power) while keeping up the mystery of information.

Utilizing Advance Encryption Standard (AES)

Some examination may infer that AES is a reasonable encryption calculation for a gigantic information collection in medical services where Edge stage assumes a significant job. Different measurements have been considered for the presentation assessment: client load against CPU time and document size against encryption/ unscrambling time and memory usage. Our case is that, encryption time will be almost the equivalent for cell phone and PC, any sort of fitbits and other computerized screens for persistent information which collects modest quantity of information, for example, 500 Kb, 5 Mb, and 10 Mb. In spite of the fact that, AES encryption is all around acknowledged and is attainable for Edge figuring, because of low equipment particulars and littler calculations, one can't contrast AES and some other accessible encryption calculation. What's more, the size of the encryption key assumes a significant function in reinforcing the encryption. Utilizing little example size probably won't give the profound knowledge to whether AES is an appropriate calculation for

Edge organizations and capacity or not. So it is suggested that, distinctive measured information must be put for AES choice. Moreover, literary information, pictures or some other information configuration can be utilized for encryption/unscrambling measures. In addition, the Edge stage comprises of heterogeneous gadgets with various details and single calculation probably won't have the option to cover every conceivable situation. Encryption is now an extra assignment for the Edge stage and furthermore devours a lot of assets. The determination of encryption calculation (regardless of whether symmetric, hilter kilter or cross breed) ought to be acted as per supplier and foundation necessities.

REFERENCES

Alabdulatif, A., Khalil, I., Yi, X., & Guizani, M. (2019). Secure Edge of Things for Smart Healthcare Surveillance Framework. *IEEE Access: Practical Innovations, Open Solutions, 7*(c), 31010–31021. doi:10.1109/ACCESS.2019.2899323

Ausanka-Crues, R. (2001). *Methods for access control : Advances and limitations.* Harvey Mudd College.

Curtis. (2020). *What are the issues with fog computing.* https://www.yourtechdiet.com/blogs/fog-computing-issues/

Dimitrievski, A., Zdravevski, E., Lameski, P., & Trajkovik, V. (2019, September). Addressing Privacy and Security in Connected Health with Fog Computing. In *Proceedings of the 5th EAI International Conference on Smart Objects and Technologies for Social Good* (pp. 255-260). 10.1145/3342428.3342654

Freedman, A. (2003). Securing the Edge. *Queue, 1*(1), 6-9.

Glikson, A., Nastic, S., & Dustdar, S. (2017, May). Deviceless edge computing: extending serverless computing to the edge of the network. In *Proceedings of the 10th ACM International Systems and Storage Conference* (pp. 1-1). 10.1145/3078468.3078497

Khan, S., Parkinson, S., & Qin, Y. (2017). Fog computing security: A review of current applications and security solutions. *Journal of Cloud Computing, 6*(1), 19. Advance online publication. doi:10.118613677-017-0090-3

Li, C., Xue, Y., Wang, J., Zhang, W., & Li, T. (2018). Edge-oriented computing paradigms: A survey on architecture design and system management. [*ACM Computing Surveys, 51*(2), 1–34. doi:10.1145/3154815

Li, N., & Tripunitara, M. V. (2005). On safety in discretionary access control. *Proceedings - IEEE Symposium on Security and Privacy*. 10.1109/SP.2005.14

Merlino, G., Dautov, R., Distefano, S., & Bruneo, D. (2019). Enabling workload engineering in edge, fog, and cloud computing through OpenStack-based middleware. *ACM Transactions on Internet Technology*, *19*(2), 1–22. doi:10.1145/3309705

Moffett, J. D. (1994). Specification of management policies and discretionary access control. *Network and Distributed Systems Management*, 455–479. http://scholar. google.com/scholar?hl=en&btnG=Search&q=intitle:The+Even+More+Irresisti ble+SROIQ#0%5Cnhttp://citeseerx.ist.psu.edu/viewdoc/download?doi=10.1.1.1 7.7145&rep=rep1&type=pdf

Osborn, S., Sandhu, R., & Munawer, Q. (2000). Configuring Role-Based Access Control to Enforce Mandatory and Discretionary Access Control Policies. *ACM Transactions on Information and System Security*, *3*(2), 85–106. Advance online publication. doi:10.1145/354876.354878

Patonico, S., Braeken, A., & Steenhaut, K. (2019). Identity-based and anonymous key agreement protocol for fog computing resistant in the Canetti–Krawczyk security model. *Wireless Networks*, *6*. Advance online publication. doi:10.100711276-019-02084-6

Ren, J., Guo, H., Xu, C., & Zhang, Y. (2017). Serving at the edge: A scalable IoT architecture based on transparent computing. *IEEE Network*, *31*(5), 96–105. doi:10.1109/MNET.2017.1700030

Ren, J., Zhang, D., He, S., Zhang, Y., & Li, T. (2019). A Survey on End-Edge-Cloud Orchestrated Network Computing Paradigms: Transparent Computing, Mobile Edge Computing, Fog Computing, and Cloudlet. *ACM Computing Surveys*, *52*(6), 1–36. doi:10.1145/3362031

Stolfo, S. J., Salem, M. B., & Keromytis, A. D. (2012, May). Fog computing: Mitigating insider data theft attacks in the cloud. In *2012 IEEE symposium on security and privacy workshops* (pp. 125-128). IEEE.

Tang, W., Ren, J., Zhang, K., Zhang, D., Zhang, Y., & Shen, X. (2019). Efficient and privacy-preserving fog-assisted health data sharing scheme. *ACM Transactions on Intelligent Systems and Technology*, *10*(6), 1–23. doi:10.1145/3341104

Wang, X., Zhang, J., Schooler, E. M., & Ion, M. (2014, June). Performance evaluation of attribute-based encryption: Toward data privacy in the IoT. In *2014 IEEE International Conference on Communications (ICC)* (pp. 725-730). IEEE. 10.1109/ICC.2014.6883405

Waters, B., & Encryption, C. P. A. B. (2011). An Expressive, Efficient, and Provably Secure Realization. Lecture Notes in Computer Science, 6571.

Xiao, Y., Jia, Y., Liu, C., Cheng, X., Yu, J., & Lv, W. (2019). Edge Computing Security: State of the Art and Challenges. *Proceedings of the IEEE, 107*(8), 1608–1631. Advance online publication. doi:10.1109/JPROC.2019.2918437

Yang, J. J., Li, J. Q., & Niu, Y. (2015). A hybrid solution for privacy preserving medical data sharing in the cloud environment. *Future Generation Computer Systems, 43*, 74–86. doi:10.1016/j.future.2014.06.004

Zhang, J., Chen, B., Zhao, Y., Cheng, X., & Hu, F. (2018). Data Security and Privacy-Preserving in Edge Computing Paradigm: Survey and Open Issues. *IEEE Access, 6*(Idc), 18209–18237. doi:10.1109/ACCESS.2018.2820162

Chapter 13
Edge Computing and IoT Technologies for Medical Applications:
A Case Study on Healthcare Monitoring

Ayshwarya B.
Kristu Jayanti College, India

Kumar R.
Kristu Jayanti College, India

Muruganantham A.
Kristu Jayanti College, India

Velmurugan R.
Kristu Jayanti College, India

EXECUTIVE SUMMARY

Dynamic observation of blood sugar levels is essential for patients diagnosed with diabetes mellitus in order to control the glycaemia. Inevitably, they must accomplish a capillary test three times per day and laboratory test once or twice per month. These regular methods make patients uncomfortable because patients have to prick their finger every time in order to measure the glucose concentration. Modern health monitoring systems rely on IoT. However, the number of advanced IoT-based continuous glucose monitoring systems is small and has several limitations. Here the authors study feasibility of invasive and continuous glucose monitoring system utilizing IoT-based approach. They designed an IoT-based system architecture from

DOI: 10.4018/978-1-7998-4873-8.ch013

a sensor device to a back-end system for presenting real-time data in various forms to end-users. The results show that the system is able to achieve continuous glucose monitoring remotely in real time, and a high level of energy efficiency can be achieved by applying the nRF compound, power management, and energy harvesting unit altogether in the sensor units.

1. INTRODUCTION

Edge computing based Internet of Things (IoT) can be viewed as a dynamic network where physical and virtual objects are interconnected together. IoT encompassing advanced technologies such as wireless sensor networks (WSN), artificial intelligence, and cloud computing play an important role in many domains comprising of robotics, logistics, transportation, and health-care. For instance, IoT-based systems for health-care consisting of sensing, WSN, smart gateways, and Cloud provide a way to remote and real-time e-health monitoring. Advances in WSNs have created an innovative ground for e-health and wellness application development. Ambient assisted living, ambient intelligence, and smart homes are becoming increasingly popular. According to the World Health Organization (WHO), the epidemic of Diabetes Mellitus (DM) in Mexico is catalogued as a national emergency. DM is a chronic non-communicable disease in which the body is unable to regulate blood glucose levels. There are two main types of diabetes: diabetes type-1 occurs when the pancreas is incapable to produce insulin, or produces only a scarce amount; insulin is essential to regulate the glucose concentration in blood and to convert glucose into energy. Diabetes type-2 takes place when the body cannot effectively use the insulin, and it is proliferating worldwide more rapidly than type-1. Standard methods for measuring the blood glucose concentration are invasive, since they require either to collect a blood sample for a laboratory test, or to prick the fingertip for a capillary test. A capillary test is often used for monitoring due to its ease of use.

However, patients require pricking their finger in different moments of the day, yielding discomfort and distress, thus hindering a proper glycaemia control. These can be combined to other health solutions such as fitness and wellness, chronic disease management and diet or nutrition monitoring applications. The new initiatives tend to be integrated into the patient information ecosystem instead of being separated into monitoring and decision processes. There are potential benefits to ageing population, where elderly people could be monitored and treated at the comfort of their own homes. Fully autonomous health monitoring wireless systems can have many useful applications. Among those applications is glucose level measurement for diabetics. Diabetes is a major health concern. According to a WHO report, the number of people with diabetes has exceeded 422 million and in 2012, over 1.5 million people died because of diabetes. The WHO classified diabetes as a top ten causes of mortality. Diabetes has serious effects on the well-being of a person and the society. Unfortunately, there is still no known permanent cure for diabetes. However, one solution to this problem is to continuously measure blood glucose levels and close the loop with appropriate insulin delivery. Hence, CGM equipped with alarm systems can help patients to take corrective action(s) such as decisions on their diet, physical exercise and when to take medication. Energy harvesters incorporated into wearable devices allow powering wireless sensor operated applications, thereby making them autonomously operated. This regime has many useful implications on patients and health-care providers, especially for implanted sensors where battery changing could cause pain and discomfort. Cautious design of both low-power electronic circuitry and efficient energy harvesting scheme is pivotal to fully autonomous wearable systems. In this chapter, the presented work aims to study the feasibility of invasive and secure CGMS using IoT. The work is to design an IoT-based system architecture from a sensor device to a back-end system for presenting real-time glucose, body temperature and contextual data (i.e. environmental temperature) in graphical and text forms to end-users such as patient and doctor. Moreover, the work customizes the nRF communication protocol for suiting to the glucose monitoring system and achieving a high level of energy efficiency.

The remainder of the chapter is organized as follows: In section 2 related works are presented. In section 3, problems are stated. In section 4, system architecture, requirements, and design of an edge computing-based healthcare system are discussed. Section 5 presents an implementation of the glucose monitoring system is shown. In section 5, experimental results are discussed. Section 6 concludes the work.

2. RELATED WORKS

Rabindra et al., (2007), He proposed that the smart health paradigms employ Internet-connected wearables for telemonitoring, diagnosis for providing inexpensive healthcare solutions. They used The Technology of Fog computing to reduce latency and increases throughput by processing data near the body sensor network. In this chapter, they described a secure service-orientated edge computing architecture that is validated on recently released public dataset. And the Results and discussions are support the applicability of proposed architecture for smart health applications. After the Discussions they proposed SoA-Fog i.e. a three-tier secure framework for efficient management of health data using fog devices. They designed the prototype by using win-win spiral model with use case and sequence diagram. Overlay analysis was performed using proposed framework on malaria vector borne disease positive maps of Maharastra state in India from 2011 to 2014. The mobile clients were taken as test case. They performed comparative analysis between proposed secure fog framework and state-of-the art cloud-based framework.

The examinations of Partha et al., (2019), The world has recently witnessed the emergence of huge technological growth in the field of data transmission and smart living through various modes of information and communication technology. The edge computing has taken a leading role to embark upon the problems related to the internetwork bandwidth minimization and service latency reduction. As per their research Inclusion of small microcontroller chips, smart sensors and actuators in the existing socio-economic sectors have paved the Internet of Things (IoT) to act upon the dissemination of smart services to the end users. They said that the crucial role of industrial standards and elements of the edge computing for the dissemination of overwhelming augmented user experience with conjunction with the IoT. In their research First they presented the taxonomical classification and the review the industrial standards and elements of the edge computing for the dissemination of overwhelming agumented user experience with conjunction with the IoT. Second, they had presented two practically implemented use cases that have recently employed the edge-IoT paradigm together to solve urban smart living problems. And that third proposed a novel edge-IoT based architecture for e-healthcare i.e. EH-IoT and developed a demo test-bed.

The test results showed promising results towards minimizing dependency over IoT cloud analytics or storage facility. They had concluded with discussion on the various parameters such as, architecture, requirement capability, functional issues, and selection criteria, related to the survival of edge-IoT ecosystem incorporation.

The study of Dubey et al (2015), the size of multi-modal, heterogeneous data collected through various sensors were growing exponentially. It was demand intelligent data reduction, data mining and analytics at edge devices. Data compression could reduce the network bandwidth and transmission power consumed by edge devices. Their proposed methodology, validates and evaluates Fog Data, a service-oriented architecture for Fog computing. And their center piece of the proposed architecture was a low power embedded computer that carries out data mining and data analytics on raw data collected from various wearable sensors used for telehealth applications. The embedded computer collects the sensed data as time series, analyzes it, and finds similar patterns present. Patterns were stored, and unique patterns are transmitted. Also, the embedded computers extract clinically relevant information that was sent to the cloud. A working prototype of the proposed architecture was built and used to carry out case studies on telehealth big data applications and specifically, their research used the data from the sensors worn by patients with either speech motor disorders or cardiovascular problems. They implemented and evaluated their application specific data mining techniques to shown orders of magnitude data reduction and hence transmission power savings.

The obtained results showed substantial improvement in system efficiency used the Fog Data architecture.

Multag et al (2019), they designed a fog computing architecture that was geographically distributed and to which a variety of heterogeneous devices were ubiquitously connected at the end of a network in order to provided collaboratively variable and flexible communication, computation, and storage services. The aim of their study that was to present a systematic review of the technologies for fog computing in the healthcare IoT systems field and analyzes the previous and that was providing motivation, limitations faced by researchers, and suggestions proposed to analysts for improving this essential research field. The taxonomy results were divided into three major classes; frameworks and models, systems (implemented or architecture), review and survey. The Fog computing was considered suitable for the applications that require real-time, low latency, and high response time, especially in healthcare applications. Those studies were demonstrating that resource sharing provides low latency, better scalability, distributed processing, better security, fault tolerance, and privacy in order to present better fog infrastructure. They concluded that the domains of Fog Computing in healthcare applications was differ, yet were equally important for the most parts and their review would help accentuating research capabilities and consequently expanding and making extra research domains.

Pasquale Pace et al., (2018)., claimed the Edge computing paradigm has attracted many interests in the last few years as a valid alternative to the standard cloud-based approaches to reduce the interaction timing and the huge amount of data coming from Internet of Things (IoT) devices toward the Internet. As per their Research In the next future, Edge-based approaches will be essential to support time-dependent applications in the Industry 4.0 context. As a consequence, this chapter proposed Body Edge, a novel architecture well suited for human-centric applications, in the context of the emerging healthcare industry.

That consists of a tiny mobile client module and a performing edge gateway supporting multiradio and MultiTech ology communication to collect and locally process data coming from different scenarios; in addition, that also exploits the facilities made available from both private and public cloud platforms to guarantee a high flexibility, robustness, and adaptive service level. The advantages of the designed software platform have been evaluated in terms of reduced transmitted data and processing time through a real implementation on different hardware platforms. They conducted study also highlighted the network conditions (data load and processing delay) in which BodyEdge is a valid and inexpensive solution for healthcare application scenarios.

Farshad et al., (2018). He described that the technology and healthcare industries have been deeply intertwined for quite some time. New opportunities, however, are now arising as a result of fast-paced expansion in the areas of the Internet of Things (IoT) and Big Data. In addition, as people across the globe have begun to adopt wearable biosensors, new applications for individualized eHealth and mHealth technologies have emerged. That they said upsides of these technologies were clear: they were highly available, easily accessible, and simple to personalize; in additionally they made it easy for providers to deliver individualized content cost-effectively, at scale. At the same time, a number of hurdles currently stand in the way of truly reliable, adaptive, safe and efficient personal healthcare devices. Major technological milestones would need to be reached in order to address and overcome these hurdles; and that would require closer collaboration between hardware and software developers and medical personnel such as physicians, nurses, and healthcare workers. And the main purpose of their special issue was to analyze the top concerns in IoT technologies that pertain to smart sensors for health care applications; particularly applications targeted at individualized tele-health interventions with the goal of enabling healthier ways of life. These applications include wearable and body sensors, advanced pervasive healthcare systems, and the Big Data analytics required to inform these devices. They conclude that these applications and these technologies were to simply the man work and easily caring or monitoring the person who used those technologies.

Cao et al., (2015)., they explained that they entering into the Biomedical research and clinical practice and there where one of the major applications of biomedical big data research is to utilize inexpensive and unobtrusive mobile biomedical sensors and cloud computing for pervasive health monitoring. However, real-world user experiences with mobile cloud-based health monitoring were poor, due to the factors such as excessive networking latency and longer response time. And they said that resting on the other hand, fog computing, a newly proposed computing paradigm, utilizes a collaborative multitude of end-user clients or near-user edge devices to conduct a substantial amount of computing, storage, communication, and etc. and this new computing paradigm, if successfully applied for pervasive health monitoring, has great potential to accelerate the discovery of early predictors and novel biomarkers to support smart care decision making in a connected health scenarios. In this chapter, they employ a real-world pervasive health monitoring application (pervasive fall detection for stroke mitigation) to demonstrate the effectiveness and worth of fog computing paradigm in health monitoring. Fall is a major source of morbidity and mortality among stroke patients. Hence, detecting falls automatically and in a timely manner becomes crucial for stroke mitigation in daily life. From their research they set to (1) investigate and develop new fall detection algorithms and (2) design and employ a real-time fall detection system employing fog computing paradigm (e.g., distributed analytics and edge intelligence), which split the detection task between the edge devices (e.g., smartphones attached to the user) and the server (e.g., servers in the cloud). Experimental results show that distributed analytics and edge intelligence, supported by fog computing paradigm, are very promising solutions for pervasive health monitoring, according to their research.

Chakraborty et al., (2016), They designed that the Fog computing is a recently proposed computing paradigm that extends Cloud computing and services to the edge of the network. And the new features offered by fog computing (e.g., distributed analytics and edge intelligence), if successfully applied for time-sensitive healthcare applications, has great potential to accelerate the discovery of early notification of emergency situations to support smart decision making. While promising, how to design and develop real-world fog computing-based data monitoring system is still an open question. As a first step to answer this question, in this research, they employ a fog-based cloud paradigm for time-sensitive medical applications and also proposed to show the practical applicability and significance of such a novel system. The ubiquitous deployment of mobile and sensor devices is creating a new environment, namely the Internet of Things (IoT) that enables a wide range of future Internet applications. In this research, they presented the dynamic Fog, a high-level programming model for time-sensitive applications that are geospatially distributed, large-scale, and latency-sensitive. They also analyzed their fog model with healthcare data, more specifically with Heartrate data that was one of the most time-sensitive medical data which deals with life and death situations. They conclude with their experiment shown that their proposed system achieves minimum delay while it also achieves the data accuracy and data consistency which are very important in many applications like medical data.

Celesti et al,(2019), They explained that they mainly focused on cloud computing, fog computing, the Internet of Things, and Big Data analytics for the future healthcare industry, or Healthcare 4.0.The Healthcare Industry 4.0 allowed to increase the flexibility in production, speeding up both manufacturing and market processes, increasing both the product quality and productivity, and changing business models modifying the interaction with value chain, competitors, and clients. Healthcare Industry 4.0 requires investments and mind-set change for cross-industry collaboration, agreements on data ownership, security, legal issue solving, product registration standards, new machine-to-machine communication protocols, and employment/skills development. Furthermore, Healthcare Industry 4.0 is revolutionizing the market of health service provisioning to patients and clinical operators.

3. PROBLEM STATEMENT

The technologies used by glucose monitoring systems addressed in recent works are mainly transdermal, thermal and optical. The transdermal glucose estimation is performed by sonophoresis, reverse iontophoresis or ultrasound. The thermal approaches aim to estimate glucose concentrations by measuring the physiological response to thermal emissions, due to glucose having absorptive effects on the heat radiation that are directly related to its concentration In optical methods, a light beam is directed to human tissue and the energy absorption, reflection or scattering is used to estimate the glucose concentration. Commonly, optical methods are preferred due to its simplicity and that small laser diodes can be used to construct portable and inexpensive devices. Besides, other technologies such as transdermal sensors need a thorough calibration process and are more susceptible to non-controlled environment. However, there is a range of factors that affect the glucose estimation, such as sweating, skin roughness, ambient temperature or pressure.

There are still many limitations. For example, some systems do not consider real-time and remote monitoring while other systems do not pay attention on energy efficiency sensor devices/nodes. In addition, they are not able to inform to medical doctors in real-time in cases of emergency. The main difference of this work from other works is to produce a new architectural design of an Edge-based IoT system that is applicable for human-centric applications, which can process massive amounts of data using model transformations. Model transformation (MT) is a mechanism of model-driven software engineering discipline that can be used here to share data between different database schemas.

4. SYSTEM ARCHITECTURE AND REQUIREMENTS

In this section, the architectural design of the recommended IoT Edge-based system is discussed. There are two main services provided by the system, namely, healthcare monitoring and medical record management service. From that, the recommended system can be organised and designed into two main subsystems: healthcare monitoring subsystem and medical record management subsystem. The widely adopted UML Deployment diagram is used to illustrate the hardware components where all software components are deployed with respect to the overall architectural design proposed in this chapter, especially for the sensing, fog and cloud storage layer.

4.1.1. Health Care Sensing Layer

This layer consists of some networked smart devices and sensors that relay complete health-related information; capturing, processing and transferring to the next layer. Some of these devices and sensors regularly monitor various health parameters, including blood sugar level, body temperature, heart rate, blood pressure, and any other parameters that come from specific medical devices such as, medical devices for diabetes or even x-ray scan.

Figure 1. A detailed Architecture IoT Edge-based System

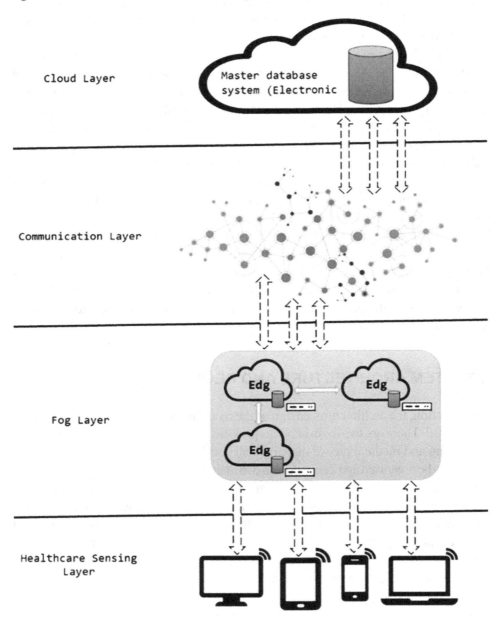

4.1.2. Fog Layer

The fog layer consists of a number of connected fog nodes. These nodes, called Edges, are responsible for receiving data from smart sensors of IoT devices, process this data locally, analyze it, then determine unusual health patterns and report to the most related party in the network to take an action. Consequently, each edge must have a communication, data storage and processing, and controlling units to achieve accelerated and low latency decision making. Figure 2 illustrates the architecture of edge nodes adopted in the system.

Figure 2. The Architecture of a Node in the proposed Edge-based System

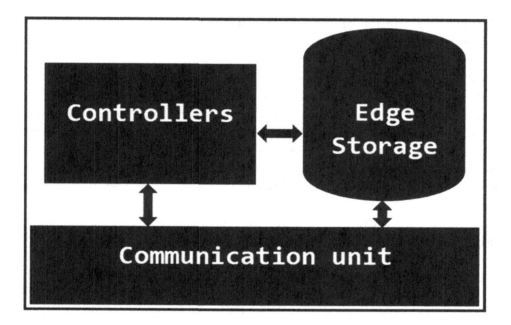

4.1.3. Communication Layer

This a typical networking layer that is responsible for managing the traffic of data and security, and other critical issues related to this type of networked system, between the fog network and the backend cloud. Some types of security threat that might be considered at this level are Man-in-the-middle, Spoofing, Confidentiality compromise and Replay attack.

4.1.4. Cloud Layer

A cloud data center is implemented at this layer, which contains the promising dynamic national repository of health data of the population. The comprehensive health record database system is constructed with three main features, namely, supporting data integration from multiple sources at the edges, long-term data analysis and processing for different points of care, and decision making support for various medical practitioners, patients and other parties. The data in the central cloud database contains data passed from fog for historical analysis of chronic diseases or other problems for early detection or treatment. To achieve this need, a database system such as relational database or data lake might be adopted at this level of the system.

4.2. Requirements of the Blood Glucose Level Monitoring System

This kind of systems aims at helping, especially diabetic patients, to better self-monitor and manage their chronic condition. It is used to optimize treatment strategies by analyzing the effect of different external factors on diabetic patients such as diet, medication and daily exercise. Monitoring glucose levels can help to understand the relation between blood glucose level, insulin, food and exercise. Besides, the usage of glucose monitoring systems can be expanded to help non-diabetic patients in detecting abnormal changes of the sugar level in their blood when performing exertion or activity, and then reporting results.

Trajectory information of measurements, including glucose level, is observed over a time to introduce disease diagnosis schemes

4.3. Energy Harvesting unit Enhancing Edge Computing

The exponential advancements in Wireless Sensor Nodes and the emerging field of IoT have opened the doors wide for numerous intelligent applications. Unfortunately, this development is not reflected at the battery capacity side. A major limitation of untethered nodes is a limited battery capacity which limits the operation time of the nodes. The finite lifetime of a node implies the mite lifetime of the applications or additional costs and complexity to regularly change batteries. In this work the RF energy harvesting system is presented, the RF energy harvesting system. A first step in designing the RF energy harvesting system is deciding on the frequencies at which power will be harvested. The wireless spectrum is full of signals with different frequencies and power levels, ranging from cellular standards, WLANs and TV signals. The criteria that control the selection of certain frequencies for the purpose of energy harvesting are wide deployment and power level.

Nodes could possibly use large batteries for longer lifetimes, but will have to deal with increased size, weight and cost. Nodes may also opt to use low-power hardware like a low-power processor and radio, at the cost of lesser computation ability and lower transmission ranges. Several solution techniques have been proposed to maximize the lifetime of battery-powered sensor nodes. Some of these include energy-aware MAC protocols, power aware storage, routing and data dissemination protocols, duty-cycling strategies, adaptive sensing rate, tiered system architectures and redundant placement of nodes. While all the above techniques optimize and adapt energy usage to maximize the lifetime of a sensor node, the lifetime remains bounded and mite. The above techniques help prolong the application lifetime and/ or the time interval between battery replacements but do not preclude energy related inhibitions 12. Energy harvesting could be a solution to the above-mentioned dilemma. Energy harvesting refers to harnessing energy from the environment or other energy sources (body heat, foot strike, finger strokes) and converting it to electrical energy. If the harvested energy source is large and periodically/continuously available, a sensor node can be powered perpetually.

Energy sources can be broadly classified into the following two categories, (i) Ambient Energy Sources: Sources of energy from the surrounding environment, e.g., solar energy, wind energy and RF energy, and (ii) Human Power: Energy harvested from body movements of humans. Passive human power sources are those which are not user controllable. Some examples are blood pressure, body heat and breath. Active human power sources are those that are under user control, and the user exerts a specific force to generate the energy for harvesting, e.g., finger motion, paddling and walking. No single energy source is ideal for all applications. The choice depends on every applications requirements and constraints. To power the glucose sensor node a combination of ambient and human powered sources is selected. Due to its ubiquitous availability RF energy is an adequate source for this application. Also, since the sensor is mounted on human body it makes sense to exploit this medium a source of energy. Through the use of a Thermoelectric Generator (TEG), thermal energy can be converted into electrical energy.

A Schottky diode which is employed in rectifier and voltage doubler as it has low forward voltage, is a rectifying metal semiconductor junction. Figure 3 illustrates the corresponding output voltage for a wide range of input power levels at 925 MHz RF input signal. The requirement proper operation of sensor node of this implementation is 2V input however, RF energy harvesting system is capable of reduction of this to 0V which corresponds to 1Mv.

Figure 3. Rectifier output voltage Vs. input power level

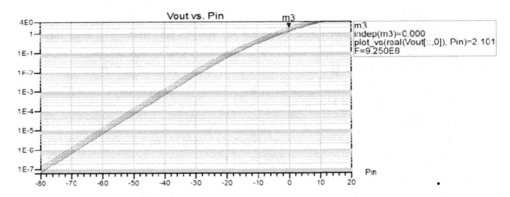

Table 1. Glucose levels

Type	Before Meals	2 hours after meals	Wake up	Risk of hypoglycaemia (low blood glucose)
Healthy Person	4 to 5.9 mmol/L	Under 7.8mmol/L		Under 4 mmol/L
Type 1 diabetes	4 to 7 mmol/L	5 to 9 mmol/L	5 to 7 mmol/L	Under 4 mmol/L
Type 2 diabetes	4 to 7 mmol/L	Under 8.5 mmol/L		Under 4 mmol/L
Children with type1 diabetes	4 to 7 mmol/L	5 to 9 mmol/L	4 to 7 mmol/L	Under 4 mmol/L

4. Effective Implementation Using Edge Computing

With the purpose of evaluating feasibility of the CGM system using edge computing, the entire system shown in Figure 1 is implemented. First, the interaction of the biological tissue under investigation is studied. Since the glucose sensor will be subcutaneous, the electrical characteristics of the biological tissue i.e. skin will be evaluated from which the amount of power loss and absorption due to propagation through the biological tissue will be estimated. It is imperative to make sure that subjecting the human body to this continuous signals is within the safe specified measures. The guidelines for Electro Magnetic Field exposure (EMF) are in terms of Specific Absorption Rate (SAR) and the equivalent plane wave power density (SW/m^2). SAR is a measure of the rate of energy absorption per unit mass due to exposure to an RF source. SAR is normalized to mass and is defined as:

$$SAR = (ef\ E_r\ ms^2)/(W/Kg)$$

Where ef is the effective conductivity of the biological material such as skin and is proportional to the frequency of the applied field, is the mass density which is approximately $1000 \, kg/m^3$ for most biological tissues, and E_r ms is the root mean square value of the electric field E at the measurement point. At an operating frequency of 2.4 GHz, the maximum E and S are 61 V/m and 10 W/m2 respectively which are well below the targeted operation power of the wireless sensor node.

Table 2. Blood glucose levels in diagnosing diabetes

Plasma glucose test	Normal	Prediabetes	Diabetes
Random	Below 11.1 mmol/l Below 200 mg/dl		11.1 mmol/l or more 200 mg/dl or more
Fasting	Below 6.1 mmol/l Below 108 mg/dl	6.1 to 6.9 mmol/l	7.0 mmol/l or more 126 mg/dl or more
2 hour post-prandial	Below 7.8 mmol/l Below 140 mg/dl	7.8 to 11.0 mmol/l 140 to 199 md/dl	11.1 mmol/l or more 200 mg/dl or more

A web page is designed for the notification which can also accessed as application in mobile devices. The application is built in the gateway for receiving data from the nRF component and performing other services. When data is available at one-end of the USB port, the app automatically reads the data and performs the data processing service. In addition, the app is capable of representing the processed data in text and graphical forms and triggering a push notification service. The push notification service is implemented by a Google push notification API. When the mobile application detects abnormal situations (i.e. too low or too high glucose level), the push notification service in the gateway is triggered for sending notification messages to Cloud which then notifies doctors and an end-user wearing the sensor device.

5. EXPERIMENTAL RESULTS AND DISCUSSIONS

In order to evaluate the proposed architecture, several experiments were designed to provide insightful results about two different aspects: (1) the throughput of the fog and cloud architecture, (2) the performance of the edge computing based (decentralized) database.

5.1. Performance of Cloud and Fog Layer Nodes

The initial tests to determine the performance of both cloud and fog nodes are organised and carried out for 4000 connection on fog node and for 800 connection on a remote node. Since there exists the possibility of network congestion issues, tests are carried out at different connection rates to determine the node maximum throughput up to the connection error occurring point. As it can be observed in the Figure 4, the desired and real rates are roughly the same up to a point when the node is not able to handle the requests and thus its performance decreases. Specifically, the fog node reaches its peak performance at 300 requests per second, while this point is at 200 requests per second for the cloud node. In the case of the fog node, this is due to its hardware constraints, while, in the case of the cloud node, it is related to the restrictions of its network (i.e., the load of the network and the characteristics of the devices involved in processing and routing the requests through the Internet).

5.2. Performance of Edge Based Database (Decentralized)

In order to estimate the throughput of the selected decentralized edge computing-based database, OrbitDB which is serverless and proper choice to decentralized edge computing, nodes were deployed locally (in fog nodes) and remotely (in a cloud). In such scenarios it was measured the average time required by an OrbitDB node for processing each REST API request. For the sake of fairness, tests were performed for four different payload sizes to evaluate their effect on network delay (for each payload size, the time required for processing 1000 requests was averaged). The obtained results are shown in Figure 5 and Figure 6. As it can be expected, the larger the payload, the larger the time response and the lower the request rate.

It is also worth noting that the difference in time response between the fog node and the cloud increases as payload size gets larger, mainly due to the communications transmission time through the network (i.e., although the processing time required by the OrbitDB node remains constant, the time required to exchange the request payload increases).

5.3 Efficient Power Consumption

Random and Predetermined data are employed in quality checking of data transmitted. Below zero-degree data at sensor and gateway are compared. The distance of one metre or few metres are maintained between sensor and gateway. We obtain the result of same sending and receiving data and there is no data loss in all of the events. However, in the case of blocked radio signals, sensor node sends the data with maximum power but the sensor's average power consumption is not varied considerably as interval time between transmission increases. Table 3 shows power consumptions of implemented components.

From the above table it is clear that nRF receiver enhance the power consumption of Android phone about 65%. When the prototype is replaced by an entire circuit device, the power consumption gets reduced further. Tests are carried out to examine functionality of the application for a maximum, moderate, and minimum value of glucose with temperature. The well organized and accurate text form of data representation is obtained as the result.

Table 3. Power consumption of nRF transceiver, sensor node and gateway

Device	Voltage supply (V)	Average Current (mA)
nRF transmitter (nRF+ATMEGA328P)	0.5	2
nRFreceiver (nRF+ATMEGA328P+FTDI board)	5	5
Sensor node	2	1.4
Gateway (Android phone without nRF receiver)	70	5
Android phone with nRF receiver	5	75

6. CONCLUSION

In this chapter, presented the design, implementation and evaluation of an IoT Edge Computing -based system for diabetes research and care. The implemented IoT-based architecture is complete system starting from sensor node to a back-end server. The system is able to collect blood glucose levels from CGMs that can be accessed remotely. Edge based computing nodes of the system are able to obtain several types of data (i.e. glucose, body temperature, and environmental data) and transmit the data wirelessly to the gateway efficiently in term of energy consumption. Thus, the system allows for monitoring patients and warn them in real-time in case a dangerous situation is detected. In order to create the proposed system, an edge computing system based on distributed mobile smartphones was devised to collect data from the CGMs and send them to a remote cloud. The sensor node is integrated with the energy harvesting unit for extending operating duration of the sensor device. With the assistance of the customized nRF receiver, a patient's smart-phone becomes a gateway for receiving data from sensor nodes. Through the system, doctors and caregivers can easily monitor their patient anytime, anywhere via a browser or a smart-phone application.

REFERENCES

Barik, R. K., Dubey, H., & Mankodiya, K. (2017, November). SOA-FOG: secure service-oriented edge computing architecture for smart health big data analytics. In *2017 IEEE Global Conference on Signal and Information Processing (GlobalSIP)* (pp. 477-481). IEEE. 10.1109/GlobalSIP.2017.8308688

Cao, Y., Hou, P., Brown, D., Wang, J., & Chen, S. (2015, June). Distributed analytics and edge intelligence: Pervasive health monitoring at the era of fog computing. In *Proceedings of the 2015 Workshop on Mobile Big Data* (pp. 43-48). 10.1145/2757384.2757398

Celesti, A., Amft, O., & Villari, M. (2019). Guest Editorial Special Section on Cloud Computing, Edge Computing, Internet of Things, and Big Data Analytics Applications for Healthcare Industry 4.0. *IEEE Transactions on Industrial Informatics*, *15*(1), 454–456. doi:10.1109/TII.2018.2883315

Chakraborty, S., Bhowmick, S., Talaga, P., & Agrawal, D. P. (2016, October). Fog networks in healthcare application. In *2016 IEEE 13th International Conference on Mobile Ad Hoc and Sensor Systems (MASS)* (pp. 386-387). IEEE. 10.1109/MASS.2016.065

Dubey, H., Yang, J., Constant, N., Amiri, A. M., Yang, Q., & Makodiya, K. (2015). Fog data: Enhancing telehealth big data through fog computing. In *Proceedings of the ASE bigdata & socialinformatics 2015* (pp. 1-6). Academic Press.

Firouzi, F., Rahmani, A. M., Mankodiya, K., Badaroglu, M., Merrett, G. V., Wong, P., & Farahani, B. (2018). *Internet-of-Things and big data for smarter healthcare: From device to architecture, applications and analytics*. Academic Press.

Gia, T. N., Ali, M., Dhaou, I. B., Rahmani, A. M., Westerlund, T., Liljeberg, P., & Tenhunen, H. (2017). IoT-based continuous glucose monitoring system: A feasibility study. *Procedia Computer Science*, *109*, 327–334. doi:10.1016/j.procs.2017.05.359

Mutlag, A. A., Ghani, M. K. A., Arunkumar, N. A., Mohammed, M. A., & Mohd, O. (2019). Enabling technologies for fog computing in healthcare IoT systems. *Future Generation Computer Systems*, *90*, 62–78. doi:10.1016/j.future.2018.07.049

Pace, P., Aloi, G., Gravina, R., Caliciuri, G., Fortino, G., & Liotta, A. (2018). An edge-based architecture to support efficient applications for healthcare industry 4.0. *IEEE Transactions on Industrial Informatics*, *15*(1), 481–489. doi:10.1109/TII.2018.2843169

Ray, P. P., Dash, D., & De, D. (2019). Edge computing for Internet of Things: A survey, e-healthcare case study and future direction. *Journal of Network and Computer Applications*, *140*, 1–22. doi:10.1016/j.jnca.2019.05.005

Compilation of References

Freedman, A. (2003). Securing the Edge. *Queue, 1*(1), 6-9.

Miraz, M. H., Ali, M., Excell, P. S., & Picking, R. (2015). *A review on Internet of Things (IoT), Internet of Everything (IoE) and Internet of Nano Things (IoNT). In 2015 Internet Technologies and Applications*. ITA. doi:10.1109/ITechA.2015.7317398

Suresh & Pattabiraman. (2016). Reduction of large database and identifying frequent patterns using enhanced high utility mining. *International Journal of Pure and Applied Mathematics, 109*(5), 161-169.

Anitha Kunari, Sudha, Sadasivam, & Akash. (2016). A secure android application with integration of wearables for healthcare monitoring system using 3D ECCDH PAKE protocol. *Journal of Medical Imaging and Heath Informatics, 6*(6), 1548-1551.

SDGlobalTech. (n.d.). https://www.sdglobaltech.com/blog/a-guide-to-iot-based-healthcare-apps

Zhang, J., Chen, B., Zhao, Y., Cheng, X., & Hu, F. (2018). Data Security and Privacy-Preserving in Edge Computing Paradigm: Survey and Open Issues. *IEEE Access, 6*(Idc), 18209–18237. doi:10.1109/ACCESS.2018.2820162

Alabdulatif, A., Khalil, I., Yi, X., & Guizani, M. (2019). Secure Edge of Things for Smart Healthcare Surveillance Framework. *IEEE Access: Practical Innovations, Open Solutions, 7*(c), 31010–31021. doi:10.1109/ACCESS.2019.2899323

Aruna, S., & Venkataswamy, R. (2018). Academic Workbench for Streetlight Powered by Solar PV System Using Internet of Everything (IoE). *International Conference on Communication, Computing and Internet of Things (IC3IoT)*, 186-190. 10.1109/IC3IoT.2018.8668152

Suresh & Pattabiraman. (2019). Developing a customer model for targeted marketing using association graph mining. *International Journal of Recent Technology and Engineering, 8*(2), 292-296.

Data Flair Training. (n.d.). https://data-flair.training/blogs/applications-of-iot-in-transportation

Demir, A. K., & Bilgili, S. (2019). Fine Tuning Distributed Divergecast Scheduling Algorithms in IEEE 802.1S.4e TSCH for Internet of Everything. *2019 International Symposium on Networks, Computers and Communications (ISNCC)*, 1-6. 10.1109/ISNCC.2019.8909093

Khan, S., Parkinson, S., & Qin, Y. (2017). Fog computing security: A review of current applications and security solutions. *Journal of Cloud Computing*, *6*(1), 19. Advance online publication. doi:10.118613677-017-0090-3

Lu, H., Su, S., Tian, Z., & Zhu, C. (2019, March). A novel search engine for Internet of Everything based on dynamic prediction. *China Communications*, *16*(3), 42–52.

Dai, C., & Song, Q. (2019, March). Heuristic computing methods for contact plan design in the spatial-node-based Internet of Everything. *China Communications*, *16*(3), 53–68.

Patonico, S., Braeken, A., & Steenhaut, K. (2019). Identity-based and anonymous key agreement protocol for fog computing resistant in the Canetti–Krawczyk security model. *Wireless Networks*, 6. Advance online publication. doi:10.100711276-019-02084-6

Moffett, J. D. (1994). Specification of management policies and discretionary access control. *Network and Distributed Systems Management*, 455–479. http://scholar.google.com/scholar?hl= en&btnG=Search&q=intitle:The+Even+More+Irresistible+SROIQ#0%5Cnhttp://citeseerx.ist. psu.edu/viewdoc/download?doi=10.1.1.17.7145&rep=rep1&type=pdf

Sergey, Nikolay, & Sergey. (2017). Cyber security concept for Internet of Everything (IoE). *Systems of Signal Synchronization, Generating and Processing in Telecommunications (SINKHROINFO)*, 1-4. . doi:10.1109/SINKHROINFO.2017.7997540

Raj, A., & Prakash, S. (2018). Internet of Everything: A survey based on Architecture, Issues and Challenges. *5th IEEE Uttar Pradesh Section International Conference on Electrical, Electronics and Computer Engineering (UPCON)*, 1-6. 10.1109/UPCON.2018.8596923

Fiaidhi, J., & Mohammed, S. (2019, January-February). Internet of Everything as a Platform for Extreme Automation. *IT Professional*, *21*(1), 21–25. doi:10.1109/MITP.2018.2876534

Li, N., & Tripunitara, M. V. (2005). On safety in discretionary access control. *Proceedings - IEEE Symposium on Security and Privacy*. 10.1109/SP.2005.14

Ausanka-Crues, R. (2001). *Methods for access control : Advances and limitations*. Harvey Mudd College.

Chauhan & Jain. (2019). A Journey from IoT to IoE. *International Journal of Innovative Technology and Exploring Engineering, 8*(11).

Liu, L., Larsson, E., Yu, W., Popovski, P., Stefanović, Č., & de Carvalho, E. (2018). Sparse Signal Processing for Grant-Free Massive Connectivity: A Future Paradigm for Random Access Protocols in the Internet of Things. *IEEE Signal Processing Magazine*, *35*(5), 88–99. Advance online publication. doi:10.1109/MSP.2018.2844952

Ren, J., Zhang, D., He, S., Zhang, Y., & Li, T. (2019). A Survey on End-Edge-Cloud Orchestrated Network Computing Paradigms: Transparent Computing, Mobile Edge Computing, Fog Computing, and Cloudlet. *ACM Computing Surveys*, *52*(6), 1–36. doi:10.1145/3362031

Osborn, S., Sandhu, R., & Munawer, Q. (2000). Configuring Role-Based Access Control to Enforce Mandatory and Discretionary Access Control Policies. *ACM Transactions on Information and System Security*, *3*(2), 85–106. Advance online publication. doi:10.1145/354876.354878

Stolfo, S. J., Salem, M. B., & Keromytis, A. D. (2012, May). Fog computing: Mitigating insider data theft attacks in the cloud. In *2012 IEEE symposium on security and privacy workshops* (pp. 125-128). IEEE.

Ren, J., Guo, H., Xu, C., & Zhang, Y. (2017). Serving at the edge: A scalable IoT architecture based on transparent computing. *IEEE Network*, *31*(5), 96–105. doi:10.1109/MNET.2017.1700030

Wang, X., Zhang, J., Schooler, E. M., & Ion, M. (2014, June). Performance evaluation of attribute-based encryption: Toward data privacy in the IoT. In *2014 IEEE International Conference on Communications (ICC)* (pp. 725-730). IEEE. 10.1109/ICC.2014.6883405

Waters, B., & Encryption, C. P. A. B. (2011). An Expressive, Efficient, and Provably Secure Realization. Lecture Notes in Computer Science, 6571.

Yang, J. J., Li, J. Q., & Niu, Y. (2015). A hybrid solution for privacy preserving medical data sharing in the cloud environment. *Future Generation Computer Systems*, *43*, 74–86. doi:10.1016/j.future.2014.06.004

Educba. (n.d.). https://www.educba.com/benefits-of-iot/

Kakkar & Shaurya. (2019). An IoT Equipped Hospital Model: A New Approach for E-governance Healthcare Framework. *International Journal of Medical Research & Health Sciences*.

Tang, W., Ren, J., Zhang, K., Zhang, D., Zhang, Y., & Shen, X. (2019). Efficient and privacy-preserving fog-assisted health data sharing scheme. *ACM Transactions on Intelligent Systems and Technology*, *10*(6), 1–23. doi:10.1145/3341104

Curtis. (2020). *What are the issues with fog computing*. https://www.yourtechdiet.com/blogs/fog-computing-issues/

Motlagh, H. (2020). Internet of Things (IoT) and the Energy Sector. *Energies*, *13*(2), 494. doi:10.3390/en13020494

Suganya & Mariappan. (2019). *IoT based Automated Medicine Dispenser for Online Health Community using Cloud*. Research Gate.

Sangeetha, Vigneshwari, Dhinakaran, Prabu, & Karpagam. (2019). Voice Controlled Autonomous Wheelchair Using IoT. *International Journal of Research in Engineering, Science and Management*, *2*(10).

Suresh, K., & Praveen, O. (2020). Extracting of Patterns Using Mining Methods Over Damped Window. *2020 Second International Conference on Inventive Research in Computing Applications (ICIRCA)*, 235-241. 10.1109/ICIRCA48905.2020.9182893

Suresh & Mohan. (2020). Development of High Utility Itemsets In Streaming Database. *Test Engineering and Management, 82*, 13052 - 13056.

Zielinski. (2015). *Internet of Everything (IoE) in Smart Grid*. Research Gate.

Embitel. (n.d.). https://www.embitel.com/blog/ecommerce-blog/how-modern-retailers-can-leverage-the-iot-benefits-in-their-supply-chain-management

Evans, D. (2012). *The Internet of Everything How More Relevant and Valuable Connections Will Change the World. Cisco Internet Business Solutions Group*. IBSG.

Glikson, A., Nastic, S., & Dustdar, S. (2017, May). Deviceless edge computing: extending serverless computing to the edge of the network. In *Proceedings of the 10th ACM International Systems and Storage Conference* (pp. 1-1). 10.1145/3078468.3078497

Masoud, Jaradat, Manasrah, & Jannoud. (2019). *Sensors of Smart Devices in Internet of Everything (IoE) Era: Big Opportunities and Massive Doubts*. Research Gate.

Suresh & Kashyap. (2020). Effectively Mining on Utility Itemset by Using Conventional Method. *Test Engineering and Management, 82*, 13062 - 13068.

Dimitrievski, A., Zdravevski, E., Lameski, P., & Trajkovik, V. (2019, September). Addressing Privacy and Security in Connected Health with Fog Computing. In *Proceedings of the 5th EAI International Conference on Smart Objects and Technologies for Social Good* (pp. 255-260). 10.1145/3342428.3342654

Evans, D. (2013). *The Internet of Everything Global Public Sector Economic Analysis. Cisco Internet Business Solutions Group*. IBSG.

Medium. (n.d.). https://medium.com/tech-lounge/the-concept-of-iot-enabled-smart-city-fe1e104e3ab

Suresh & Pattabiraman. (2015). An improved utility itemsets mining with respect to positive and negative values using mathematical model. *International Journal of Pure and Applied Mathematics, 101*(5).

Taştan, M. (2018). IoT Based Wearable Smart Health Monitoring System. *IoT Based Wearable Smart Health Monitoring System*, (September), 343–350. Advance online publication. doi:10.18466/cbayarfbe.451076

Abdul, R., Khan, M. M., Lodhi, M. A., & Hussain, F. B. (2016). Rank attack using objective function in RPL for low power and lossy networks. *International Conference on Industrial Informatics and Computer Systems (CIICS)*, 1-5.

Abomhara, M., & Koien, G. M. (2014). Security and privacy in the Internet of Things: Current status and open issues. *Privacy and Security in Mobile Systems (PRISMS), 2014 International Conference on IEEE*, 1-8. 10.1109/PRISMS.2014.6970594

Agbehadji, I. E., Frimpong, S. O., Millham, R. C., Fong, S. J., & Jung, J. J. (2020). Intelligent energy optimization for advanced IoT analytics edge computing on wireless sensor networks. *International Journal of Distributed Sensor Networks*, *16*(7), 1550147720908772.

Ai, Y., Peng, M., & Zhang, K. (2017). Edge cloud computing technologies for Internet of things: A primer. *Digital Communications and Networks*, *4*(2), 77–86. doi:10.1016/j.dcan.2017.07.001

Al-Fuqaha, A., Guizani, M., Mohammadi, M., Aledhari, M., & Ayyash, M. (2015). Internet of things: A survey on enabling technologies, protocols, and applications. *IEEE Communications Surveys and Tutorials*, *17*(4), 2347–2376. doi:10.1109/COMST.2015.2444095

Ali, R., Lasebae, A., & Loo, J. (2014). A secure authentication protocol for IP-based wireless sensor communications using the Location/ID Split Protocol (LISP). *Trust, security and privacy in computing and communications (TrustCom), 2014 IEEE 13th international conference on IEEE*, 840-845.

Amos, B. (2015). Edge analytics in the internet of things. *IEEE Pervasive Computing*, *14*(2), 24–31.

Anagnostopoulos, C. (2020). Edge-centric inferential modeling & analytics. *Journal of Network and Computer Applications*.

Areej, A., Ji, H., Gong, T., Nixon, M., Ammar, R., & Han, S. (2017). ARM: A hybrid specification-based intrusion detection system for rank attacks in 6TiSCH networks. *Emerging Technologies and Factory Automation (ETFA), 22nd IEEE International Conference on IEEE*, 1-8.

Ashton, K. (2009). That Internet of Things thing. *RFiD J.*, *22*(7), 97–114.

Asim, M., Wang, Y., Wang, K., & Huang, P. (2020). *A Review on Computational Intelligence Techniques in Cloud and Edge Computing*. ArXiv, abs/2007.14215.

Baktir, A. C., Ozgovde, A., & Ersoy, C. (2017). How Can Edge Computing Benefit from Software-Defined Networking: A Survey, Use Cases & Future Directions. *IEEE Communications Surveys and Tutorials*, *1*. Advance online publication. doi:10.1109/COMST.2017.2717482

Baktir, A. C., Sonmez, C., Ersoy, C., Ozgovde, A., & Varghese, B. (2019). *Addressing the Challenges in Federating Edge Resources*. Fog and Edge Computing. doi:10.1002/9781119525080.ch2

Barik, R. K., Dubey, H., & Mankodiya, K. (2017, November). SOA-FOG: secure service-oriented edge computing architecture for smart health big data analytics. In *2017 IEEE Global Conference on Signal and Information Processing (GlobalSIP)* (pp. 477-481). IEEE. 10.1109/GlobalSIP.2017.8308688

Bojanova, I., & Samba, A. (2011). Analysis of Cloud Computing Delivery Architecture Models. *2011 IEEE Workshops of International Conference on Advanced Information Networking and Applications*, 453-458.

Cao, Y., Hou, P., Brown, D., Wang, J., & Chen, S. (2015, June). Distributed analytics and edge intelligence: Pervasive health monitoring at the era of fog computing. In *Proceedings of the 2015 Workshop on Mobile Big Data* (pp. 43-48). 10.1145/2757384.2757398

Caprolu, D. P., Lombardi, & Raponi. (2019). Edge Computing Perspectives: Architectures, Technologies, and Open Security Issues. *2019 IEEE International Conference on Edge Computing (EDGE)*, 116-123. doi: 10.1109/EDGE.2019.00035

Carvalho, & O' Mahony, Krpalkova, Campbell, Walsh, & Doody (2019). Edge Computing Applied to Industrial Machines. *Procedia Manufacturing, 38*, 178–185.

Celesti, A., Amft, O., & Villari, M. (2019). Guest Editorial Special Section on Cloud Computing, Edge Computing, Internet of Things, and Big Data Analytics Applications for Healthcare Industry 4.0. *IEEE Transactions on Industrial Informatics, 15*(1), 454–456. doi:10.1109/TII.2018.2883315

Chakraborty, S., Bhowmick, S., Talaga, P., & Agrawal, D. P. (2016, October). Fog networks in healthcare application. In *2016 IEEE 13th International Conference on Mobile Ad Hoc and Sensor Systems (MASS)* (pp. 386-387). IEEE. 10.1109/MASS.2016.065

Chang, Z., Gong, J., Li, Y., Zhou, Z., Ristaniemi, T., Shi, G., Han, Z., & Niu, Z. (2016, December). Energy efficient resource allocation for wireless power transfer enabled collaborative mobile clouds. *IEEE Journal on Selected Areas in Communications, 34*(12), 3438–3450. doi:10.1109/JSAC.2016.2611843

Chen & Wan. (2018). Edge Computing in IoT-Based Manufacturing. *IEEE Communications Magazine, 56*(9). Advance online publication. doi:10.1109/MCOM.2018.1701231

Chiang, M., & Zhang, T. (2016). Fog and IoT: An overview of research opportunities. *IEEE Internet of Things Journal, 3*(6), 854–864. doi:10.1109/JIOT.2016.2584538

Chinnasamy & Deepalakshmi. (2018b). A Survey on Enhancing Cloud Security through Access Control Models and Technologies. *International Journal on Computer Science and Engineering, 9*(5), 326–331.

Chinnasamy, Deepalakshmi, & Praveena, Rajakumari, & Hamsagayathri. (2019). Blockchain Technology: A Step Towards Sustainable Development. *International Journal of Innovative Technology and Exploring Engineering, 9*(S2).

Chinnasamy, P., & Deepalakshmi, P. (2018a). A scalable multilabel-based access control as a service for the cloud (SMBACaaS). *Transactions on Emerging Telecommunications Technologies, 29*(8), e3458. doi:10.1002/ett.3458

Crăciunescu, M., Chenaru, O., Dobrescu, R., Florea, G., & Mocanu, Ş. (2020). IIoT Gateway for Edge Computing Applications. In T. Borangiu, D. Trentesaux, P. Leitão, A. Giret Boggino, & V. Botti (Eds.), *Service Oriented, Holonic and Multi-agent Manufacturing Systems for Industry of the Future. SOHOMA 2019. Studies in Computational Intelligence* (Vol. 853). Springer.

Cziva, R., & Pezaros, D. P. (2017, June). Container Network Functions: Bringing NFV to the Network Edge. *IEEE Communications Magazine, 55*(6), 24–31. doi:10.1109/MCOM.2017.1601039

Dey, A. (2019). *Internet Of Things (IoT), Security, privacy, application and trends*. Retrieved 5 Nov 2020 from https://medium.com/@arindey/internet-of-things-iot-security-privacy-applications-trends-3708953c6200

Donald, A. C., & Arockiam, L. (2016). Key Based Mutual Authentication (KBMA) Mechanism for Secured Access in MobiCloud Environment. In *MATEC Web of Conferences* (Vol. 40, p. 09002). EDP Sciences.

Donno & Ronchieri. (2009). *The Impact of Grid on Health Care Digital Repositories.* Doi:10.1109/HICSS.2009.435

Dubey, H., Yang, J., Constant, N., Amiri, A. M., Yang, Q., & Makodiya, K. (2015). Fog data: Enhancing telehealth big data through fog computing. In *Proceedings of the ASE bigdata & socialinformatics 2015* (pp. 1-6). Academic Press.

Eleonora, B. (2014). The Internet of Things vision: Key features, applications and open issues. *Computer Communications, 54,* 1–31. doi:10.1016/j.comcom.2014.09.008

El-Sayed, Sankar, Prasad, Puthal, Gupta, Mohanty, & Lin. (2018). Edge of things: The big picture on the integration of edge, IoT and the cloud in a distributed computing environment. *IEEE Access, 6,* 1706-1717.

Evans, D. (2011). The internet of things: How the next evolution of the internet is changing everything. *CISCO White Paper, 1*(2011), 1-11.

Evans, D. (2014). Cisco global cloud index: Forecast and methodology, 2014–2019 white paper. In *The Internet of Things: How the next evolution of the Internet is changing everything.* CISCO White Paper.

Evans, D. (n.d.). *The Internet of Things How The Next Evolution of the Internet is Changing Everything.* Available: https://www.researchgate.net/publication/30612290

Fan Liang, W. Y., He, X., & Hatcher, W. G. (2017). A Survey on the Edge Computing for the Internet of Things. IEEE Access, 6. doi:10.1109/ACCESS.2017.2778504

Fatemeh, T., Samdanis, K., Mada, B., Flinck, H., Dutta, S., & Sabella, D. (2017). On Multi-Access Edge Computing: A Survey of the Emerging 5G Network Edge Cloud Architecture and Orchestration. *IEEE Communications Surveys and Tutorials, 19*(3), 1657–1681. doi:10.1109/COMST.2017.2705720

Firouzi, F., Rahmani, A. M., Mankodiya, K., Badaroglu, M., Merrett, G. V., Wong, P., & Farahani, B. (2018). *Internet-of-Things and big data for smarter healthcare: From device to architecture, applications and analytics.* Academic Press.

Gabbouj & Stouraitis. (n.d.). Building Blocks for IoT Analytics. *River Publishers.*

Gamundani Attlee, M. (2015). An impact review on internet of things attacks. *Emerging Trends in Networks and Computer Communications (ETNCC), 2015 International Conference on, IEEE,* 114-118. 10.1109/ETNCC.2015.7184819

Ganz, F., Puschmann, D., Barnaghi, P. M., & Carrez, F. (2015). A Practical Evaluation of Information Processing and Abstraction Techniques for the Internet of Things. *IEEE Internet of Things Journal, 2*(4), 340–354. doi:10.1109/JIOT.2015.2411227

Gao, Y. Q., Bguan, H., & Qi, Z. W. (2014). Service level agreement based energy-Effificient resource man agreement in cloud data centers. Comput. Elect. Eng., 40(5), 1621–1633. doi: .compeleceng.2013.11.001 doi:10.1016/j

Gheorghe, A.-G., Crecana, C.-C., Negru, C., Pop, F., & Dobre, C. (2019). Decentralized Storage System for Edge Computing. *2019 18th International Symposium on Parallel and Distributed Computing (ISPDC)*, 41–49. doi:10.1109/ISPDC.2019.00009

Ghobaei-Arani, M., Souri, A., & Rahmanian, A. A. (2020). Resource Management Approaches in Fog Computing: A Comprehensive Review. *Journal of Grid Computing*, *18*(1), 1–42. doi:10.100710723-019-09491-1

Gia, T. N., Ali, M., Dhaou, I. B., Rahmani, A. M., Westerlund, T., Liljeberg, P., & Tenhunen, H. (2017). IoT-based continuous glucose monitoring system: A feasibility study. *Procedia Computer Science*, *109*, 327–334. doi:10.1016/j.procs.2017.05.359

Gislason. (2008). *Zigbee Wireless Networking* (1st ed.). Zigbee Alliance.

Gomes, A. S., Sousa, B., Palma, D., Fonseca, V., Zhao, Z., Monteiro, E., Braun, T., Simoes, P., & Cordeiro, L. (2017, May). Edge caching with mobility prediction in virtualized LTE mobile networks. *Future Generation Computer Systems*, *70*, 148–162. doi:10.1016/j.future.2016.06.022

Gracie, M. (2019). *The Case for Computing at the Edge*. Retrieved, 2 Nov 2020 https://www.kdnuggets.com/2016/09/evolution-iot-edge-analytics.html

Greenberg, A., Hamilton, J., Maltz, D. A., & Patel, P. (2008). The cost of a cloud: Research problems in data center networks. *SIGCOMM Comput. Commun. Rev., 39*(1), 68–73. Available: https://doi.acm.org/10.1145/1496091.1496103

Grewe, D., Wagner, M., Arumaithurai, M., Psaras, I., & Kutscher, D. (2017). Information-Centric Mobile Edge Computing for Connected Vehicle Environments: Challenges and Research Directions. *Proceedings of the Workshop on Mobile Edge Communication*, 7-12. 10.1145/3098208.3098210

Guan, Zhang, Si, Zhou, Wu, Mumtaz, & Rodriguez. (2019). ECOSECURITY: Tackling challenges related to data exchange and security: An edge-computing-enabled secure and efficient data exchange architecture for the energy Internet. *IEEE Consum. Electron. Mag., 8*(2), 61-65.

Gubbi, J., Buyya, R., Marusic, S., & Palaniswami, M. (2013). Internet of Things (IoT): A vision, architectural elements, and future directions. *Future Generation Computer Systems*, *29*(7), 1645–1660. doi:10.1016/j.future.2013.01.010

Gupta, A., & Jha, R. (2015). A Survey of 5G Network: Architecture and Emerging Technologies. *IEEE Access : Practical Innovations, Open Solutions*, *1*. Advance online publication. doi:10.1109/access.2015.2461602

Habak, K., Zegura, E., Ammar, M., & Harras, K. A. (2017). Workload management for dynamic mobile device clusters in edge Femtoclouds. *Proceedings of the Second ACM/IEEE Symposium on Edge Computing*, 1-14. 10.1145/3132211.3134455

Han, Z. (2016). Dynamic virtual machine management via approximate Markov decision process. *Proc. IEEE Int. Conf. Comput. Commun. (INFOCOM)*, 1–9. 10.1109/INFOCOM.2016.7524384

Han, Y., Park, B., & Jeong, J. (2019). Fog Based IIoT Architecture Based on Big Data Analytics for 5G-networked Smart Factory. In Lecture Notes in Computer Science: Vol. 11620. *Computational Science and Its Applications – ICCSA 2019. ICCSA 2019.* Springer. doi:10.1007/978-3-030-24296-1_5

Hong, C., & Varghese, B. (2019). Resource Management in Fog/Edge Computing: A Survey on Architectures, Infrastructure, and Algorithms. *ACM Comput. Surv., 52*, 97:1-97:37.

Hossein, S., & Hithnawi, A. (2014). Security comes first, a public-key cryptography framework for the internet of things. *Distributed Computing in Sensor Systems (DCOSS), 2014 IEEE International Conference on IEEE*, 135-136.

Israa, A., & Svetinovic, D. (2014). A taxonomy of security and privacy requirements for the Internet of Things (IoT). *Industrial Engineering and Engineering Management (IEEM), 2014 IEEE International Conference on IEEE*, 1244-1248.

Jalali, F., Hinton, K., Ayre, R., Alpcan, T., & Tucker, R. (2016). Fog Computing May Help to Save Energy in Cloud Computing. *IEEE Journal on Selected Areas in Communications, 34*(5), 1728–1739. doi:10.1109/JSAC.2016.2545559

Jang, M., Schwan, K., Bhardwaj, K., Gavrilovska, A., & Avasthi, A. (2014). Personal clouds: Sharing and integrating networked resources to enhance end-user experiences. *IEEE INFOCOM 2014 - IEEE Conference on Computer Communications*, 2220-2228.

Jha, D. N., Alwasel, K., Alshoshan, A., Huang, X., Naha, R. K., Battula, S. K., Garg, S., Puthal, D., James, P., Zomaya, A. Y., Dustdar, S., & Ranjan, R. (2020). IoTSim-Edge: A simulation framework for modeling the behavior of Internet of Things and edge computing environments. *Software, Practice & Experience, 50*(6), 844–867. doi:10.1002pe.2787

Jošilo, S., & Dán, G. (2018). Decentralized algorithm for randomized task allocation in fog computing systems. *IEEE/ACM Transactions on Networking, 27*(1), 85–97. doi:10.1109/TNET.2018.2880874

Khan. (2019). Edge computing. *Survey.*

Khan, Ahmed, & Hakak, Yaqoob, & Ahmed. (2019). Edge computing: A survey. *Future Generation Computer Systems, 97*, 219–235.

Ko, S.-W., Huang, K., Kim, S.-L., & Chae, H. (2017, May). Live prefetching for mobile computation offloading. *IEEE Transactions on Wireless Communications, 16*(5), 3057–3071. doi:10.1109/TWC.2017.2674665

Li, X., Zhu, L., Chu, X., & Fu, H. (2020). Edge Computing-Enabled Wireless Sensor Networks for Multiple Data Collection Tasks in Smart Agriculture. *J. Sensors, 2020*, 4398061:1-4398061:9.

Li, A., Yang, X., Kandula, S., & Zhang, M. (2010). *CloudCmp: Comparing public cloud providers. In Proc. 10th ACM SIGCOMM Conf. Internet Meas.* doi:10.1145/1879141.1879143

Li, C., Xue, Y., Wang, J., Zhang, W., & Li, T. (2018, April). Edge-oriented computing paradigms: A survey on architecture design and system management. *ACM Computing Surveys, 51*(2), 1–34. doi:10.1145/3154815

Linus, W., Raza, S., & Voigt, T. (2013). Routing Attacks and Countermeasures in the RPL-based Internet of Things. *International Journal of Distributed Sensor Networks.*

Liu, L., Chen, C., & Pei, Q. (2020). Vehicular Edge Computing and Networking: A Survey. *Mobile Netw Appl.* doi:10.100711036-020-01624-1

Loong, K. S., Kumar, S. S., & Tschofenig, H. (2014). Securing the internet of things: A standardization perspective. *IEEE Internet of Things Journal, 1*(3), 265–275. doi:10.1109/JIOT.2014.2323395

López, P., Montresor, A., Epema, D., Datta, A., Higashino, T., Iamnitchi, A., Barcellos, M. P., Felber, P., & Rivière, E. (2015). Edge-centric Computing: Vision and Challenges. *Computer Communication Review, 45*(5), 37–42. doi:10.1145/2831347.2831354

Luigi, A., Iera, A., & Morabito, G. (2010). The internet of things: A survey. *Computer Networks, 54*(15), 2787–2805.

Lu, R., Heung, K., Lashkari, A., & Ghorbani, A. (2017). A Lightweight Privacy-Preserving Data Aggregation Scheme for Fog Computing-Enhanced IoT. *IEEE Access: Practical Innovations, Open Solutions, 5*, 3302–3312. doi:10.1109/ACCESS.2017.2677520

Mach, P., & Becvar, Z. (2017). Mobile Edge Computing: A Survey on Architecture and Computation Offloading. *IEEE Communications Surveys and Tutorials, 19*(3), 1628–1656. doi:10.1109/COMST.2017.2682318

Mahmud, H. M., Fotouhi, M., & Hasan, R. (2015). Towards an analysis of security issues, challenges, and open problems in the internet of things. *Services (SERVICES), 2015 IEEE World Congress on IEEE*, 21-28.

Manish. (2020). *IoT Analytics – 3 Major Uses Cases of Internet of Things Analytics.* Retrieved, 2 Nov 2020 from https://data-flair.training/blogs/iot-analytics

Mao, Y., You, C., Zhang, J., Huang, K., & Letaief, K. (2017). A Survey on Mobile Edge Computing: The Communication Perspective. *IEEE Communications Surveys and Tutorials, 19*(4), 2322–2358. doi:10.1109/COMST.2017.2745201

Merlino, G., Dautov, R., Distefano, S., & Bruneo, D. (2019). Enabling Workload Engineering in Edge, Fog, and Cloud Computing through OpenStack-based Middleware. *ACM Transactions on Internet Technology, 19*(2), 28. doi:10.1145/3309705

Minteer. (2017). *Analytics for the Internet of Things (IoT).* Academic Press.

Mirkhanzadeh, B., Shakeri, A., Shao, C., Razo, M., Tacca, M., Galimberti, G., Martinelli, G., Cardani, M., & Fumagalli, A. (2018). An SDN-enabled multi-layer protection and restoration mechanism. *Optical Switching and Networking, 30,* 23–32. doi:10.1016/j.osn.2018.05.005

Moghaddam, F. F., Ahmadi, M., Sarvari, S., Eslami, M., & Golkar, A. (2015). Cloud computing challenges and opportunities: A survey. *2015 1st International Conference on Telematics and Future Generation Networks (TAFGEN),* 34-38.

Mohammad, A., Khan, I., Alsaffar, A. A., & Huh, E.-N. (2014). Cloud of Things: Integrating Internet of Things and cloud computing and the issues involved. *Applied Sciences and Technology (IBCAST), 11th International Bhurban Conference on IEEE,* 414-419.

Muñoz, Vilalta, Yoshikane, Casellas, Martínez, Tsuritani, & Morita. (2018). *Integration of IoT, Transport SDN, and Edge/Cloud Computing for Dynamic Distribution of IoT Analytics and Efficient Use of Network Resources.* Academic Press.

Mur. (1994). Edge Elements, their Advantages and their Disadvantages. *IEEE Transactions on Magnetics, 30*(5).

Mutlag, A. A., Ghani, M. K. A., Arunkumar, N. A., Mohammed, M. A., & Mohd, O. (2019). Enabling technologies for fog computing in healthcare IoT systems. *Future Generation Computer Systems, 90,* 62–78. doi:10.1016/j.future.2018.07.049

Nagashree, R. N., Rao, V., & Aswini, N. (2014). Near field communication. *Int. J. Wirel. Microw. Technol., 2014*(4), 20.

Naha, R. K., Garg, S., Georgakopoulos, D., Jayaraman, P., Gao, L., Xiang, Y., & Ranjan, R. (2018). Fog computing: Survey of trends, architectures, requirements, and research directions. *IEEE Access: Practical Innovations, Open Solutions, 6*(47), 980–009. doi:10.1109/ACCESS.2018.2866491

Newman, D. M. (2020). *Bayesian edge analytics of machine process and health status in an IoT framework* (Doctoral dissertation). Georgia Institute of Technology.

Ni, J., Zhang, A., Lin, X., & Shen, X. (2017). Security, Privacy, and Fairness in Fog-Based Vehicular Crowdsensing. *IEEE Communications Magazine, 55*(6), 146–152. doi:10.1109/MCOM.2017.1600679

O'Grady, M., Langton, D., & O'Hare, G. (2019). *Edge computing: A tractable model for smart agriculture?* Academic Press.

OpenFogConsortium. (2017). *Openfog reference architecture for fog computing.* https://www.openfogconsortium.org/ra/

Pace, P., Aloi, G., Gravina, R., Caliciuri, G., Fortino, G., & Liotta, A. (2018). An edge-based architecture to support efficient applications for healthcare industry 4.0. *IEEE Transactions on Industrial Informatics, 15*(1), 481–489. doi:10.1109/TII.2018.2843169

Pan & McElhannon. (2018). Future Edge Cloud and Edge Computing for Internet of Things Applications. *IEEE Internet of Things Journal, 5*(1). Advance online publication. doi:10.1109/JIOT.2017.2767608

Pavan, P., & Chavan, G. (2015). A survey: Attacks on RPL and 6LoWPAN in IoT. In *Pervasive Computing (ICPC), 2015 International Conference on.* IEEE.

Peng, K., Leung, V., Xu, X., Zheng, L., Wang, J., & Huang, Q. (2018). A Survey on Mobile Edge Computing: Focusing on Service Adoption and Provision. *Wireless Communications and Mobile Computing, 2018*, 2018. doi:10.1155/2018/8267838

Peng, M., & Zhang, K. (2016). Recent advances in fog radio access networks: Performance analysis and radio resource allocation. *IEEE Access: Practical Innovations, Open Solutions, 4*, 5003–5009. doi:10.1109/ACCESS.2016.2603996

Premsankar, G., Francesco, M. D., & Taleb, T. (2018). Edge Computing for the Internet of Things: A Case Study. *IEEE Internet of Things Journal, 5*(2), 1275–1284. doi:10.1109/JIOT.2018.2805263

Pu. (n.d.). *Low Latency Geo-distributed Data Analytics.* doi:10.1145/2829988.2787505

Raj & Raman. (2017). *The Internet of Things.* Enabling Technologies, Platforms, and Use Cases.

Rapuzzi & Repetto. (2018). Building situational awareness for network threats in fog/edge computing: Emerging paradigms beyond the security perimeter model. *Future Gener. Comput. Syst., 85*, 235-249.

Ray, P. P., Dash, D., & De, D. (2019). Edge computing for Internet of Things: A survey, e-healthcare case study and future direction. *Journal of Network and Computer Applications, 140*, 1–22. doi:10.1016/j.jnca.2019.05.005

Ren, Bajic, Cosic, Katalinic, Moraca, Lazarevic, & Rikalovic. (n.d.). *Edge computing vs. cloud computing: Challenges and opportunities in Industry 4.0.* Doi:10.2507/30th.daaam. proceedings.120

Ren. (2019). *Collaborative Cloud and Edge Computing for Latency Minimization.* doi:10.1109/TVT.2019.2904244

Roman, Lopez, & Mambo. (2018). Mobile edge computing, fog et al.: A survey and analysis of security threats and challenges. *Future Gener. Comput. Syst., 78*, 680-698.

Salguerio, Barton, & Henry. (2017). *IoT Fundamentals: Networking Technologies, Protocols, and Use Cases for the Internet of Things.* Cisco.

Satyanarayanan, M. (2011). Mobile computing: The next decade. *SIGMOBILE Mobile Comput. Commun. Rev., 15*(2), 2–10. Available: http://doi.acm.org/ 10.1145/2016598.2016600

Satyanarayanan, M. (2019). The emergence of edge computing. *Computer, 50*(1), 30–39.

Satyanarayanan, M., Bahl, P., Cáceres, R., & Davies, N. (2009). The Case for VM-Based Cloudlets in Mobile Computing. *IEEE Pervasive Computing, 8*(4), 14–23. doi:10.1109/MPRV.2009.82

Sehrawat & Gill. (2018). Data Mining in IoT and its Challenges. *International Journal of Computer Sciences and Engineering, 289 – 293*, 2347 – 2693.

Serpanos & Wolf. (2018). *Internet-of-Things (IoT) Systems Architectures, Algorithms, Methodologies.* Springer.

Sethi, P., & Sarangi, S. R. (2017). Internet of Things: Architectures, Protocols, and Applications. *Journal of Electrical and Computer Engineering, 1-4.* doi:10.1155/2017/9324035

Shankar, B. S., Tripathy, S., & Chowdhury, A. R. (2015). Design challenges and security issues in the Internet of Things. *Region 10 Symposium (TENSYMP), 2015 IEEE,* 90-93.

Shaw, K. (2019). *What is edge computing and why it matters.* Retrieved, 14 Nov 2020 from https://www.networkworld.com/article/3224893/what-is-edge-computing-and-how-it-s-changing-the-network.html

Shi & Dustdar. (2016). The Promise of Edge Computing. *Computer, 49*(5). Advance online publication. doi:10.1109/MC.2016.145

Shi, Cao, Zhang, Li, & Xu. (n.d.). Edge computing: Vision and challenges. IEEE Internet of Things Journal, 3(5), 637–646. doi:10.1109/JIOT.2016.2579198

Shi, Zhang, & Wang. (n.d.). Edgecomputing:State-of-the-art and future directions. J. Comput. Res. Develop., 56(1), 1–21.

Shi, F., Tang, G., Li, Y., Cai, Z., Zhang, X., & Zhou, T. (2019). A Survey on Edge Computing Systems and Tools. *Proceedings of the IEEE, 107*(8), 1537–1562. doi:10.1109/JPROC.2019.2920341

Shi, W., Cao, J., Zhang, Q., Li, Y., & Xu, L. (2016). Edge Computing: Vision and Challenges. *IEEE Internet of Things Journal, 3*(5), 637–646. doi:10.1109/JIOT.2016.2579198

Shi, W., Sun, H., Cao, J., Zhang, Q., & Liu, W. (2016, October). Edge computing-an emergingcomputingmodelfortheInternetofeverythingera. *J. Comput. Res. Develop., 54*(5), 907–924.

Singh, M. G., Upadhyay, P., & Chaudhary, L. (2014). The internet of things: Challenges and security issues. *Emerging Technologies (ICET), 2014 International Conference on IEEE,* 54-59.

Sittón-Candanedo, I. & Corchado Rodríguez, J. (2019). An Edge Computing Tutorial. *Oriental Journal of Computer Science and Technology, 12,* 34-38. . doi:10.13005/ojcst12.02.02

Sodhro, A. H., Pirbhulal, S., & de Albuquerque, V. H. C. (2019). Artificial intelligence driven mechanism for edge computing based industrial applications. *IEEE Transactions on Industrial Informatics, 15*(7), 4235–4243. doi:10.1109/TII.2019.2902878

Sonmez, C., Ozgovde, A., & Ersoy, C. (2019). Fuzzy Workload Orchestration for Edge Computing. *IEEE eTransactions on Network and Service Management, 16*(2), 769–782. doi:10.1109/TNSM.2019.2901346

Stojanovic, L. (2020). Intelligent edge processing. In Machine Learning for Cyber Physical Systems. Technologien für die intelligente Automation (Technologies for Intelligent Automation) (vol. 11). Springer Vieweg. doi:10.1007/978-3-662-59084-3_5

Sundmaeker, H., Guillemin, P., Friess, P., & Woelfflé, S. (2010). Vision and challenges for realising the Internet of things. Academic Press.

Sun, X., & Ansari, N. (2017, January/February). Green cloudlet network: A distributed green mobile cloud network. *IEEE Network*, *31*(1), 64–70. doi:10.1109/MNET.2017.1500293NM

Tang, L., Tang, B., Kang, L., & Zhang, L. (2019). A Novel Task Caching and Migration Strategy in Multi-Access Edge Computing Based on the Genetic Algorithm. *Future Internet*, *11*(8), 1–14. doi:10.3390/fi11080181

Turner, V., Gantz, J. F., & Reinsel, D. (2018). *The digital universe of opportunities: Rich Data and the Increasing Value of the Internet of Things*. Available: https://www.emc.com/leadership/digitaluniverse/2014iview/index.htm

Varghese, B. (2016). Challenges and Opportunities in Edge Computing. Academic Press.

Varghese, B., Wang, N., Barbhuiya, S., Kilpatrick, P., & Nikolopoulos, D. S. (2016). Challenges and Opportunities in Edge Computing. *2016 IEEE International Conference on Smart Cloud (SmartCloud)*. 10.1109/SmartCloud.2016.18

vonStietencron, M., Lewandowski, M., Lepenioti, K., Bousdekis, A., Hribernik, K., Apostolou, D., & Mentzas, G. (2020, August). Streaming Analytics in Edge-Cloud Environment for Logistics Processes. In *IFIP International Conference on Advances in Production Management Systems* (pp. 245-253). Springer.

Walter De Gruyter. (2017). *IoT Energy Storage – A Forecast*. Author.

Wang, von Laszewski, Younge, He, Kunze, Tao, & Fu. (2010). *Cloud Computing: a Perspective Study*. doi:10.100700354-008-0081-5

Wang, J., Pan, J., Esposito, F., Calyam, P., Yang, Z., & Mohapatra, P. (2018). *Edge Cloud Offloading Algorithms: Issues, Methods, and Perspectives*. Networking and Internet Architecture.

Wang, R., Peng, X., Zhang, J., & Letaief, K. B. (2016, August). Mobilityaware caching for content-centric wireless networks: Modeling and methodology. *IEEE Communications Magazine*, *54*(8), 77–83. doi:10.1109/MCOM.2016.7537180

Wu, H., Hu, J., Sun, J., & Sun, D. (2019). Edge Computing in an IoT Base Station System: Reprogramming and Real-Time Tasks. *Complexity*, *2019*, 2019. doi:10.1155/2019/4027638

Xiao, Y., Jia, Y., Liu, C., Cheng, X., Yu, J., & Lv, W. (2019). Edge Computing Security: State of the Art and Challenges. *Proceedings of the IEEE*, 107(8), 1608-1631. 10.1109/JPROC.2019.2918437

Xu, J., & Ren, S. (2016). Online learning for offloading and autoscaling in renewable-powered mobile edge computing. *Proc. IEEE Glob. Commun. Conf. (GLOBECOM)*, 1–6. 10.1109/GLOCOM.2016.7842069

Yadav & Mittal. (2018). *IoT, Challenges and issues in Indian Perspective*. Cornell University Library.

Yang, Yu, Si, Yang, & Zhang. (2019). Integrated Blockchain and Edge Computing Systems: A Survey, Some Research Issues and Challenges. *IEEE Communications Surveys and Tutorials*, *21*(2), 1508–1532. doi:10.1109/COMST.2019.2894727

Yi, L., & Li. (2015). A Survey of Fog Computing: Concepts, Applications and Issues. *Proceedings of Workshop on Mobile Big Data*, 37-42.

Yousefpour, A., Fung, C., Nguyen, T., Kadiyala, K.P., Jalali, F., Niakanlahiji, A., Kong, J., & Jue, J. (2019). *All One Needs to Know about Fog Computing and Related Edge Computing Paradigms: A Complete Survey*. ArXiv, abs/1808.05283.

Yousefpour, Fung, Nguyen, Kadiyala, Jalali, Niakanlahiji, … Jue. (2019). *All one needs to know about fog computing and related edge computing paradigms: A complete survey*. Academic Press.

Yousefpour, A., Fung, C., Nguyen, T., Kadiyala, K., Jalali, F., Niakanlahiji, A., Kong, J., & Jue, J. P. (2019). All One Needs to Know about Fog Computing and Related Edge Computing Paradigms. *Journal of Systems Architecture*, *98*, 289–330. doi:10.1016/j.sysarc.2019.02.009

Yousefpour, Fung, Nguyen, Kadiyala, & Jalali, Niakanlahiji, Kong, & Jue. (2019). All one needs to know about fog computing and related edge computing paradigms: A complete survey. *Journal of Systems Architecture*, *98*, 289–330.

Yu, T., & Zha, Z., Song, & Han. (2020). An EPEC Analysis among Mobile Edge Caching, Content Delivery Network and Data Center. 2020 IEEE Wireless Communications and Networking Conference (WCNC), 1-6. doi: 10.1109/WCNC45663.2020.9120613

ZAID, M. A., Faizal, M., Maheswar, R., & Abdullaziz, O. I. (2020). Toward Smart Urban Development Through Intelligent Edge Analytics. In *Integration of WSN and IoT for Smart Cities* (pp. 129–150). Springer. doi:10.1007/978-3-030-38516-3_8

Zhang, Chen, Zhao, Cheng, & Hu. (2018). Data security and privacy-preserving in edge computing paradigm: Survey and open issues. *IEEE Access, 6*, 18209-18237.

Zhang, D., Yang, L. T., Chen, M., Zhao, S., Guo, M., & Zhang, Y. (2016). Real-time locating systems using active RFID for Internet of Things. *IEEE Systems Journal*, *10*(3), 1226–1235. doi:10.1109/JSYST.2014.2346625

Zhang, Q., Cheng, L., & Boutaba, R. (2010). Cloud computing: State-of-the-art and research challenges. *Journal of Internet Services and Applications*, *1*(1), 7–18. doi:10.100713174-010-0007-6

Compilation of References

Zha, Z. M., & Liu, F. (2018). Edgecomputing:Platforms;Applications and challenges. *J. Comput. Res. Develop.*, *55*(2), 327–337.

Zhong, S., & Wang, X. (2018). Energy Allocation and Utilization for Wirelessly Powered IoT Networks. *IEEE Internet of Things Journal*, *5*(4), 2781–2792.

Zhou, Y., Tian, L., Liu, L., & Qi, Y. (2019). Fog Computing Enabled Future Mobile Communication Networks: A Convergence of Communication and Computing. IEEE Communications Magazine, 57(5), 20-27. doi:10.1109/MCOM.2019.1800235

About the Contributors

Muruganantham A. is serving as the Associate Professor in the Department of Computer Science at Kristu Jayanti College (Autonomous), Bangalore. He has 24 years in the field of education holding various academic roles. He has pursued his research in web mining. Exceptional track record of research success with multiple published articles. His expertise and interests are in Web mining, Data mining, Object-oriented Programming, Middleware Technologies and various high-level programming languages. He has won the Teacher Innovation Award from ZIIEI in the year 2019 and his achievements are listed in Asian Biographies website. Highly committed person who goes beyond the call of duty and inspires students to pursue academic and personal excellence.

Neeraja Lakshmi A. is pursuing her Master's degree at PSG College of Technology and she has completed her B.E. in Electronics and Communication Engineering from Saranathan College of Engineering in the year 2017. She has published papers on the automotive domain at International Conferences. Her main research interest includes IoT, In-vehicle software development and Autonomous or connected vehicle.

Ben Sujin B., PhD, is Professor in the Department of Engineering at University of Technology and Applied Sciences- Nizwa, Sultanate of Oman. Dr. Ben Sujin is a Fellow of the IEEE and Counsellor for the University Student Branch. He is awarded the Best Active Researcher Award by the University in the year 2018. He authored many research papers, books and also presented various research papers in several conferences. Dr. Ben Sujin secured many funded projects from the Research Council of Oman and the Institution of Engineers. He also enlightened the young engineering minds in the field of robotics, Internet of Things, Artificial Intelligence and other emerging computer engineering topics through various seminars and webinars.

Vinoth Kumar B. is working as an Associate Professor with 16 years of experience in the Department of Information Technology at PSG College of Technology. His research interests include Soft Computing, Blockchain, and Digital Image Processing. He is author of more than 26 papers in refereed journals and international conferences. He has edited three books with reputed publishers such as Springer and CRC Press. He serves as a Guest Editor/Reviewer of many journals with leading publishers such as Inderscience, Springer.

Kamalanathan Chandran completed his research in the area of cloud computing. He is presently working as an Associate professor in the Department of Electrical, Electronics and Communication Engineering, GITAM University, Bengaluru Campus. He is having 15 years of teaching experience in engineering. His research interest focus on Cloud Computing, Wired & Wireless Network, Network Security.

Rojaramani D. is an Information Technology professional in a Sethu Institute of Technology in India. She received his Ph.D (Information and Communication Engineering) Anna University at Chennai in 2020. She received her Bachelor's degree in Information Technology Sethu Institute of Technology, India in 2007. She has more than twelve years of professional experience in Information Technology. She has published 5 books in the area of Information Technology. She has published 15 research articles in leading journals, conference proceedings and books.

Shantha Mary Joshitta is working as Head and Assistant Professor in the Department of Computer Science, Jayaraj Annapackiam College (Autonomous), Periyakulam, Theni, India. She has 13 years of experience in teaching and 7 years in research. She has published 20 research articles in the National / International Conferences and Journals and served as a resource person for an adequate number of colleges. Her research interests are the Internet of Things, Blockchain, Data Mining, and Big Data.

Anitha Kumari K. is working as an Associate Professor in Department of IT for past 10 Years in PSG College of Technology, India. She is Highly Passionate and curious about Learning New stuffs in New Generation Computing Technologies. As an Independent Researcher, she had an Opportunity to present her UGC sponsored paper based on Quantum Cryptography in USA and visited a few Foreign Universities. To her credit, she had Published a PATENT and 55 Technical Papers in refereed and Impact Factored International/National Journals/Conferences published by IEEE, Elsevier, Springer, T&F, etc.,.Also, she's been an Active Reviewer for Prestigious Journals published by IEEE (IEEE Communications Surveys and Tutorials (IF: 20.230), IEEE Transactions on Industrial Informatics (IF: 5.43)), IEEE Access, Springer, Wiley, etc., and Technical Program Committee (TPC) for CECNet 2017, NGCT-2017 WICC-2018 and NCCI-2018 conferences. Her areas of interest include Cloud & IoT Security, Design and Analysis of Security Protocols, Attacks

& Defense, Security in Computing, Bioinformatics, Quantum Cryptography, Web Service Security, Network Security, Cognitive Security and Analysis of Algorithms. Currently she's being the Programme Coordinator for PSG CARE Sponsored One Year Certification Course on Cyber Security. Out of her research interest, she had contributed book chapters published by T & F, Springer and delivered ample Guest Lectures. Her security project is sanctioned and granted by AICTE for a sum of Rs.11,80,000/-. She's been the mentor for Technovator Projects (2019, 2018 & 2014) and 'MEDROIDZ', an ICICI – Trinity 2014 funded project that was selected as one among the 6 projects in India. She also mentored 5 projects exhibited in NST Fair and AICTE Vishwakrama Awarded Project. Academically, she has secured RANK-I and awarded Gold Medal in ME (SE) & in BE (CSE) from Anna University and from Avinashilingam University. As a Supervisor, she is currently guiding PhD scholars in her research area.

Sivakumar P. received his B.E. degree in Electrical and Electronics with I class in 2006 from Anna University. He completed his M.E. degree in Embedded System technologies with I class in 2009 from Anna University Coimbatore. He completed his Ph.D. in Electrical Engineering with a specialization in Automotive Embedded Software in the year 2018 from Anna University, PSG College of Technology. His research interests include Embedded System, Model-Based Design, Model-Based Testing of Automotive Software, Automotive Software Development, Fog, and Edge Computing. He has around 14 years of teaching experience. He has published 14 papers in reputed International Journals. He has also published 20 National and International conferences papers and has organized National seminar, workshop funded by DRDO, DST, and MNRE

Sunita Panda is presently working as Assistant Professor in the department of Electronics and communication Engg, GITAM Deemed To be University, Bengaluru Campus. She has published many research papers in national and international journals. having 16 years of experience in the field of teaching, research. Her area of interest include soft computing, Channel equalization, digital Signal processing.

Chinnasamy Ponnusamy received his both Bachelor's in Computer Science and Engineering from Anna University, Chennai and Master's degree in Computer Science and Engineering from Kalasalingam University. He also received Doctor of Philosophy in computer science during the year 2019. He was an Assistant Professor of Information Technology at Sri Shakthi Institute of Engineering and Technology. His research interest includes cloud security, Access control, Blockchain Technology and cryptography. Moreover, he has also published 6 papers in International Journal, 6 papers in International Conferences and 5 book chapters.

Kumar R. is Associate Professor in the Department of Computer Science, at Kristu Jayanti College (Autonomous), Bangalore. He has 25+ years of experience in teaching and 2 years of industry experience in software development. His broad area of research is Data Mining. He has published many research papers in International Journals and chaired National and International Conferences. He is an active member of IEEE and also convenor for national and international conferences.

Velmurugan R. is Associate Professor in the Department of Computer Science at Kristu Jayanti College (Autonomous), Bangalore. He has 21+ years in the field of education holding various academic roles. He has pursued his research in Web Mining. His areas of interests are Web mining, Data mining, Object-oriented technologies, Simulation, Software Engineering and various high-level programming languages. An enthusiast always strives for achieving his passion for innovation and keeping up-to-date in the emerging trends of Information Technology.

Sandhya Devi R. S. received her B.E (Electronics and Communication Engineering) from Avinashilingam University, Coimbatore Tamilnadu, India. She completed her M.E (Embedded Systems) at the Anna University of Technology, Coimbatore, Tamilnadu, India. She is Asst. Professor at Kumaraguru College of Technology. Her areas of interest include Embedded System Design and ARM processor. She published her project in a journal and international conference.

Annlin Jeba S. V. pursued a Bachelor of Engineering from MS University. She received her master's degree and PhD. degree from Anna University. She is currently working as an Associate Professor in the Computer Science and Engineering department of Sree Buddha College of Engineering. She has published more than 10 research papers in reputed international journals. Her areas of research focus on Network Security, Privacy in communication, wireless sensor networks. She has more than 18 years of teaching experience and 6 years of research experience.

Padma Charan Sahu is presently doing PhD in the department of Electronics and Telecommunication Engg., GIET, Odisha. He has published many research papers in national and international journals. having 11 years of experience in the field of teaching, research. His areas of interest include soft computing, Channel equalization, digital Signal processing and Microprocessor & Microcontroller.

Kavita Srivastava is currently working as an Associate Professor in the Department of Computer Science, Institute of Information Technology & Management affiliated to GGSIPU, New Delhi, India. She obtained an M.Tech degree in IT in 2007 from USICT, GGSIPU, Delhi, India. She has an interest in Machine Learning, Wireless Sensor Networks, Internet of Things and Image Processing.

Praveena V. obtained her both Bachelor's in Computer Science and Engineering from Bharathiyar University, Coimbatore and Master's degree in Computer Science and Engineering from Karpagam University, Coimbatore. She also received Doctor of Philosophy in Network Security during the year 2017. She was a dynamic professor of Information Technology at Sri Shakthi Institute of Engineering and Technology. Her talents were soon recognized and propelled her in academic ladder. After 16+ years of experience both in academics and industry. She organized several workshops and seminars for the benefit of both students and professors as well. Her area of specialization includes IoT Application, Cloud Computing technologies, cybersecurity and cyber forensics. Moreover, she has also published 16 papers in International and 4 papers in National Conference. During 2018, she had published the book entitled "Fundamentals of Computer and Computer programming, Web Technology, Operating system". She is also a member of Institute of Electrical and Electronics Engineers (IEEE), Universal Association of Computer and Electronics Engineer (UACEE), International Association of Engineers (IAENG), Indian Society for Technical Education (ISTE).

Vijay Kumar V. R. is currently working as an Associate Professor in the Department of Electronics and Communication Engineering, Anna University Regional Campus, Coimbatore. He received his Ph.D. degree from Anna University Chennai in the area of nonlinear filtering and Masters and Bachelors from Thiayarajar College of Engineering, Madurai, and Thanthai Periyar Govt. College of Technology, Vellore respectively. He has 20 years of teaching experience and his area of research includes Image Processing, Signal Processing, and VLSI Design. He has published more than 85 research papers in International Journals and Conferences.

Index

Ensure Quality Research is Introduced to the Academic Community

Become an IGI Global Reviewer for Authored Book Projects

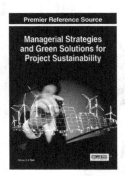

The overall success of an authored book project is dependent on quality and timely reviews.

In this competitive age of scholarly publishing, constructive and timely feedback significantly expedites the turnaround time of manuscripts from submission to acceptance, allowing the publication and discovery of forward-thinking research at a much more expeditious rate. Several IGI Global authored book projects are currently seeking highly-qualified experts in the field to fill vacancies on their respective editorial review boards:

Applications and Inquiries may be sent to:
development@igi-global.com

Applicants must have a doctorate (or an equivalent degree) as well as publishing and reviewing experience. Reviewers are asked to complete the open-ended evaluation questions with as much detail as possible in a timely, collegial, and constructive manner. All reviewers' tenures run for one-year terms on the editorial review boards and are expected to complete at least three reviews per term. Upon successful completion of this term, reviewers can be considered for an additional term.

If you have a colleague that may be interested in this opportunity, we encourage you to share this information with them.

InfoSci®-OnDemand

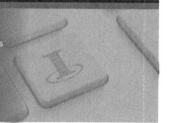

Continuously updated with new material on a weekly basis, InfoSci®-OnDemand offers the ability to search through thousands of quality full-text research papers. Users can narrow each search by identifying key topic areas of interest, then display a complete listing of relevant papers, and purchase materials specific to their research needs.

Comprehensive Service

• Over 125,000+ journal articles, book chapters, and case studies.

• All content is downloadable in PDF and HTML format and can be stored locally for future use.

No Subscription Fees

• One time fee of $37.50 per PDF download.

Instant Access

• Receive a download link immediately after order completion!

"It really provides an excellent entry into the research literature of the field. It presents a manageable number of highly relevant sources on topics of interest to a wide range of researchers. The sources are scholarly, but also accessible to 'practitioners'."

– Lisa Stimatz, MLS, University of North Carolina at Chapel Hill, USA

"It is an excellent and well designed database which will facilitate research, publication, and teaching. It is a very useful tool to have."

– George Ditsa, PhD, University of Wollongong, Australia

"I have accessed the database and find it to be a valuable tool to the IT/IS community. I found valuable articles meeting my search criteria 95% of the time."

– Prof. Lynda Louis, Xavier University of Louisiana, USA

Recommended for use by researchers who wish to immediately download PDFs of individual chapters or articles.
www.igi-global.com/e-resources/infosci-ondemand

IGI Global
DISSEMINATOR OF KNOWLEDGE
www.igi-global.com

Printed in the United States
By Bookmasters